Lecture Notes in Computer Science 14061

The series Lecture Notes in Computer Science (LNCS), including its subseries Lecture Notes in Artificial Intelligence (LNAI) and Lecture Notes in Bioinformatics (LNBI), has established itself as a medium for the publication of new developments in computer science and information technology research, teaching, and education.

LNCS enjoys close cooperation with the computer science R & D community, the series counts many renowned academics among its volume editors and paper authors, and collaborates with prestigious societies. Its mission is to serve this international community by providing an invaluable service, mainly focused on the publication of conference and workshop proceedings and postproceedings. LNCS commenced publication in 1973.

Konstantinos Georgiou · Evangelos Kranakis
Editors

Algorithmics of Wireless Networks

19th International Symposium, ALGOWIN 2023
Amsterdam, The Netherlands, September 7–8, 2023
Revised Selected Papers

Editors
Konstantinos Georgiou
Toronto Metropolitan University
Toronto, ON, Canada

Evangelos Kranakis 🆔
Carleton University
Ottawa, ON, Canada

ISSN 0302-9743 ISSN 1611-3349 (electronic)
Lecture Notes in Computer Science
ISBN 978-3-031-48881-8 ISBN 978-3-031-48882-5 (eBook)
https://doi.org/10.1007/978-3-031-48882-5

This Springer imprint is published by the registered company Springer Nature Switzerland AG
The registered company address is: Gewerbestrasse 11, 6330 Cham, Switzerland

Paper in this product is recyclable.

Preface

This volume contains the papers presented at ALGOWIN 2023: the 19th International Symposium on Algorithmics of Wireless Networks, held during September 7–8, 2023, at the CWI (Centrum Wiskunde en Informatica), Amsterdam, the Netherlands, as part of ALGO 2023.

ALGOWIN is an international symposium dedicated to algorithmic aspects of wireless networks. Founded in 2004, it originally focused on sensor networks. It was formerly known as ALGOSENSORS and now covers algorithmic issues arising in wireless networks of all types of computational entities, static or mobile, including sensor networks, sensor-actuator networks and systems of autonomous robots. The focus is on the design and analysis of algorithms, models of computation and experimental analysis. The new title of the conference, the International Symposium on Algorithmics of Wireless Networks, reflects this broader scope.

In response to the Call for Papers, 15 submissions were received. Each submission was reviewed by at least four Program Committee members and some trusted external reviewers, and evaluated on its quality, originality and relevance to the symposium. The committee decided to accept 10 papers for presentation at ALGOWIN 2023 and inclusion in these proceedings. The program of ALGOWIN 2023 also included an invited talk by Sándor Fakete, Technische Universität Braunschweig, entitled, "Coordinated Motion Planning: Reconfiguring a Swarm of Robots".

The Program Committee selected the following contribution for the Best Paper and Best Student Paper Award, both kindly sponsored by Springer:

Temporal Reachability Dominating Sets: contagion in temporal graphs,
by David C. Kutner and Laura Larios-Jones.

We would like to thank the Steering Committee, chaired by Sotiris Nikoletseas, for giving us the opportunity to serve as Program Chairs of ALGOWIN 2023. Furthermore, we would like to thank all the authors who responded to the Call for Papers, the invited speaker for enriching the program of the event, and the Program Committee members and external reviewers for their fundamental contributions to the paper selection process, resulting in a strong program. We would also like to warmly thank the ALGO 2023 organizing committee, chaired by Solon Pissis, for enabling us to hold ALGOWIN as part of the ALGO symposium and taking care of all organizational matters. We would like to thank Springer for publishing the proceedings of ALGOWIN 2023 in the LNCS series and for their support and sponsorship.

Finally, we would like to acknowledge the use of EasyChair for handling the submission of papers, and managing the review process.

October 2023

Konstantinos Georgiou
Evangelos Kranakis

Organization

Steering Committee

Josep Díaz	Universitat Politècnica de Catalunya, Spain
Magnús M. Halldórsson	Reykjavik University, Iceland
Panganamala R. Kumar	Texas A&M University, USA
Sotiris Nikoletseas (Chair)	University of Patras and CTI, Greece
José Rolim	University of Geneva, Switzerland
Paul Spirakis	University of Liverpool, UK and University of Patras, Greece
Adam Wolisz	Technical University of Berlin, Germany

Program Committee Co-chairs

Konstantinos Georgiou	Toronto Metropolitan University, Canada
Evangelos Kranakis	Carleton University, Canada

Program Committee

Evangelos Bampas	Université Paris-Saclay, France
Jérémie Chalopin	CNRS-LIS, France
Marek Chrobak	University of California Riverside, USA
Stefan Dobrev	Slovak Academy, Slovakia
Shlomi Dolev	Ben-Gurion University of the Negev, Israel
Olga Goussevskaia	Federal University of Minas Gerais, Brazil
Ralf Klasing	CNRS Bordeaux, France
Dariusz Kowalski	Augusta University, USA
Danny Krizanc	Wesleyan University, USA
Arnaud Labourel	Aix-Marseille Université, France
Flaminia Luccio	Ca'Foscari University, Italy
Euripides Markou	University of Thessaly, Greece
Conrado Martinez	Univ. Politècnica de Catalunya, Spain
Othon Michail	University of Liverpool, UK
Avery Miller	University of Manitoba, Canada
Nathalie Mitton	Inria Lille-Nord Europe, France
Aris Pagourtzis	National Technical University of Athens, Greece

Boaz Patt-Shamir	Tel Aviv University, Israel
Cristina M. Pinotti	University of Perugia, Italy
Giuseppe Prencipe	University of Pisa, Italy
Sergio Rajsbaum	Universidaó Nacional Autónoma de México, Mexico
Christian Scheideler	Paderborn University, Germany
Jukka Suomela	Aalto University, Finland
Sebastian Tixeuil	Sorbonne Université, France
Prudence Wong	University of Liverpool, UK

External Reviewers

Nada Almalki	University of Liverpool, UK
Sajjad Ghobadi	University of Perugia, Italy
Nikolaos Giachoudis	University of Crete, Greece
Alkis Kalavasis	National Technical University of Athens, Greece
Nikos Leonardos	National Technical University of Athens, Greece
Augusto Modanese	University of Aalto, Finland
Ling Ren	University of Illinois, Urbana-Champaign, USA
Jason Schoeters	University of Cambridge, UK
Gokarna Sharma	Kent State University, USA
Marianna Spyrakou	National Technical University of Athens, Greece

Contents

Segment Visibility for k-Transmitters

Yeganeh Bahoo$^{(\boxtimes)}$, Somnath Kundu, and Kody Manastyrski

Toronto Metropolitan University, Toronto, ON, Canada
{bahoo,somnath.kundu,kody.a.manastyrski}@torontomu.ca

Abstract. Given a simple polygon P and a segment e of P, we define the terms completely k-visible, strongly k-visible, and weakly k-visible with respect to P. Two points x and y are said to be k-visible when the line segment xy intersects the boundary of the polygon at most k times. If all of P is k-visible to all of e, then P is completely k-visible from e, but if the entirety of P is k-visible from a subset of e, then P is strongly k-visible from e. Conversely, if e can only see all of P through a set of disjoint intervals, then e is weakly visible. We propose two methods to determine whether P is completely, and strongly k-visible. We also develop an algorithm to calculate the weakly k-visible part of P from e in $O(kn^4)$ time complexity.

Keywords: Visibility · k-modem · k-transmitter · segment visibility · weak visibility · strong visibility · complete visibility

1 Introduction

Given a simple polygon P, two points p and q are said to be visible if the line segment $\overline{pq}$ does not cross the edges of P. The concept of visibility was first introduced by Klee [8]. He asked what number of stationary guards are necessary such that each point in P is at least visible for one guard, known as *art gallery* problem. Naturally, this provides applications in guarding and lighting.

When we allow for obstacles to intersect with the line between two points, we arrive at what is called k-visibility. The definition of k-visibility is formally stated as follows: given a polygon, and two points within the polygon, p and q, p is k-visible to q (and vice versa) when the line segment $\overline{pq}$ intersects with the boundary of P at most k times. This paradigm was first proposed in 1988 by Dean et al. [9], which considered infrared cameras which are capable of penetrating at most through one wall. This was further elaborated on by Mouawad and Shermer in 1994 [16]. In either work the value of k is 1, which means that visibility stops when a second intersection is encountered.

Subsequent work has dealt with values of k larger than 1, usually focusing on even values. The focus on even values follows from the intuition that odd values will inevitably result in visibility ending on the exterior of a polygon, which acts as a redundancy for the $k - 1$ even case immediately prior to a given odd case (i.e. the case of $k = 3$ would be redundancy for $k = 2$). This extends the

K. Georgiou and E. Kranakis (Eds.): ALGOWIN 2023, LNCS 14061, pp. 1–12, 2023.
https://doi.org/10.1007/978-3-031-48882-5_1

application of visibility to include optimal placement of transmitters which can penetrate obstacles such as walls, for example wifi routers and other wireless transmitters, and has implications and applications in robotics. Some of the previous works showed the sufficient/necessary number of guards needed to see all of a given polygon or plane with different polygonal obstacles [5, 7, 15]. While others developed algorithms to calculate the k-visible areas for a given point [2–4]. In the art gallery problem, guards may be stationary, either located at any point in the plane or polygon or located at vertices, or guards may be mobile. Mobile guards may move on an edges, a segment, or some paths. As such, edge or segment visibility was defined.

In wireless transmissions, segment visibility may be used for cases where a mobile transmitter is used to communicate with a group or area. An example of such would be swarms of drones operating autonomously in an environment with a single control drone. In such a case, an operator would only need to directly control one drone, but ensure that the drone remains within an area to maintain communications. An additional example is in maintaining, and maximizing, the area of communication blocking with radio jamming technologies attached to military vehicles. In this case, a vehicle with some wireless communication signal jamming or blocking technology is attached to a patrol in order to thwart attempts by hostile forces to either reconnoitre the patrol remotely, use improvised explosive devices to begin an ambush, or otherwise coordinate when taking hostile actions against the patrol. Examples of this technology have limited range, generally only enough to cover a convoy of vehicles, so significant thought must be given to where to place them.

Examples of work in segment visibility and patrolling guards are presented by different researchers [1, 13]. Some work on edge or segment visibility considered k-visibility in particular [6, 14]. On the topic of k-visibility, Biedl shows NP-hardness to discover the optimal placement of sliding k-transmitters, where the line of visibility is constrained to be orthogonal to the edge, and give upper and lower bounds for the number needed, both in orthogonal polygons [6]. Finally, Mahdavi et al. deal with the orthogonal art gallery problem for line segments which are also orthogonal. This problem considers polygons which have edges aligned parallel or perpendicular to either axis in 2D, and treats guards as sliding cameras on line segments, while considering k-visibility [14]. Mahdavi et al. show optimal placement of guards is NP-hard for $k = 2$, and provides an approximation algorithm.

There are three types of visibility that were studied for edge or segment visibility: strong, complete, and weak visibility. A given polygon P is called completely visible from a segment e if the entire P is visible to all of e. For strong visibility, a polygon P is considered strongly visible from e if at least one interval of the edge e can see all of the polygon P. The weak visibility polygon for a segment in P is constructed of all points in the plane which are visible to at least one point along the segment. The polygon P is called weakly visible with respect to a segment e if the weak visibility polygon of e includes P entirely. Note that weak visibility is the super set of strong visibility, and strong the super set of complete. The first examples of edge visibility originate in 1981 with Toussaint and Avis [1] under the context of normal visibility where they introduced the concept of complete, strong, and weak visibility. Avis and Toussaint provided an $O(n)$ algorithm for deciding whether the polygon P is completely, strongly, weakly visible from an edge or not under the context of *normal* visibility ($k = 0$). The weak visible area of P from a segment can be determined in $O(n \log n)$ [13]. We focus on line segments in this paper, since they are analogous to edges.

There is no direct work available on segment visibility, considering k-visibility. Considering k-visibility, Evans and Sember in 2010 [10] showed how to calculate the set of points which can see the entire P, called k-kernel. They showed that the complexity (number of vertices) of the $k - kernel$ is $O(n^2)$ for $k \leq 2$, and $O(n^4)$ for all other cases. This means that naively attempting to decide whether an edge is completely, strongly, or weakly visible to an edge by calculating the $k - kernel$ will require $O(n^2)$ at best, or $O(n^4)$ in the worse case in most case of k.

Considering k-visibility, given a simple polygon P and a segment e in P, we determine if P is completely and strongly from e. We also propose an algorithm to calculate the weakly visible polygon from e in P.

1.1 Organization of the Paper

We structure our forthcoming discussion as follows: Sect. 2 defines the terms relevant to our discussion. Section 3 discusses complete and strong visibility including details of previous methods and the relationship with the k-kernel. Section 4 outlines two methods which we combine to create our weak visibility solution. In Sect. 5 we discuss the difference between normal and k-visibility, and the difficulties present in k-visibility. Finally, in Sect. 6, we provide concluding remarks.

2 Preliminaries and Definitions

In this section we define the terms and context upon which our results are derived. We start with basic definitions, and build to more complex definitions as we proceed.

Let P be a simple polygon in 2D space, which means P has n unique vertices, with degree 2. An edge is a straight line segment connecting two vertices. As P is a simple polygon, no two edges intersect. We label the vertices of P in ascending clockwise order and label an edge by the two end vertices it connects.

Definition 1. *Given a simple polygon P, two points in the same plane of P, are k-visible to each other when the line connecting the two points intersects boundary of P with at most k points.*

Consider Fig. 1a. The shaded region is 2-visible to the point q, while the unshaded isn't.

Definition 2. *Given a simple polygon P, a point q is said to be weakly k-visible from a segment e when there exists a point p on e which is k-visible to q.*

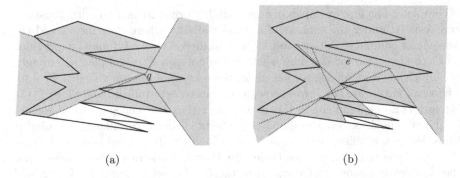

(a)   (b)

Fig. 1. (a) A sample polygon with the corresponding 2-visibility polygon relative to the point q. (b) A sample polygon with a line segment e, and the weak k-visible part of P for e where $k = 2$.

Definition 3. *The set of points in P which the entirety of P is k-visible from is called the $k - kernel$ of P.*

Definition 4. *A given polygon P is said to be completely k-visible from a given segment e when all of P is k-visible to all of the points along e. P is said to be strongly k-visible from e when there is a subset of e from which the entire P is k-visible. P is said to be weakly k-visible from e when for any point in P, q, there is a point along e that is k-visible from q.*

3   Complete Visibility and Strong Visibility

In this section we discuss the relationship between the k-kernel, complete, and strong k-visibility. We begin by laying out the theoretical groundwork of relationship on the k-kernel and the visibility categories.

The k-kernel is defined as the set of points $p_i \in P$ which are k-visible to all of P. For something to be completely k-visible it must exist within the k-kernel as shown by Evans and Sember [10].

Lemma 1. *The simple polygon P is strongly visible from a segment e for any value of k if and only if e intersects the k-kernel. If and only if e lies completely within the k-kernel, then the polygon P is completely k-visible from e.*

Proof. Any point in the k-kernel can see all of the polygon P for any arbitrary value of k. If e intersects, the k-kernel at any point s, it means that s on e can see the entire of P. This means that there is at least one point s on e that all of P is k-visible from. In other words, P is strongly visible from e. In other way, if P is strongly visible from e, then there is at least one point s on e that all of P is k-visible from. That means, there exists a point of e, which resides on the k-kernel. That means in this case e, intersects with k-kernel.

Similarly, if e lies completely within the k-kernel, then from all the point of e the polygon P is completely k-visible, i.e., P is completely visible from e. In other way, if P is completely visible from e, then from all the points of e entire P is k-visible. That means, there exists a point of e, which resides on the k-kernel. That means in this case e, intersects with k-kernel.

Having the above lemma, we describe our first approach to determine if P is completely or strongly visible from e.

3.1 $O(n^4)$-Time Algorithm

In this approach to determine if the polygon P is completely or strongly visible from e, we first calculate the k-kernel. We then check if e lies completely within the kernel or intersects with it. By Lemma 1, if e is completely in the k-kernel, then P is completely k-visible from e. If e intersects the k-kernel at some point, P is strongly visible for e. In this context we derive the following lemma:

Theorem 1. *Calculating if the polygon P is completely visible or strongly visible from a segment e can be done in $O(n^2 \log n + h)$, where h refers to the complexity of the k-kernel and can be $O(n^4)$.*

Proof. By Lemma 1 P is completely k-visible from e, if e lies completely in the k-kernel of P. P is strongly k-visible from e, if e intersects with k-kernel of P.

As such we fist calculate the k-kernel for P using the algorithm described by Evans and Sember [10]. This algorithm takes $O(n^2 \log n + h)$ where h refers to the complexity of the k-kernel. The complexity of the k-kernel is the count of vertices and is $O(n^2)$ when $k = 2$ and $O(n^4)$ for $k \geq 4$ [10].

Further, determining if e lies in the k-kernel can be done in $O(h)$ time. When combined, the overall time complexity is $O(n^2 \log n + h) + O(h) = O(n^2 \log n + h)$. It can be $O(n^4) + O(h) = O(n^4)$, if $h \leq n$.

For our purposes, the k-kernel may be encoded as one or more simple polygons. Encoding the k-kernel in this way, we may test if a segment is within the k-kernel by checking if both endpoints are in the k-kernel (or one polygon of the k-kernel), then perform intersection testing with the segment and the k-kernel. If either endpoint is outside of the k-kernel, or there exists an intersection not at the endpoints of e or a vertex of the k-kernl, then e is completely within the k-kernel. There are multiple algorithms for point location and intersection testing which run with time complexity less than $O(n^4)$ any of which would suffice.

3.2 $O(n^2 \log n)$-Time Algorithm

Next, we describe our proposed algorithm to reduce the time complexity of the decision version of the problem to $O(n^2 \log n)$ for determining if P is completely or strongly k-visible. To do so, first we bring the following definition from [10]:

Definition 5. v_k-*region:* *Given a polygon P a point x is said to be in the v_k-region of the vertex u of P, when any point in P on the ray $\vec{xu}$ is k-visible for x. In other words, x is in the v_k-region of the vertex u, if u is not an obstacle of k-visibility for x; see Fig. 2.*

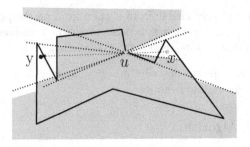

Fig. 2. The v_k-region of the vertex u is shaded as gray where $k = 2$. Point x is not in the v_2-region of u, as the point y on the ray xu is not 2-visible for x. Note that x is 2-visible for the vertex u.

The k-kernel of the polygon is constructed by calculating the intersection of the v_k-regions of all the vertices of the polygon P as shown in [10].

Lemma 2. *If and only if the intersection of the v_k-regions of all vertices of the simple polygon P covers the segment e, P is completely visible from e. If and only if the intersection of the v_k-regions of all vertices of the simple polygon P intersects with the segment e, P is strongly visible from e.*

Proof. The intersection of the v_k-regions of all vertices of P is a part of the k-kernel [10]. So using Lemma 1, the proof follows automatically.

Considering Lemma 2, we can calculate the v_k-region of each vertex of P, and find the intersection of each v_k-region with the segment e. If and only if the intersection of the v_k-regions of all vertices of P intersect with e, P is strongly visible from e. If and only if such intersection completely covers e, P is completely visible from e.

Lemma 3. *Any segment e crosses the boundary of the v_k-regions of the vertices of the simple polygon P, $O(n^2)$ times.*

Proof. Each v_k-region has $O(n)$ vertices. As such, a v_k-region may intersect a line segment $O(n)$ times. There exist n, v_k-regions, one per vertex in P. As a result, the number of intersections between v_k-regions and the line segment e is in the order of $O(n^2)$.

Lemma 4. *The intersections of a v_k-region with any line segment is a set of at most n disjoint intervals.*

Proof. Consider a bounding box enclosing the polygon P. The v_k-region for a vertex of P is a simple polygon with $O(n)$ vertices. The intersection of a simple polygon with n vertices and a given line segment is a set of n intervals. As such, the set of intersections of a v_k-region and a segment includes $O(n)$ intervals.

Consider a segment e and its intersection with the v_k-region of vertices v_1, $v_2, \ldots,$ and v_n of polygon P. Let the set of intersections of v_k-region of the vertex v_i of polygon P with e be shown as Int_{v_i}; see Fig. 3. Each point in Int_{v_i} has at most n disjoint elements; see Lemma 4. The intersection of the k-kernel with the segment e is the subset of intervals which intersect all n number of v_k-regions, called *depth-n* intervals.

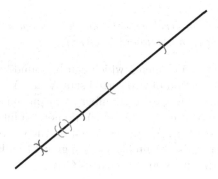

Fig. 3. The intersections of the v_k-regions with the segment e.

Lemma 5. *The simple polygon P is strongly k-visible for the segment e if there exist a depth-n interval on e.*

Proof. The intervals of the intersections of the v_k-region of a specific vertex do not self intersect. As such, an intersection of such intervals is between the intervals of different v-regions. As a result, a depth-n interval represents the interval which is the intersection of n different v_k-regions. If such an interval exists on e, e intersects with the k-kernel. Therefore, P is strongly visible from e by Lemma 1.

Given a set of n intervals which overlap, a depth-n interval is a subinterval which represents the intersection of n intervals.

Lemma 6. *The simple polygon P is completely k-visible for the segment e if e is a depth-n interval.*

Proof. By Lemma 1, e has to be completely inside the k-kernel in order for P to be completely visible from e. As shown in the proof of Lemma 5, a depth-n interval is the intersection of k-kernel with the line segment e. If e is completely in the depth-n interval, e is completely in the k-kernel. Then P is completely k-visible from e.

Lemma 7. *Given a v_k-region of a vertex of the polygon P, finding and sorting the intersection points of this v_k-region with a given line segment takes $O(n)$.*

Proof. The v_k-region has $O(n)$ vertices. As such finding the intersections of the v_k-region of a vertex with a given line segment takes $O(n)$. Sorting these intersection points can be done also in $O(n)$ as the v_k-region is a Jordan arc [11].

Based on Lemma 7, we can determine and sort the intersection points of each v_k-region with the line segment e in $O(n)$ time. There are n vertices. The sorted intersection points of v_k-regions of the vertices with e takes $O(n^2)$ time complexity.

Lemma 8. *The deepest interval with the depth n, for a set of $O(n^2)$ intervals on a given line segment e can be found in $O(n^2)$ time.*

Proof. Each Int_{v_i} has $O(n)$ elements which can be found7 and sorted in $O(n)$; see Lemma 7. The intersection of two sorted sets X and Y can be calculated in $O(|X| + |Y| + h)$ where h refers to the number of output intervals [18]. X and Y are both v_k-regions and of size $O(n)$. X and Y do not self intersect, which means h has the size of at most $O(n)$. As such, calculating the intersection of Int_{v_i} and Int_{v_j} takes $O(n)$. There exist n number of v_k-regions. Finding the intersections of all v_k-regions with the line segment e takes $O(n^2)$.

Theorem 2. *Determining if P is completely or strongly visible from a line segment e can be done in $O(n^2 \log n)$.*

Proof. We first find the v_k-region of each vertex. Calculating the v_k-region of each vertex takes $O(n \log n)$ [10]. There are n vertices. Calculating the v_k-region for all vertices takes $O(n^2 \log n)$. The intersection points of each v_k-region with the segment e can be calculated and sorted based on the location of the intersection on the segment e in $O(n)$ by Lemma 7. There are n number of v_k-regions, so this step takes $O(n^2)$ time complexity overall. When the intersection intervals are sorted for each v_k-region, the depth-n interval can be calculated in $O(n^2)$ by Lemma 8.

4   Weak Visibility

In this section we discuss weak k-visibility. Weak visibility is a loosened form of complete or strong visibility under our context. We still require that the entire polygon be visible, but not in the same contiguous interval(s). Instead, a disjoint set of intervals is acceptable to determine if a polygon P is weakly k-visible from an edge, or calculate the weakly k-visible polygon for e. Note that a contiguous interval is still able to be considered weakly visible.

Guibas et al. proposed a linear time algorithm to calculate the weakly 0-visible area from a given segment e [12]. Later, Suri and O'Rourke developed an algorithm with $O(n^4)$ time complexity [17]. We use these past findings to propose our algorithm. We have the following observation:

Observation 1. *From the definition of k-visibility, the area that is weakly k'-visible from e when $k' \leq k$ includes in the weakly k-visible area from e.*

Given a simple polygon P and a line segment e in P, the weakly k-visible area can be determine as follows:

1. Calculate the weakly 0-visible polygon from e, using Guibas et al. method [12].
2. Remove the parts of P that are weakly 0-visible from e.
3. Repeat the following process $k - 1$ times:
   (a) Find the weakly 0-visible region from e when there is a set of segments in the plane using Suri and O'Rourke's approach [17].
   (b) Remove the parts that are detected to be visible.

Suri and O'Rourke's method [17] requires an arrangement of line segments on a 2D plane. Their method deconstructs the polygon into triangles of visibility. This is doen by iterating over the vertices of the polygon, and checking if the endpoints of each edge are close to the current vertex than to a comparison vertex. In the case that an endpoint is closer, and the comparison vertex is to the right of the edge, then update the visibility region with the segment between the endpoint and the vertex, and add the triangle of the edge with the vertex to the output. In the case that the comparison vertex is to the left or in line with the edge, construct a segment with the comparison vertex as an endpoint and output the triangle between it, and the current vertex. Finally, if the comparison vertex is closer to an endpoint than the current vertex and to the left of the edge, output the triangle between the edge and the comparison vertex. The comparison vertices are iterated over the list of vertices in a nested for loop.

Repeating this process guarantees that all region that are weakly k-visible from the segment e are being reported. Step 1 takes $O(n)$ time complexity as P has n vertices. To calculate the time complexity of the rest of the algorithm we first bring the following lemmas.

Lemma 9. *Given a simple polygon P and a line segment e, the weakly visible polygon of e will intersect P at most $O(n)$ times.*

Proof. The weakly 0-visible polygon of P, P', has $O(n)$ number of vertices. Each edge of P' continues until it hits an edge of P or the bounding box. Hence, the number of intersections between P and P' is $O(n)$.

Lemma 10. *Given simple polygon P with n vertices and a line segment e, if the weakly 0-visible region of e be removed, a set of disjoint line segments (where they may intersects at their endpoints) with $O(2n)$ end points will remain in the plane.*

Proof. Based on the Lemma 9, the weakly visibility polygon has the size of $O(n)$. As such after removing, the weakly 0-visible part of the simple polygon P, it may create $O(n)$ new points as the end points of the remaining segments. There may exist $O(n)$ points that were the vertices of P which also were the end points of the line segments. This creates overall $O(n + n) = O(2n)$ vertices (end points of the line segments).

Based on Lemma 10, after removing, the weakly 0-visible part of the simple polygon P, the first repeat of the loop of the algorithm takes $O((2n)^4)$, as the overall number of end points of the segments is $2n$. To calculate the rest of the time complexity we bring the following definitions and lemma.

Consider a simple polygon $P \in \mathbb{R}^2$, with n number of vertices and a point $q \in \mathbb{R}^2$. The visibility region of any point $q \in \mathbb{R}^2$, with respect to any polygon $P \in \mathbb{R}^2$ is denoted by $V_q(P)$. We denote

$$P_0 = P,$$
$$P_1 = P_0 \backslash V_q(P),$$
$$P_2 = P_1 \backslash V_q(P_1),$$
$$\ldots \ldots$$
$$P_i = P_{i-1} \backslash V_q(P_{i-1}).$$

It is clear that $\forall i \in \mathbb{N}, P_i$ could be a disjointed polygon.

Lemma 11. *Given a simple polygon $P \in \mathbb{R}^2$, with n number of vertices and a point $q \in \mathbb{R}^2$, $\forall i \in \mathbb{N}, P_i$ has a maximum of $2n$ vertices.*

Proof. Consider a boundary line l of a visible region $V_q(P_{i-1})$ of q, which intersects with an edge e of the polygon P_{i-1} at point s. The line connecting the points q and s, touches at least one vertex of the polygon P_{i-1}. So all the vertices which are on line qs will be in $V_q(P_{i-1})$. So, when the region $V_q(P_{i-1})$ is removed from the polygon P_{i-1}, all the vertices which are on line qs are removed and all the lines that are connected with each of those points that many number of vertices will be added back to the polygon P_i. Now because we started with a simple polygon each vertex will have 2 connecting edges. But once an original vertex is removed then no new connected vertex is created. So $\forall i \in \mathbb{N}, P_i$, for each n number of vertices there can only be maximum extra 1 number of vertices $\forall i \in \mathbb{N}$. So considering only the n number of vertices there can be maximum of $2n$ vertices in P_i, $\forall i \in \mathbb{N}$.

Now we consider the edge e of P_{i-1}. If the part of edge e between point s and one of the end points of e is visible, then that end point will be removed, and in place of that another point (vertex) just next to s will appear on the new polygon P_i. So, in that case no extra vertex will be added to the polygon P_i. If the part of edge e between point s and any of the end point of e is not visible, then some mid part of the edge e will be removed. In that case there must be an edge between the edge e and the point s, which will be completely removed. For that removed edge two end points will be removed for the two extra vertices that will be created on edge e. So, for every edges in P_{i-1} there won't be any extra vertices that will appear in P_i.

Combining all of the cases, it follows that there can be $O(n)$ vertices in P_i, $\forall i \in \mathbb{N}$.

Lemma 11 shows that each repeat of the loop of our algorithm takes $O((2n)^4)$. This provide us the following theorem.

Theorem 3. *The weakly k-visible polygon for a segment in a given simple polygon P can be calculated in $O(kn^4)$.*

Proof. We can calculate the weakly k-visible polygon from e based on our proposed approach in this section. Calculating the weakly 0-visible polygon from e is a simple polygon P takes $O(n)$ time. After this step we have segments with $O(n)$ end points at each step. As a result, to calculate the weakly k-visible polygon from e at each repeat we need $O((n)^4)$. We repeat this process $k - 1$ times. As such the overall time complexity is $O(n + k(n)^4) = O(kn^4)$.

5   Comparison Between 0-Visibility vs k-Visibility

Before we conclude, it is worth outlining the difference in the nature of the problem of k-visibility and normal visibility (0-visibility). In normal visibility, we may rely on requirements such as the vertices of our segment being required to see the vertices of each edge of the polygon in order to consider that edge is normally visible to the given segment. However, since k-visibility allows obstacles to intercept the line between points, it is possible that obstacles may overlap to hide some region within the area between an edge and the given segment. Detecting these events is where the difficulty of k-visibility comes from for segment visibility. To compound this problem, we have to consider the difference in perspective that is brought on by moving the transmitter along the segment. It may be the case that neither endpoint of the segment can see the vertices of the edge, but somewhere in between the endpoints there is an interval that can see the vertices.

When we look at properties which may provide scaleability, we find that complexity is either the same as we have presented, or worse. For example, locations along the segment where the visibility polygon changes. So called *inflection points* along the segment happen at locations where the line between a point along the segment and two critical vertices (vertices which have both adjacent edges on one side of the line passing through a point on the segment. In this case the mentioned point). Discovering where on the segment these points exist is possible in $O(n^2)$ time, because we potentially have to consider every combination of non-adjacent vertices in the polygon. A method we had considered for making use of these inflection points involved calculating the visibility polygons at these points. This results an algorithm with $O(n^3 \log(n))$ time in the best case and $O(n^4 \log(n))$ for worst case, which clearly requires improvement.

Another possible approach is to bring methods from normal visibility into k-visibility. While this seems promising, trying it with Avis and Toussaint's work [1] does not provide with strong enough lemmas. This is because the ability of k-visibility to create disjointed visibility intervals on a single segment mean that the lemmas become quite restrictive, or mean that the lemmas cannot be adapted. This means that adapting Avis and Toussaint's method for k-visibility is not possible without adding in significant overhead from either attempting to maintain an internal k-convex path or detecting intersections with k edges.

6   Conclusion

In this paper we have presented an algorithm categorizing a segment to a category of visibility for a given polygon. We showed that the vertices of a polygon are necessary and sufficient for calculating weak visibility, and the relationship between the k-kernel and both strong and complete visibility. It remains to be seen if this methodology transfers to 3 dimensions.

References

1. Avis, D., Toussaint, G.T.: An optimal algorithm for determining the visibility of a polygon from an edge. IEEE Trans. Comput. C-**30**, 910–914 (1981)
2. Bahoo, Y., Bose, P., Durocher, S.: Watchtower for k-crossing visibility. In: CCCG (2019)
3. Bahoo, Y., Bose, P., Durocher, S., Shermer, T.C.: Computing the k-visibility region of a point in a polygon. Theory Comput. Syst. **64**, 1292–1306 (2020)
4. Bahoo, Y., Khorasani, A.M., Eskandari, M., Sorouri, M.: 2-modem pursuit-evasion problem. In: EuroCG (2013)
5. Biedl, T., et al.: Guarding orthogonal art galleries with sliding k-transmitters: hardness and approximation. Algorithmica **81**, 69–97 (2019)
6. Biedl, T., Mehrabi, S., Yu, Z.: Sliding k-transmitters: hardness and approximation. arXiv preprint arXiv:1607.07364 (2016)
7. Cannon, S., Fai, T.G., Iwerks, J., Leopold, U., Schmidt, C.: Combinatorics and complexity of guarding polygons with edge and point 2-transmitters. Comput. Geom. **68**, 89–100 (2018)
8. Chvátal, V.: A combinatorial theorem in plane geometry. J. Comb. Theory Seri. B **18**, 39–41 (1975)
9. Dean, J.A., Lingas, A., Sack, J.R.: Recognizing polygons, or how to spy. Visual Comput. **3**, 344–355 (1988)
10. Evans, W., Sember, J.: k-star-shaped polygons. In: CCCG, pp. 215–218 (2010)
11. Fung, K.Y., Nicholl, T.M., Tarjan, R.E., Van Wyk, C.J.: Simplified linear-time Jordan sorting and polygon clipping. Inf. Process. Lett. **35**(2), 85–92 (1990)
12. Guibas, L., Hershberger, J., Leven, D., Sharir, M., Tarjan, R.: Linear time algorithms for visibility and shortest path problems inside simple polygons. In: Proceedings of the Second Annual Symposium on Computational Geometry, pp. 1–13 (1986)
13. Lee, D., Lin, A.: Computing the visibility polygon from an edge. Comput. Vision Graph. Image Process. **34**, 1–19 (1986)
14. Mahdavi, S.S., Seddighin, S., Ghodsi, M.: Covering orthogonal polygons with sliding k-transmitters. Theor. Comput. Sci. **815**, 163–181 (2020)
15. Monroy, R.F., Vargas, A.R., Fucugauchi, J.U.: On modem illumination problems. In: XIII Encuentros de Geometría Computacional: Zaragoza, del 29 de junio al 1 de julio de 2009, pp. 9–19. Prensas Universitarias de Zaragoza (2009)
16. Mouawad, N., Shermer, T.: The superman problem. Visual Comput. **10**, 459–473 (1994)
17. Suri, S., O'Rourke, J.: Worst-case optimal algorithms for constructing visibility polygons with holes. In: Proceedings of the Second Annual Symposium on Computational Geometry, pp. 14–23 (1986)
18. Zomorodian, A., Edelsbrunner, H.: Fast software for box intersections. In: Proceedings of the Sixteenth Annual Symposium on Computational Geometry, pp. 129–138 (2000)

Conflict Resolution in Arbitrary Hypergraphs

Annalisa De Bonis[(✉)]

Dipartimento di Informatica, Università di Salerno, Fisciano, SA, Italy
adebonis@unisa.it

Abstract. We study conflict resolution algorithms in a multiple-access system in which there are n stations, and at any time only members of specified subsets of stations might need to transmit simultaneously on the same channel. This corresponds to saying that there is a hypergraph $\mathcal{F}$ such that stations $i_1, \ldots, i_k$ may attempt to transmit at the same time on the channel if and only if $i_1, \ldots, i_k$ are contained in some member of $\mathcal{F}$. To the best of our knowledge, in the literature there are no papers studying the conflict resolution problem under the conflict model considered in this paper. When $\mathcal{F}$ is the family of all possible subsets of up to a certain number d of stations in $\{1, \ldots, n\}$, our conflict model corresponds to the *classical* conflict model. In this paper, we focus on non-adaptive algorithms, that is, algorithms that schedule all transmissions in advance so that all stations transmit according to a predetermined protocol. It is well known that there exists a correspondence between superimposed codes and non-adaptive algorithms for conflict resolution in the classical conflict model [18]. In order to design our algorithms for the problem considered in the present paper, we introduce new combinatorial structures that generalize the notions of strongly selective families [4,5,18] and classical selectors [8], and are parameterized by the particular hypergraph at hand.

1 Introduction

Conflict resolution is the problem of solving conflicts among a set of stations that compete to transmit on a shared channel that, at each time, allows only a single station to successfully transmit its message. Commonly, this problem is studied under the assumption that conflicts may arise among any subset of up to a certain number d of stations. Here, we consider a multiple-access system in which there are n stations and at any time only specified subsets of stations might need to transmit simultaneously on the same channel. By denoting the n stations by integers $1, \ldots, n$, this corresponds to saying that there is a family (hypergraph) $\mathcal{F} = (V, E)$ of subsets of stations (hyperedges) such that stations $i_1, \ldots, i_k$ may attempt to transmit at the same time on the channel if and only if $\{i_1, \ldots, i_k\} \subseteq e$, for some $e \in E$. When $\mathcal{F}$ is the family of all possible subsets of up to a certain number d of stations in $\{1, \ldots, n\}$, our conflict model corresponds to the *classical* conflict model. We study conflict resolution algorithms, i.e., algorithms that schedule the transmissions of the n stations so that all *active* stations, i.e., all stations that need to send a message on the channel, transmit successfully. The parameter to be optimized is the number of time steps needed to allow all active stations to transmit successfully. The algorithms proposed in this paper find application in situations where fixed channels are assigned in a way such that conflicts may arise only among certain groups of nodes as a result of a preliminary channel assignment. Situations like these arise in wireless communication where an efficient use of the radium spectrum calls for channel assignments techniques to avoid interferences due to simultaneous transmissions that may affect the communication. In the first instance, interferences are reduced by appropriate channel allocations algorithms by leveraging on the physical characteristics of the system that critically interfere with radio propagation [15,17,20]. Another application of our algorithms is in distributed multi-user secret sharing [9,10,22]. In this problem, the goal is to enable the dealer to securely communicate with each user via storage nodes (servers). The dealer encodes secrets into several secret shares and distributes them to users so that only qualified groups of users belonging to a given collection are allowed to reconstruct the secrets. In a distributed storage scenario, the dealer behaves as a master node that loads the shares on the storage nodes and, in order to recover the secret, each user needs to access a certain subset of servers. On the other hand, each server might be loaded with secret shares that need to be distributed to several users. If a group of users that need to obtain their secret shares send a request to the same server simultaneously, then a conflict occurs on the secure channel toward that node. In such a scenario, a hyperedge of the input hypergraph corresponds to a subset of users that need to access a same node.

2   Related Work and Our Contribution

Our version of the conflict resolution problem consists in solving conflicts among groups of potentially active stations that correspond to the members of a given hypergraph. To the best of our knowledge, in the literature, there are no papers studying the conflict resolution problem under the conflict model considered herein. We investigate conflict resolution under two different channel models: the multiple-access channel with feedback where active stations receive feedback on whether their transmissions have been successful and the multiple-access channel without feedback where such feedback is not provided. We focus on non-adaptive conflict resolution algorithms, i.e., algorithms that schedule all transmissions in advance, and aim at optimizing the number of steps needed to solve conflicts among all active stations.

If the stations receive no feedback from the channel, then the conflict resolution algorithm must schedule transmissions in such a way that each active station transmits singly to the channel at some step, i.e., in such a way that no other active station is scheduled to transmit at that same step. In the classical conflict model, in which the set of conflicting stations might be any subset of up to d stations of the given set of n stations, the best upper and lower bounds on the minimum number of steps needed to solve conflicts non-adaptively follow from those on the length of classical superimposed codes [18], also known under the name of cover free families [13], disjunct codes [11], and strongly selective families [4,5], and therefore are $O(d^2 \log n)$ and $\Omega((d^2/\log d) \log n)$ [1,12,21], respectively.

In the multiple access model with feedback, an active station becomes *inactive* (i.e., stops transmitting) after it has transmitted successfully. As in the previous model, a non-adaptive conflict resolution algorithm should guarantee that, for each active station, there is a step at which it transmits singly. However, in this scenario, an active station transmits singly to the channel also when it is scheduled to transmit simultaneously with some of the other stations that were initially active, provided that these stations transmitted successfully in one of the previous steps. For the classical conflict model, Komlós and Greenberg [16] proved an $O\left(d \log \frac{n}{d}\right)$ upper bound on the number of steps needed to solve conflicts among any subset of up to d active stations. Interestingly, the above bound is tight with the lower bound $\Omega\left(d \log \frac{n}{d}\right)$, first proved by the author of [2], and subsequently and independently, in [3,5].

In order to design non-adaptive algorithms that solve conflicts under the hypothesis that conflicts arise among groups specified by the members of a given hypergraph, we introduce a new generalized version of strongly selective families [4,5] and selectors [8], the former to be applied to the multiple-access model without feedback, and the latter to the multiple-access model with feedback. The non-adaptive algorithm for the no-feedback case achieves an $O(d \log |E|)$ upper bound. If E is the set of all possible subsets of at most d stations, then our upper bound is the same as the above mentioned $O(d^2 \log n)$ upper bound holding in the classical conflict model. For the multiple-access system with feedback, we present a non-adaptive algorithm that uses $O(\min\{(\log d)(\log |E|) + d \log d, d \log n\})$ steps.

3   Notations and Terminology

For any positive integer m, we denote by $[m]$ the set of integers $\{1, \ldots, m\}$. Given a finite set V and a family E of subsets of V, a hypergraph is a pair $\mathcal{F} = (V, E)$. The elements of E will be called hyperedges. If all hyperedges of E have the same size d, then the hypergraph is said to be d-uniform. Unless specified differently, the set of vertices of the input hypergraph is $[n]$. Let $\mathcal{F} = ([n], E)$ be a d-uniform hypergraph. For any hyperedge $e \in E$, we will denote by S_e the d-tuple consisting of all integers in e, and given a matrix M with entries in $\{0, 1\}$, we will denote by $M[e]$ the submatrix of the columns of M with indices in S_e.

We remark that we assume that, given an input hypergraph $\mathcal{F} = ([n], E)$, every vertex of $[n]$ is contained in at least one hyperedge of E. If otherwise, one could remove the vertex from the set of vertices of the hypergraph without changing the groups of potentially active stations. As a consequence, for a given hypergraph $\mathcal{F} = ([n], E)$ we need only to specify its set of hyperedges E to designate both the input of the problem and the parameter of the related combinatorial tools.

4   The Multiple-Access Model

We consider a multiple-access system in which n stations have access to the channel and only specified subsets of the set of the stations are willing to transmit at the same time. We call these stations *active* stations. By denoting the n stations by integers $1, \ldots, n$, this corresponds to saying that there is a set E of hyperedges with vertices in $\{1, \ldots, n\}$ such that stations $i_1, \ldots, i_k$ may be active at the same time if and only if $\{i_1, \ldots, i_k\} \subseteq e$, for some $e \in E$.

If only one active station transmits to the channel, then this station succeeds to transmit its message, whereas if two or more stations transmit then all messages are lost. In this latter case, we say that a *conflict* occurs. We assume that time is divided into time slots and that transmissions occur during these time slots. We also assume that all stations have a global clock and that active stations start transmitting at the same time slot. A scheduling algorithm for such a multiple-access system is a protocol that schedules the transmissions of the n stations over a certain number t of time slots (*steps*) identified by integers $1, 2, \ldots, t$. A *conflict resolution* algorithm is a scheduling algorithm that schedules transmissions so that all active stations transmit successfully. In the present paper, we study conflict resolution algorithms under the conflict model described above and in the context of two different kinds of multiple-access channels we describe in the following section.

4.1   Multiple-Access Channels with Feedback and Without Feedback

In the model of multiple-access channel with feedback, whenever an active station transmits to the channel, it receives *feedback* from the channel on whether its transmission has been successful. As soon as an active station becomes aware that its message has been successfully transmitted, it becomes *inactive* and does not transmit in the following time slots, even though it is scheduled to transmit by the protocol. In other words, if a station succeeds to transmit its message in a certain time slot, it stops participating in the algorithm thereafter. Consequently, a *still* active station results in transmitting singly to a channel also in the case when it is scheduled to transmit simultaneously on the channel with stations that, though were originally active, have transmitted successfully in one of the previous time steps. For the particular case when E is the family of all sets of up to a certain number d of stations, our multiple-access model with feedback corresponds to the multiple-access model with feedback considered by Komlós and Greenberg in [16].

In the multiple-access model without feedback, stations receive no feedback from the channel, and therefore, even if a station has already transmitted with success in some time slot, it keeps transmitting in the next time slots if it is scheduled to do so. In this model, the conflict resolution algorithm must schedule transmissions in such a way that each active station transmits singly over the channel, i.e., no other active station is scheduled to transmit on the channel at that same time slot. For the particular case when E is the family of all sets of up to a certain number d of stations, our multiple-access model without feedback corresponds to the classical multiple-access model without feedback.

5   Non-adaptive Algorithms

In this paper, we focus on non-adaptive scheduling algorithms, that is, algorithms that schedule all transmissions in advance so that all stations transmit according to a predetermined protocol known to them from the very beginning. Please notice that, in the non-adaptive setting, the knowledge of the feedback cannot affect the schedule of transmissions but can only signal a station to become inactive after it has successfully transmitted. Indeed, the non-adaptive algorithm decides from the very beginning which stations are allowed to transmit in each time slot and possibly schedule a station s to transmit in a certain time slot i even though that station has already transmitted successfully in a previous time slot. As we have already remarked, in this eventuality the station s does not transmit in time slot i because it has become inactive in the meantime.

When the channel does not provide any feedback to the active stations, then a conflict resolution algorithm must ensure that for each active station j, there is a time slot in which j is the only active station scheduled to transmit at that time slot. Indeed, in this model, when active stations transmit with success they are not aware of that and keep transmitting at any time slot they are scheduled to do so.

A non-adaptive scheduling algorithm is represented by a $t \times n$ Boolean matrix where each column is associated with a distinct station and a station j is scheduled to transmit at step i if and only if entry (i, j) of the matrix is 1. In fact, station j really transmits at step i if and only if it is active and is scheduled to transmit at that step. We are interested in minimizing the number of time slots over which the conflict resolution algorithm schedules the transmissions. This number corresponds to the number of rows of the Boolean matrix associated with the algorithm.

6 E-Superimposed Codes and (E, m)-Selectors

In this section, we introduce the combinatorial structures we need to design our non-adaptive conflict resolution algorithms. The combinatorial structures in the following definition are employed in the design of our non-adaptive conflict resolution algorithm for the multiple access model without feedback.

Definition 1. *Let d and n be positive integers such that $d \leq n$. Given a d-uniform hypergraph $G = (V, E)$ with $V = [n]$, we say that a $t \times n$ matrix M with entries in $\{0, 1\}$ is an E-superimposed code of length t if, for any hyperedge $e \in E$, the submatrix $M[e]$ contains all the rows of the identity matrix I_d.*

One can see that if E consists of all subsets of $[n]$ of size d, the combinatorial structures in Definition 1 correspond to classical d-superimposed codes [18], or equivalently to disjunct codes and strongly selective family [4,5,11,13].

Obviously, the non-adaptive algorithms for multiple-access without feedback work also in the case when stations receive feedback from the channel. However, in order to improve on the number of steps in this latter case, we need to generalize the above definition as follows.

Definition 2. *Let m, d, and n be positive integers such that $m \leq d \leq n$. Given a d-uniform hypergraph $G = (V, E)$ with $V = [n]$, we say that a $t \times n$ matrix M with entries in $\{0, 1\}$ is an (E, m)-selector of size t if, for any hyperedge $e \in E$, the submatrix $M[e]$ contains at least m distinct rows of the identity matrix I_d.*

If E consists of all subsets of $[n]$ of size d then the selectors defined in Definition 2 correspond to the (d, m, n)-selectors introduced in [8]. Moreover, for $m = d$, an (E, m)-selector is indeed an E-superimposed code. Notice that we refer to the number of rows of an (E, m)-selector as its size, whereas we refer to the number of rows of an E-superimposed code as its length. The different terminology is only due to a convention in use when dealing with the classical versions of our combinatorial structures. The following theorem furnishes the upper bound we will exploit to derive our existential results.

Theorem 1. *Let d and n be positive integers with $2d \leq n$, and let $G = (V, E)$ be a d-uniform hypergraph with $V = [n]$. Moreover, let m be an integer such that $1 \leq m \leq d$. There exists an (E, m)-selector of size t with*

$$t < \frac{2ed}{d - m + 1} \left(1 + \ln \left(\binom{d-1}{d-m} \min \left\{ |E|, \left\lfloor \frac{n}{d} \right\rfloor \binom{n - \lfloor \frac{n}{d} \rfloor}{d-1} \right\} \right) \right),$$

where $e = 2.7182\ldots$ is the base of the natural logarithm.

Proof. We will show that (E, m)-selectors are covers of properly defined hypergraphs and exploit Lovász's well known upper bound on the maximum size of covers [19] to prove our upper bound on the size of (E, m)-selectors.

Given a hypergraph $\mathcal{H} = (X, \mathcal{R})$ with set of vertices X and set of hyperedges $\mathcal{R}$, a *cover* of $\mathcal{H}$ is a subset $T \subseteq X$ such that for any hyperedge $R \in \mathcal{R}$ we have $T \cap R \neq \emptyset$. The minimum size of a cover of $\mathcal{H}$ will be denoted by $\tau(\mathcal{H})$. Lovász [19] proved that

$$\tau(\mathcal{H}) < \frac{|X|}{\min_{R \in \mathcal{R}} |R|} (1 + \ln \Delta), \tag{1}$$

where $\Delta = \max_{x \in X} |\{R : R \in \mathcal{R} \text{ and } x \in R\}|$.

Let X be the set of all binary vectors $\mathbf{x} = (x_1, \ldots, x_n)$ of length n containing $\lfloor \frac{n}{d} \rfloor$ 1's. For any integer i, $1 \leq i \leq d$, let us denote by $\mathbf{a}_i$ the binary vector of length d having all components equal to zero but that in position i, that is, $\mathbf{a}_1 = (1, 0, \ldots, 0)$, $\mathbf{a}_2 = (0, 1, \ldots, 0)$, $\ldots$, $\mathbf{a}_d = (0, 0, \ldots, 1)$. For any $e \in E$ and for any binary vector $\mathbf{a} = (a_1, \ldots, a_d) \in \{\mathbf{a}_1, \ldots, \mathbf{a}_d\}$, let us define the set of binary vectors $R_{\mathbf{a}, e} = \{\mathbf{x} = (x_1, \ldots, x_n) \in X : x_{i_1} = a_1, \ldots, x_{i_d} = $

a_d, with $(i_1, \ldots, i_d) = S_e$}. For any set $A \subseteq \{a_1, \ldots, a_d\}$ of size r, $1 \leq r \leq d$, and any set S_e, for $e \in E$, let us define $R_{A,e} = \bigcup_{a \in A} R_{a,e}$. For any $b = 1, \ldots, d$, let us define the set of hyperedges $\mathcal{R}_b = \{R_{A,e} : A \subseteq \{a_1, \ldots, a_d\}, |A| = b$, and $e \in E\}$, and let us denote with $\mathcal{H}_b$ the hypergraph $\mathcal{H}_b = (X, \mathcal{R}_b)$. Let T be *any* cover of $\mathcal{H}_{d-m+1}$. Notice that the vertices of X are in fact binary vectors of length n, and therefore they can be regarded as the rows of an n-column binary matrix. With a little abuse of notation, we denote with T both the cover and its associated binary matrix. We claim that *any* cover T of $\mathcal{H}_{d-m+1}$ is an (E, m)-selector, that is, for any $e \in E$, the submatrix of d columns of T with indices in S_e contains at least m distinct rows of the identity matrix I_d. The proof is by contradiction. Suppose that there exists a hyperedge $e \in E$ such that the submatrix $T[e]$ of the columns of T with indices in $S_e = (i_1, \ldots, i_d)$ contains *at most* $m - 1$ distinct rows of I_d. Let such rows be $a_{j_1}, \ldots, a_{j_s}$, with $s \leq m - 1$, let A be *any* subset of $\{a_1, \ldots, a_k\} \setminus \{a_{j_1}, \ldots, a_{j_s}\}$ of cardinality $|A| = d - m + 1$, and let $R_{A,e}$ be the corresponding hyperedge of $\mathcal{H}_{d-m+1}$. By the contradiction hypothesis and by construction of $R_{A,e}$, we have that $T \cap R_{A,e} = \emptyset$, contradicting the fact that T is a cover for $\mathcal{H}_{d-m+1}$.

In the following, we exploit upper bound (1) to derive an upper bound on the minimum size of a cover of the hypergraph $\mathcal{H}_{d-m+1}$. By taking X as the set of all binary vectors $\mathbf{x} = (x_1, \ldots, x_n)$ of length n containing $\lfloor \frac{n}{d} \rfloor$ 1's, and replacing $\mathcal{H}$ with $\mathcal{H}_{d-m+1}$ and $\mathcal{R}$ with $\mathcal{R}_{d-m+1}$, in upper bound (1), we get the following upper bound on $\tau(\mathcal{H}_{d-m+1})$:

$$\tau(\mathcal{H}_{d-m+1}) < \frac{|X|}{\min_{R \in \mathcal{R}_{d-m+1}} |R|} (1 + \ln \Delta), \qquad (2)$$

where $\Delta = \max_{x \in X} |\{R : R \in \mathcal{R}_{d-m+1} \text{ and } x \in R\}|$.

In order to derive an upper bound on the minimum size of (E, m) selectors, we need only to evaluate the following quantities for the hypergraph $\mathcal{H}_{d-m+1}$:

$$|X|, \quad \min\{|R| : R \in \mathcal{R}_{d-m+1}\} \quad \text{and} \quad \Delta.$$

Since X is the set of all binary vectors of length n containing $\lfloor \frac{n}{d} \rfloor$ entries equal to 1, it holds that $|X| = \binom{n}{\lfloor \frac{n}{d} \rfloor}$. Moreover, each hyperedge $R_{A,e}$ of $\mathcal{H}_{d-m+1}$ is the union of $d - m + 1$ disjoint sets $R_{a,e}$, and therefore it has cardinality

$$|R_{A,e}| = (d - m + 1) \cdot |R_{a,e}| = (d - m + 1) \binom{n-d}{\lfloor \frac{n}{d} \rfloor - 1}.$$

To compute Δ, observe that each $\mathbf{x} \in X$ belongs to at most

$$\min \left\{ |E|, \binom{\lfloor \frac{n}{d} \rfloor}{1} \binom{n - \lfloor \frac{n}{d} \rfloor}{d - 1} \right\} \qquad (3)$$

distinct sets $R_{a,e}$'s. Indeed, $|E|$ is the number of distinct d-tuples S_e's. For a vector $\mathbf{a} = (a_1, \ldots, a_d)$, the actual number of d-tuples $S_e = (i_1, \ldots, i_d)$ for which $x_{i_1} = a_1, \ldots, x_{i_d} = a_d$ might be significantly smaller than the total number of d-tuples S_e's. However, this estimation turns out to be good enough to obtain the first term appearing in the min of the stated upper bound. On the other hand, if $|E|$ is close to $\binom{n}{d}$, then it is convenient to upper bound the number of distinct sets $R_{\mathbf{a},e}$'s containing a given vector $\mathbf{x}$ by $\binom{\lfloor \frac{n}{d} \rfloor}{1}\binom{n-\lfloor \frac{n}{d} \rfloor}{d-1}$ which is obtained by considering all possible subvectors of $\mathbf{x}$ of lenght d and with exactly one entry equal to 1.

Now observe that each $R_{\mathbf{a},e}$ belongs to $\binom{d-1}{d-m}$ distinct hyperedges $R_{A,e}$'s. Therefore, (3) implies that the maximum degree of vertices in $\mathcal{H}_{d-m+1}$ is

$$\Delta \le \binom{d-1}{d-m} \min\left\{|E|, \binom{\lfloor \frac{n}{d} \rfloor}{1}\binom{n-\lfloor \frac{n}{d} \rfloor}{d-1}\right\}. \tag{4}$$

Now, let us limit from above $\dfrac{|X|}{\min\{|R| : R \in \mathcal{R}_{d-m+1}\}} = \dfrac{\binom{n}{\lfloor \frac{n}{d} \rfloor}}{(d-m+1)\binom{n-d}{\lfloor \frac{n}{d} \rfloor - 1}}$. For $d \in$

$\{1,2\}$, it is $\dfrac{\binom{n}{\lfloor \frac{n}{d} \rfloor}}{\binom{n-d}{\lfloor \frac{n}{d} \rfloor - 1}} < 2d$, whereas for $d \ge 3$ it is

$$\frac{\binom{n}{\lfloor \frac{n}{d} \rfloor}}{\binom{n-d}{\lfloor \frac{n}{d} \rfloor - 1}} = \frac{n}{\lfloor \frac{n}{d} \rfloor} \cdot \frac{n-1}{n-\lfloor \frac{n}{d} \rfloor} \cdot \frac{n-2}{n-\lfloor \frac{n}{d} \rfloor - 1} \cdots \frac{n-d+1}{n-d-\lfloor \frac{n}{d} \rfloor + 2}.$$

It holds that

$$\frac{n-1}{n-\lfloor \frac{n}{d} \rfloor} \cdot \frac{n-2}{n-\lfloor \frac{n}{d} \rfloor - 1} \cdots \frac{n-d+1}{n-d-\lfloor \frac{n}{d} \rfloor + 2} \le \left(\frac{n-d+1}{n-d-\lfloor \frac{n}{d} \rfloor + 2}\right)^{d-1}$$

$$\le \left(\frac{n-d+1}{n-d-\frac{n}{d}+2}\right)^{d-1}$$

$$\le \left(\frac{d(n-d+1)}{d(n-d+1)-(n-d)}\right)^{d-1}$$

$$= \left(1 + \frac{n-d}{d(n-d+1)-(n-d)}\right)^{d-1}$$

$$\le \left(1 + \frac{1}{d-1}\right)^{d-1}$$

$$< e.$$

Moreover, it holds that $\frac{n}{\lfloor \frac{n}{d} \rfloor} < \frac{n}{\frac{n}{d}-1} = \frac{dn}{n-d} \le 2d$, with the last inequality being a consequence of the assumption $d \le n/2$.

The above inequalities imply

$$\frac{|X|}{\min\{|R| : R \in \mathcal{R}_{d-m+1}\}} \le \frac{2ed}{d-m-1}. \tag{5}$$

By plugging into (2) the upper bound (4) on Δ and the upper bound (5) on $\frac{|X|}{\min\{|R| : R \in \mathcal{R}_{d-m+1}\}}$, we obtain the upper bound in the statement of the theorem.

By setting $m = d$ in the upper bound of the above theorem, we get the following corollary.

Corollary 1. *Let d and n be positive integers with $2d \leq n$, and let $G = (V, E)$ be a d-uniform hypergraph with $V = [n]$. There exists an E-superimposed code of length t with*

$$t < 2ed \left(1 + \ln \left(\min \left\{ |E|, \left\lfloor \frac{n}{d} \right\rfloor \binom{n - \lfloor \frac{n}{d} \rfloor}{d - 1} \right\} \right) \right),$$

where $e = 2.7182...$ is the base of the natural logarithm.

7 A Non-adaptive Algorithm for the Multiple-Access Channel Without Feedback

We recall that, if the channel does not provide any feedback to the active stations, then a conflict resolution algorithm must ensure that for each active station j there is a time slot i in which j is scheduled to transmit singly over the channel. Let E be the set of hyperedges of stations that may be active at the same time, and let d be the maximum cardinality of any such subset. For any member e of E, we denote with $\hat{e}$ the subset of the $d - |e|$ smallest vertices in $[n] \setminus e$, and define E' as $E' = \{e \cup \hat{e} : \text{for } e \in E\}$. One can see that the scheduling algorithm associated with an E'-superimposed code is a conflict resolution algorithm for E under the no-feedback model. Indeed, let M be an E'-superimposed code, and suppose that $e \in E$ contains the subset of active users. Let $e' = e \cup \hat{e}$ be the hyperedge of E' associated with e. By Definition 2, the submatrix $M[e']$ formed by the columns of M with indices in e' contains all rows of the identity matrix I_d. This implies that for any $j \in e'$, there is a row index $i \in \{1, \ldots, t\}$ such that entry (i, j) of M is equal to 1, whereas for each $j' \in e' \setminus \{j\}$, entry (i, j') of M is equal to 0. In terms of the scheduling algorithm, this means that for each station $j \in e'$ there is a time slot in which j is scheduled to transmit whereas all other stations in e' are not allowed to transmit in that time slot. Since the subset of active stations e is contained in e', for each active station $j \in e$ there is a time slot in which j is the only active station that is scheduled to transmit in that time slot and, as a consequence, all active stations transmit successfully. Notice that there might exist more than one hyperedge of E associated with the same hyperedge of E', since for two distinct hyperedges e_1 and e_2 of E, it might be $e_1 \cup \hat{e}_1 = e_2 \cup \hat{e}_2$. However, this does not affect our conflict resolution algorithm. By Corollary 1, it follows that there exists an E'-superimposed code of with t rows, where

$$t < 2ed \left(1 + \ln \left(\min \left\{ |E'|, \left\lfloor \frac{n}{d} \right\rfloor \binom{n - \lfloor \frac{n}{d} \rfloor}{d - 1} \right\} \right) \right). \tag{6}$$

Since $|E'| \leq |E|$, the following theorem holds.

Theorem 2. *Let d and n be positive integers, with $2d \leq n$, and let E be a set of hyperedges on $[n]$ of size at most d. There exists a non-adaptive conflict resolution algorithm for a multiple-access channel without feedback that schedules the transmissions of n stations in such a way that, if the active stations are contained in a member of E, then all active stations transmit with success. The number of time slots t used by this algorithm is*

$$t < 2ed \left(1 + \ln \left(\min \left\{ |E|, \left\lfloor \frac{n}{d} \right\rfloor \binom{n - \lfloor \frac{n}{d} \rfloor}{d-1} \right\} \right) \right),$$

where $e = 2.7182...$ is the base of the natural logarithm.

8   A Non-adaptive Algorithm for the Multiple-Access Channel with Feedback

The algorithm for the multiple-access channel without feedback presented in the previous section, of course, can be used to solve conflicts also in the multiple-access model with feedback. In the present section, we give a non-adaptive algorithm for the multiple-access model with feedback that improves on the number of time slots used by the algorithm in the previous section. We exploit (E, m)-selectors and resort on the parameter m to tune these combinatorial tools so as to gradually reduce the number of active users. Let E be the set of hyperedges corresponding to the subsets of stations that may be active at the same time, and let d be the maximum cardinality of any hyperedge in E. Let E' be defined as $E' = \{e' = e \cup \hat{e} : \text{for } e \in E\}$, with $\hat{e}$ being the subset of the $d - |e|$ smallest vertices in $[n] \setminus e$. One can see that the scheduling algorithm associated with an (E', m)-selector is a scheduling algorithm for E, under the no-feedback model, that allows all but at most $d - m$ active stations to transmit successfully. Indeed, let M be an (E', m)-selector, and let us suppose that $e \in E$ contains the subset of active users. Let e' be the hyperedge of E' associated to e, i.e., $e' = e \cup \hat{e}$. By Definition 2, the submatrix $M[e']$ formed by the columns of M with indices in e' contains at least m rows of the identity matrix I_d. In other words, there are at least $h \geq m$ columns with indices in e', say $j_1, \ldots, j_h$ and h distinct row indices $i_1, \ldots, i_h$ such that, for each $r \in \{1, \ldots, h\}$, entry (i_r, j_r) of M is 1, whereas for each $j \in e' \setminus \{j_r\}$, entry (i_r, j) of M is equal to 0. In terms of the scheduling algorithm, this means that, for each station $j_r \in \{j_1, \ldots, j_h\}$, there is a time slot in which j_r is scheduled to transmit over the channel, whereas all other stations in e' are not allowed to transmit. Notice that if $|e| > d - h$, then the number of active stations that transmit with success is at least $|e \cap \{j_1, \ldots, j_h\}| \geq |e| - (d - h)$. If otherwise $|e| \leq d - h$, then it might be the case that none of $j_1, \ldots, j_h$ belong to e, and consequently, none of the active stations transmit singly on the channel. However, what matters here is that, in both cases, we are left with at most $d - h \leq d - m$ active stations that do not succeed to transmit.

Now, let us define the set of hyperedges E_i as follows:

$$E_i = \begin{cases} \{e' = e \cup \hat{e} : \text{for } e \in E\}, & \text{if } i = \lceil \log d \rceil. \\ \{e' : |e'| = 2^i \text{ and } e' \subseteq e \text{ for some } e \in E_{i+1}\}, & \text{for } i = 1, \ldots, \lceil \log d \rceil - 1, \end{cases}$$

and let M_i denote an $(E_i, 2^{i-1})$-selector of size t_i, for $i = 1, \ldots, \lceil \log d \rceil$. By replacing m with $2^{\lceil \log d \rceil - 1}$ in the discussion preceding the definition of E_i, we have that the scheduling algorithm associated with $M_{\lceil \log d \rceil}$ schedules transmissions so that at most $d - 2^{\lceil \log d \rceil - 1} \leq 2^{\lceil \log d \rceil - 1}$ active stations do not transmit successfully. Since each set of still potentially active stations is a subset of a member of $E_{\lceil \log d \rceil}$ and has size at most $2^{\lceil \log d \rceil - 1}$, it follows that each set of potentially active stations is a subset of a member of $E_{\lceil \log d \rceil - 1}$. Continuing in this way, by replacing d with 2^i and m with 2^{i-1}, for $i = \lceil \log d \rceil - 1, \ldots, 1$, in the discussion preceding the definition of E_i, we see that the scheduling algorithm associated with M_i schedules transmissions so that, if the subset of active stations is contained in some hyperedge $e' \in E_i$, then at most $2^i - 2^{i-1} = 2^{i-1}$ active stations do not transmit successfully and all these still active stations are contained in a member of E_{i-1}.

Now, let us consider the non-adaptive scheduling algorithm associated with the matrix obtained by concatenating matrices M_i's, one on the top of the other, starting from $i = \lceil \log d \rceil$ through $i = 1$, with the rows of M_i placed on the top of M_{i-1}, and then placing an all-one row at the bottom. Let $t_1, \ldots, t_{\lceil \log d \rceil}$ denote the number of rows of selectors $M_1, \ldots, M_{\lceil \log d \rceil}$. By the above argument, in the first $t_{\lceil \log d \rceil}$ time slots, at most $d - 2^{\lceil \log d \rceil - 1} \leq 2^{\lceil \log d \rceil - 1}$ active stations fail to transmit and will attempt to do that in the following time slots. After the first $t_{\lceil \log d \rceil}$ time slots, each set of potentially active stations is a subset of some hyperedge in $E_{\lceil \log d \rceil - 1}$. Therefore, the scheduling algorithm associated to $M_{\lceil \log d \rceil - 1}$ takes care of these stations and schedule transmissions in $t_{\lceil \log d \rceil - 1}$ time slots so that at most $2^{\lceil \log d \rceil - 2}$ are still active afterward. Each such subset of still potentially active stations is a subset of some member of $E_{\lceil \log d \rceil - 2}$. Continuing in this way, one can see that after time slots $t_{\lceil \log d \rceil} + t_{\lceil \log d \rceil - 1} + \cdots + t_i$, there are at most 2^{i-1} stations that are still attempting to transmit. For $i = 1$, this means that we are left with at most one active station that is still trying to transmit. This station transmits successfully in the last step (associated with the all-one row) when all stations are scheduled to transmit but, in fact, only the active station transmits.

The total number of time steps used by the algorithm is equal to

$$1 + \sum_{i=1}^{\lceil \log d \rceil} t_i. \tag{7}$$

Let $t(E_i, 2^{i-1})$ denote the minimum size of an $(E_i, 2^{i-1})$-selector, and assume that, for $i = 1, \ldots, \lceil \log d \rceil$, the number of rows t_i of M_i is equal to $t(E_i, 2^{i-1})$. By replacing d with 2^i and m with 2^{i-1} in the upper bound of Theorem 1, we get that $t(E_i, 2^{i-1})$ is smaller than

$$\frac{e 2^{i+1}}{2^i - 2^{i-1} + 1} \left(1 + \ln \left(\binom{2^i - 1}{2^{i-1}} \min \left\{ |E_i|, \left\lfloor \frac{n}{2^i} \right\rfloor \binom{n - \lfloor \frac{n}{2^i} \rfloor}{2^i - 1} \right\} \right) \right). \tag{8}$$

For the sake of simplicity, for $i = \lceil \log d \rceil$, we have replaced d with $2^{\lceil \log d \rceil}$ in the upper bound of Theorem 1 on $t(E_{\lceil \log d \rceil}, 2^{\lceil \log d \rceil - 1})$, so that we can use (8) for any $i = 1, \ldots, \lceil \log d \rceil$. This increases the upper bound on $t(E_{\lceil \log d \rceil}, 2^{\lceil \log d \rceil - 1})$ only by a constant factor smaller than 2.

Notice that, for $i = 1, \ldots, \lceil \log d \rceil$, the size of E_i is

$$|E_i| \leq \binom{2^{\lceil \log d \rceil}}{2^i} |E| \leq \binom{2^{\lceil \log d \rceil}}{2^{\lceil \log d \rceil - 1}} |E| \tag{9}$$

The first inequality is due to the fact that, for any member of $E_{\lceil \log d \rceil}$, there are at most $\binom{2^{\lceil \log d \rceil}}{2^i}$ pairwise distinct members of E_i. We have replaced $E_{\lceil \log d \rceil}$ with $|E|$ in that inequality, since $|E_{\lceil \log d \rceil}| \leq |E|$. The second inequality follows from taking the largest of the binomial coefficients $\binom{2^{\lceil \log d \rceil}}{2^i}$'s.

The upper bound (8) on $t(E_i, 2^{i-1})$, along with upper bound (9) on the cardinality of E_i, implies that $t(E_i, 2^{i-1})$ is smaller than

$$4e \left(1 + \ln \left(\binom{2^i - 1}{2^{i-1}} \min \left\{ \binom{2^{\lceil \log d \rceil}}{2^{\lceil \log d \rceil - 1}} |E|, \left\lfloor \frac{n}{2^i} \right\rfloor \binom{n - \lfloor \frac{n}{2^i} \rfloor}{2^i - 1} \right\} \right) \right). \tag{10}$$

The already mentioned upper bound $\binom{a}{b} \leq (ea/b)^b$ on the binomial coefficient implies the following three inequalities:

$$\binom{2^i - 1}{2^{i-1}} \leq \left(\frac{e(2^i - 1)}{2^{i-1}} \right)^{2^{i-1}} < (2e)^{2^{i-1}},$$

$$\binom{2^{\lceil \log d \rceil}}{2^{\lceil \log d \rceil - 1}} \leq (2e)^{2^{\lceil \log d \rceil - 1}} < (2e)^d,$$

$$\binom{n - \lfloor \frac{n}{2^i} \rfloor}{2^i - 1} \leq \left(\frac{e \left(n - \lfloor \frac{n}{2^i} \rfloor \right)}{2^i - 1} \right)^{2^i - 1} < \left(\frac{en}{2^i - 1} \right)^{2^i - 1}.$$

These three inequalities, along with upper bound (10), imply the following:

$$t(E_i, 2^{i-1}) < 4e \left(1 + \ln \left((2e)^{2^{i-1}} \min \left\{ (2e)^d |E|, \left\lfloor \frac{n}{2^i} \right\rfloor \left(\frac{en}{2^i - 1} \right)^{2^i - 1} \right\} \right) \right).$$

By (7) and by the above upper bound on $t(E_i, 2^{i-1})$, the number of rows of the matrix obtained by concatenating matrices M_i's and placing an all-one row at the bottom is smaller than

$$1 + \sum_{i=1}^{\lceil \log d \rceil} 4e \left(1 + \ln \left((2e)^{2^{i-1}} \min \left\{ (2e)^d |E|, \left\lfloor \frac{n}{2^i} \right\rfloor \left(\frac{en}{2^i - 1} \right)^{2^i - 1} \right\} \right) \right)$$

$$< 1 + \min \left\{ \sum_{i=1}^{\lceil \log d \rceil} 4e(1 + \ln \left((2e)^{2d} |E| \right)), \sum_{i=1}^{\lceil \log d \rceil} 4e \left(1 + \ln \left((2e)^d e^{2d-1} n^{2^i} \right) \right) \right\}.$$

The first summation in the above min is

$$\sum_{i=1}^{\lceil \log d \rceil} 4e(1 + \ln \left((2e)^{2d} |E| \right)) = O(d \log d + (\log d)(\log |E|)),$$

whereas the second summation is

$$\sum_{i=1}^{\lceil \log d \rceil} 4e \left(1 + \ln \left(2^d e^{3d-1} n^{2^i} \right) \right)$$

$$= 4e \sum_{i=1}^{\lceil \log d \rceil} \left(1 + \ln \left(2^d e^{3d-1} \right) \right) + 4e \ln n \sum_{i=1}^{\lceil \log d \rceil} 2^i$$

$$= 4e \lceil \log d \rceil \left(1 + \ln \left(2^d e^{3d-1} \right) \right) + 4e(\ln n) \left(2^{\lceil \log d \rceil + 1} - 2 \right)$$

$$< 4e \lceil \log d \rceil \left(1 + \ln \left(2^d e^{3d-1} \right) \right) + 4e(\ln n)(4d - 2)$$

$$= O(d \log n).$$

Therefore, the following theorem holds.

Theorem 3. *Let d and n be positive integers with $2d \leq n$, and let E be a hypergraph of hyperedges on $[n]$ of size at most d. There exists a non-adaptive conflict resolution algorithm for a multiple-access channel with feedback that schedules the transmissions of n stations in such a way that, if the active stations are contained in a member of E, then all active stations transmit with success. The number of time slots t used by this algorithm is*

$$t = O(\min\{(\log d)(\log |E|) + d \log d, d \log n\})$$

9 Conclusions and Future Work

In this paper we have studied the conflict resolution problem in communication systems where the subsets of possibly active stations are contained in the members of a given hypergraph. We have given non-adaptive conflict resolution algorithms for both the multiple-access model with feedback and the multiple-access model without feedback. Our results show that it is possible to improve on the time needed by the corresponding non-adaptive algorithms for the classical conflict model, working under the hypothesis that the subset of active stations might be any subset of up to a certain number d of stations. In particular, the algorithm for the no-feedback communication model uses $O(d \log |E|)$ time steps, and therefore, outperforms the $O(d^2 \log n)$ non-adaptive algorithm for the classical conflict model. When $|E|$ consists in all possible subsets of size at most d, it attains the same performance of the algorithm for the classical model. As far as it concerns the channel model with feedback, our non-adaptive algorithm achieves an $O(\min\{(\log d)(\log |E|) + d \log d, d \log n\})$ upper bound, and therefore, outperforms the best algorithm for the classical conflict model when $|E| < n^{\frac{d}{\log d}}$, and achieves the same performance otherwise. An interesting future research goal would be to see whether it is possible to design an $O(\log |E|)$ time non-adaptive algorithm for the multiple-access model with feedback, i.e., an algorithm that would compare to the algorithm for the classical conflict model in a way similar to the way our algorithm for the no-feedback channel compares with its counterpart for the classical conflict model.

Acknowledgments. This work was partially supported by project SERICS (PE00000014) under the NRRP MUR program funded by the EU - NGEU.

References

1. Alon, N., Asodi, V.: Learning a hidden subgraph. SIAM J. Discrete Math. **18**(4), 697–712 (2005)
2. Cohen, G.D.: Applications of coding theory to communication combinatorial problems. Discret. Math. **83**(2–3), 237–248 (1990)
3. Csűrös, M., Ruszinkó, M.: Single-user tracing and disjointly superimposed codes. IEEE Trans. Inf. Theory **51**(4), 1606–1611 (2005)
4. Chrobak, M., Gąsieniec, L., Rytter, W.: Fast broadcasting and gossiping in radio networks, fast broadcasting and gossiping in radio networks. J. Algorithms **43**(2), 177–189 (2002)
5. Clementi, A.E.F., Monti, A., Silvestri, R.: Selective families, superimposed codes, and broadcasting on unknown radio networks. In: Twelfth Annual ACM-SIAM Symposium on Discrete Algorithms, pp. 709–718 (2001)
6. De Bonis, A.: Theoretical computer science new selectors and locally thin families with applications to multi-access channels supporting simultaneous transmissions. Theor. Comput. Sci. **796**(3), 35–40 (2019)
7. De Bonis, A., Vaccaro, U.: A new kind of selectors and their applications to conflict resolution in wireless multichannels networks. In: Chrobak, M., Fernández Anta, A., Gąsieniec, L., Klasing, R. (eds.) ALGOSENSORS 2016. LNCS, vol. 10050, pp. 45–61. Springer, Cham (2017). https://doi.org/10.1007/978-3-319-53058-1_4
8. De Bonis, A., Gąsieniec, L., Vaccaro, U.: Optimal two-stage algorithms for group testing problems. SIAM J. Comput. **34**(5), 1253–1270 (2005)
9. De Prisco, R., De Santis, A., Palmieri, F.: Improved protocols for distributed secret sharing. IEEE Transactions on Dependable and Secure Computing (2022)
10. De Santis, A., Masucci, B.: New results on distributed secret sharing protocols. In: Proceedings of the 37th Annual IFIP WG 11.3 Conference on Data and Applications Security and Privacy - DBSec 2023, pp. 51–68 (2023)
11. Du, D.Z., Hwang, F.K.: Combinatorial Group Testing and Its Applications. World Scientific, River Edge (2000)
12. D'yachkov, A.G., Rykov, V.V.: A survey of superimposed code theory. Probl. Control Inform. Theory **12**, 229–242 (1983)
13. Erdös, P., Frankl, P., Füredi, Z.: Families of finite sets in which no set is covered by the union of r others. Israel J. Math. **51**, 79–89 (1985)
14. Gonen, M., Langberg, M., Sprintson, A.: Group testing on general set-systems. IEEE Trans. Inf. Theory **2022**, 874–879 (2022)
15. Idoudi, H., Mabrouk, O., Minet, P., et al.: Cluster-based scheduling for cognitive radio sensor networks. J Ambient Intell. Human Comput. **10**, 47–489 (2019)
16. Komlos, J., Greenberg, A.: An asymptotically fast non-adaptive algorithm for conflict resolution in multiple-access channels. IEEE Trans. Inf. Theory **31**(2), 302–306 (1985)
17. Liu, S., Lazos, L., Krunz, M.: Cluster-based control channel allocation in opportunistic cognitive radio networks. IEEE Trans. Mob. Comput. **11**(10), 1436–1449 (2012)
18. Kautz, W.H., Singleton, R.C.: Nonrandom binary superimposed codes. IEEE Trans. Inf. Theory **10**, 363–377 (1964)

19. Lovàsz, L.: On the ratio of optimal integral and fractional covers. Discrete Math. **13**, 383–390 (1975)
20. Mabrouk, O., Idoudi, H., Amdouni, I., Soua, R., Minet P., Saidane, L.: OTICOR: opportunistic time slot assignment in cognitive radio sensor networks. In: 2014 IEEE 28th International Conference on Advanced Information Networking and Applications, Victoria, BC, Canada, 2014, pp. 790–797 (2014)
21. Ruszinkó, M.: On the upper bound of the size of the r-cover-free families. J. Comb. Theory Ser. A **66**, 302–310 (1994)
22. Soleymani, M., Mahdavifar, H.: Distributed multi-user secret sharing. IEEE Trans. Inf. Theory **67**(1), 164–178 (2021)

Dispatching the Minimum Number of UAVs in Neighborhood IoT Networks

Sajjad Ghobadi[(✉)] [ID] and Cristina M. Pinotti[ID]

University of Perugia, Perugia, Italy
{sajjad.ghobadibabi,cristina.pinotti}@unipg.it

Abstract. In this paper, we investigate the problem of deploying the minimum number of Unmanned Aerial Vehicles (UAVs) and finding their flying tours to collect data of all Internet of Things (IoT) sensors. Since UAVs are powered by a battery that has a limited amount of energy, we assume that the total energy consumed in the flying tour of each UAV is bounded by a given budget B. We study this problem in a scenario with neighbourhoods where a UAV can collect the data of an IoT sensor if the Euclidean distance between the UAV and the IoT sensor is less than the wireless communication range of the IoT sensor. For the problem, we propose two approximation algorithms, where the second algorithm is a bicriteria approximation algorithm, i.e., it returns an approximate solution while the cost of obtained tours are violated by a factor of $1 + \epsilon$, for any $\epsilon > 0$.

Keywords: Unmanned aerial vehicles · Wireless sensor network · Approximation algorithms

1 Introduction

Unmanned Aerial Vehicles (UAVs), such as drones, are widely used in many applications such as search and rescue operations to localize a person in an area after natural disasters like earthquake [4], delivering goods to reduce delivery cost [3,23], target tracking [32], weather and field monitoring [5–7,24]. Search and rescue applications and field monitoring collect data from Internet of Things (IoT) devices on the ground as part of their final goal, whereas target tracking and delivering goods applications can opportunistically collect data from the IoT devices scattered in the operational area. Hence, all these applications face the problem of efficiently collecting data from IoT sensors, which are devices that can be queried and can transmit their sensed data with a limited radio communication range. In data collection, the UAVs act as mobile sinks. Specifically, UAVs reside at a fixed location, called *depot*, and at the occurrence of

---

This work was partially supported by "HALY-ID" project funded by the European Union's Horizon 2020 under grant agreement ICT-AGRI-FOOD no. 862665, no. 862671, and by MIPAAF.

K. Georgiou and E. Kranakis (Eds.): ALGOWIN 2023, LNCS 14061, pp. 28–40, 2023.
https://doi.org/10.1007/978-3-031-48882-5_3

a triggering event (like, an accident at a junction, an alarm, an earthquake) or periodically (like, in field-, weather-monitoring), they visit the IoT sensors in order to receive and collect the sensed data for further analysis. The UAVs are powered by batteries. Since they deplete energy for flying and for receiving data, the UAV paths must take into account the amount of energy available.

Usually, for the sake of simplicity, one assumes that the UAV is at the Zenith of the IoT when it establishes the UAV-IoT data communications. However, it is sufficient that the Euclidean distance between the IoT sensor and the UAV is no greater than the communication range of the sensor to be able to establish the data transfer. Namely, assuming that the IoT sensor is equipped with an omnidirectional antenna, the UAV can receive the data whenever it is in any point of the communication sphere, centered at the IoT sensor, with radius equal to the sensor communication range[1]. Assuming that the UAV flies at a fixed altitude ℓ, the data can be received by the UAV from any point of the disk obtained by intersecting the communication sphere with the plane at altitude ℓ. Such a disk will be called the collection region of the IoT sensor, or the IoT *neighborhood*.

In this paper, we present an optimization problem, called *Minimum r-Rooted UAV Deployment Problem with Neighborhoods* (MRDPN), described as follows. We assume that a set of IoT sensors are randomly deployed in a large IoT network. These sensors can monitor the area and collect the required information or data. Since the sensors may be sparsely deployed in the area and they have limited energy, sometimes it is unrealistic to assume that they can communicate with each other or directly transmit the data to the base station r, called *depot*. Then, an effective way of collecting data is to use a fleet of UAVs that fly at a fixed altitude and collect the data of all sensors and return to the depot. Specifically, the sensors will be partitioned in groups. Each group will be assigned to a single UAV which follows a path that starts and finishes at the depot, and intersects at least at one point of the neighborhood of each sensor in the group. Since UAVs are limited in terms of energy battery, we assume that we are given a budget B and the amount of consumed energy in the flying tour, including hovering cost, of every UAV cannot exceed this budget B. The objective of MRDPN is to determine the minimum number of UAVs to serve all the sensors and to find their flying tours originating from depot r whose energy cost is bounded by a given budget B.

1.1   Our Contributions

We define the *Minimum r-Rooted UAV Deployment Problem with Neighborhoods*. For the problem, we propose two approximation algorithms, where the second algorithm is a bicriteria approximation algorithm, that is, the budget B is violated within a limited amount. The approximation guarantees of the proposed algorithms depend on a parameter ϵ $(0 < \epsilon < 1)$, R_0^f that is the flying

---

[1] In this discussion, we assume that the communication radius of the IoT sensor is always smaller than or equal to the communication range of the UAV.

energy cost of a UAV for a distance R_0, A that is the maximum amount of required energy by a UAV to collect data of a sensor using its neighborhoods, and a given budget B.

The rest of this paper is organized as follows. Section 2 consists of the related works. Section 3 contains preliminaries and problem definition. Section 4 presents two approximation algorithms for the problem. Section 5 includes the conclusion and future research directions.

2   Related Work

Many papers have been proposed in the realm of data collection in IoT sensor networks with the help of drones. In this section, we review the previous works that are closely related to the present paper. We concentrate on works that aim to collect the data from all the IoT sensors of the deployed network, instead of just collecting the data from a subset of IoT sensors that maximizes a reward function [24]. The literature related to the collection of all the data sensed by IoTs with UAVs can be partitioned in two groups: without and with neighborhoods. When the data collection problem is studied without neighborhoods, the UAV must be in the sensor communication range, directly at the Zenith of the IoT in order to communicate with it. When the data collection problem is studied with neighborhoods, it is sufficient that the UAV intersects at least at one point the IoT neighborhood.

Silva and Caillouet [21] studied the problem of deploying a set of drones in a dynamic graph in order to connect each mobile sensor to a depot through drones. In their setting, for each time step t, the position of sensors change and the objective is to minimize the total traveled distance and energy consumption of drones while maintaining the connectivity of the sensors with the depot. They model the problem as a mixed integer linear program and experimentally evaluated the proposed approach. The disadvantage of the proposed approach is that it cannot be applied for large instances. So, in [22], the authors proposed a column generation model to improve the time complexity of the mixed integer linear program in [21].

Several papers have studied the minimum cycle cover problem without neighborhoods, where the objective is to find the minimum number of cycles/tours of length/cost at most B that cover all nodes. Arkin et al. [1] proposed a 6-approximation algorithm for the problem. Yu et al. [30] improved the previous results by proposing a 32/7-approximation algorithm. Recently, Xu et al. [27] presented an algorithm with an approximation factor of 4. The minimum cycle cover problem without neighborhoods is also studied in a case where each cycle/tour should contain a root node or a depot. Nagarajan and Ravi [19] proposed a 2-approximation algorithm for the problem on tree metrics. For the problem on general metrics, they also presented $\left(O(\log \frac{1}{\epsilon}), 1 + \epsilon\right)$-bicriteria approximation algorithm, for any $\epsilon > 0$, where the size of each cycle/tour is violated by a factor of $1 + \epsilon$. Li and Zhang [17] investigated the same problem with single and multiple depots. For the single depot, they gave an $O(\log \frac{B}{\mu})$-approximation algorithm, where μ is the minimum difference of any two different distances of sensors from the depot. For the multiple depots, they gave an $O(\log n)$-approximation algorithm. Khuller et al. [15] studied single gas station problem that is equivalent to the single-depot minimum cycle cover problem without neighborhoods. The authors proposed a greedy algorithm with an approximation factor of $O(\log n)$. Zhang et al. [31] also devised an algorithm with an approximation factor of $\frac{1.5}{1-\frac{A}{B}}$, where A is the maximum amount of required energy to charge or collect the data of any sensor of the network and B is the UAV energy budget.

Our work is also related to a slightly different problem, called the min-max cycle cover problem without neighborhoods. In such a problem, the number k of UAVs/cycles is given. The objective is to find a limited number of k cycles such that the length of the longest cycle among the k cycles is minimized and all sensors are covered [1]. Yu and Liu [29] proposed the best approximation algorithm with a factor of 5. For the min-max cycle cover problem without neighborhoods and with single-depot, that is, a version of the problem in which every cycle has to pass through a single depot, there is a $\frac{5}{2}$ approximation algorithm [11]. There are also some papers that studied multi-depot min-max cycle cover problem without neighborhoods [26, 28, 29]. The best known approximation algorithm for the multi-depot min-max cycle cover problem without neighborhoods is $5\frac{1}{3}$ [12].

Most closely related works to our work are the papers that consider to collect all the IoT data with the neighborhoods. Xu et al. [27] studied the minimum cycle cover problem with neighborhoods and present a $(27+108\gamma)$ OPT $-(67.2\gamma+12.5)$ approximation algorithm, where $\gamma = \frac{R_0^f}{B}$ and R_0^f is the flying time/cost of a UAV for a distance R_0 and B is the maximum flying time/cost allowed for each UAV.

Kim et al. [16] devised an approximation algorithm for the multi-depot min-max cycle cover problem with neighborhoods with the approximation factor of $(369 + \epsilon)$ OPT $+c \cdot \gamma$, where c is a positive constant. Deng et al. [8] investigated different variants of min-max cycle cover problem with neighborhoods and proposed different approximation algorithms. For the unrooted (without depot) and single depot case, they gave $(27 + \epsilon)$ OPT$_u$ $+108\gamma$ and 7.75 OPT$_r$ $+20.4\gamma$ approximation algorithms, where OPT$_u$ and OPT$_r$ are the optimal values of the respective problems. The authors also improved the result obtained in [16] for the min-max cycle cover problem with neighborhoods and multiple depots to $(28 + \epsilon)$ OPT$_m$ $+112\gamma$, where OPT$_m$ is the optimal value of the problem.

Our work is also related to the Travel Salesman Problem with Neighborhoods (TSPN) for which there are different approximation algorithms by considering different constraints, like the neighborhood regions are disjoint disks, identical disks, and non-overlapping disks. In a case that the disks can overlap with each other and the radius of the disks are the same, Dumitrescu and Mitchell [9] proposed a 7.62 approximation algorithm. Then, the authors improved the result to 6.75 [10].

To the best of our knowledge, we are the first to study the problem of finding the minimum number of UAVs for collecting the data of all IoT sensors with single depot and with neighborhoods.

Note that the approaches used in previous works in a scenario without neighborhoods cannot be directly applied to our problem. Moreover, the problem studied in [27] with neighborhoods does not consider any depot.

3   Preliminaries

In this section, we introduce network and data collection models and define our problem.

3.1   Network and Data Collection Models

Assume that a set of n homogeneous IoT ground sensors $V = \{v_1, v_2, \ldots, v_n\}$ and a depot $r = v_0$ are randomly deployed on an area to monitor some points or collect information from the area. Let, the coordinates of the sensors/vertices be $v_i = (x_i, y_i, 0)$ for $v_i \in V$ and the coordinates of the depot be $v_0 = (x_0, y_0, 0)$. We assume that for each pair of vertices v_i and v_j in $V \cup \{r\}$, with $i \neq j$ and $0 \leq i \leq n$, there exists an edge $e = (v_i, v_j)$ in E. The UAV fleet consists of homogeneous UAVs and fly at a fixed altitude ℓ. A UAV can collect the data of the sensor $v_i \in V$ if the Euclidean distance between the position of the UAV and the sensor v_i is within the given communication range R. Hence the neighborhood C_i of sensor v_i consists of the points at altitude ℓ at Euclidean distance at most R from v_i, i.e., $C_i = \{(x, y, \ell) : \sqrt{(x - x_i)^2 + (y - y_i)^2 + (\ell - 0)^2} \leq R\}$. More precisely, C_i is a disk with radius $R_0 = \sqrt{R^2 - \ell^2}$ centered at point (x_i, y_i, ℓ). We also denote with R_0^f the flying energy cost of a UAV for a distance R_0.

Given a UAV, we denote by $f(p_i, p_j)$ the flying energy cost, which is the amount of energy that UAV consumes to fly from one point p_i of the neighborhood C_i to any point p_j of the neighborhood C_j, following the shortest path. Moreover, let $h(v_i)$ be the hovering energy cost (data collection cost) that UAVs consume to collect the data of sensor v_i. Note that $h(v_0) = h(r) = 0^2$.

Specifically, assume that there is a UAV u placed at the depot r that collects, in this order, the data of sensors $v_1, v_2, \ldots, v_k$ and returns to the depot. Since we are in a scenario with neighborhoods, first UAV u flies to a point p_1 in C_1 where it can collect the data of sensor v_1, then it flies to a point p_2 in C_2 in order to collect the data of sensor v_2, and so on. Finally, the UAV u returns to the depot $r = v_0$ after collecting the data of sensor v_k at point $p_k \in C_k$. The flying tour T_u of the UAV u can be represented as $T_u = r \to p_1 \to \cdots \to p_k \to r$, where we refer to it as r-*rooted* flying tour of the UAV u. The total energy consumed by UAV u in its flying r-rooted tour T_u is

$$w(T_u) = \sum_{i=0}^{k} f(p_i, p_{i+1}) + \sum_{i=0}^{k} h(v_i),$$

where $p_0 = p_{k+1} = r$, and $h(r) = 0$. We assume that $h(p_i) = h(v_i)$ for any point $p_i \in C_i$, i.e., the data collection cost of a UAV for the sensor v_i is the same at any point $p_i \in C_i$. Instead, the energy cost to traverse the edge $e = (p_i, p_j)$ varies with the positions $p_i \in C_i$ and $p_j \in C_j$ from where the data of v_i and v_j are collected.

---

[2] We consider negligible the energy spent for the takeoff and landing at v_0.

3.2   Problem Definition

We now define the *Minimum r-Rooted UAV Deployment Problem with Neighborhoods* (MRDPN) using the network model and data collection model. Given an IoT network $G = (V \cup \{r\}; E; f : E \rightarrow \mathbb{R}^{\geq 0}; h : V \rightarrow \mathbb{R}^{\geq 0})$, a budget B, and the neighborhood C_i for each sensor $v_i \in V$. We assume that the edge function f satisfies the triangle inequality. Here, the objective is to determine the minimum number of UAVs and find their r-rooted flying tours to collect the data of all sensors, such that the amount of energy consumed by each UAV in its r-rooted flying tour is at most B. The MRDPN is NP-hard, since it can be viewed as the minimum cycle cover problem with a single depot when the neighborhood radius R_0 and the hovering cost of each sensor is set to 0 [17].

4   Approximation Algorithms

In this section, we propose two approximation algorithms for the MRDPN which use an auxiliary graph G' which associates the hovering vertex cost to the cost of the edges. Specifically, given a complete graph $G = (V \cup \{r\}; E; f : E \rightarrow \mathbb{R}^{\geq 0}; h : V \rightarrow \mathbb{R}^{\geq 0})$, it can be transformed into another graph $G' = (V \cup \{r\}; E; f' : E \rightarrow \mathbb{R}^{\geq 0})$ with $f'(p_i, p_j) = f(p_i, p_j) + \frac{h(v_i) + h(v_j)}{2}$ for any $e = (v_i, v_j) \in E$, where $p_i \in C_i$ and $p_j \in C_j$. Then, the optimal solutions to the MRDPN in G and G' are equivalent [31].

Recall that the energy cost to traverse the edge $e = (v_i, v_j)$ depends on the neighborhood positions from where the data of sensors v_i and v_j are collected. For every sensor $v_i \in V$, we define d_{v_i} as the maximum energy cost to traverse the edge (r, v_i), which corresponds to the energy consumed to collect the data of v_i from the point $\bar{p}_i$ which is the point of C_i furthest from r. Let $d(r, v)$ be the Euclidean distance between the depot r and any sensor v. Since for any sensor v_i, $d(r, v_i) - d(r, \bar{p}_i)$ is equal to R_0, it holds: $d_{v_i} = f'(r, (x_i, y_i, \ell)) + R_0^f$, where $f'(r, (x_i, y_i, \ell)) = f(r, (x_i, y_i, \ell)) + \frac{h(v_i)}{2}$, (x_i, y_i, ℓ) is the projection of v_i at altitude ℓ, and $h(v_i)$ is the hovering cost of a UAV for sensor v_i.

4.1   The ApproxTSPN Algorithm

We now propose the first approximation algorithm for the MRDPN, called *Approximation using the TSPN* (ApproxTSPN), that is inspired by [31]. Let

$$A = \max_{v_i \in V} \begin{cases} h(v_i) & \text{if } \| r - (x_i, y_i, \ell) \|_2 \leq R_0 \\ 2 \cdot d_{v_i} & \text{otherwise} \end{cases}$$

be the maximum amount of energy consumed by a UAV to collect the data of any sensor using its neighborhoods. We also assume that B is large enough, i.e., $B \geq A$. The proposed approximation algorithm works as follows. It first transforms the graph $G = (V \cup \{r\}; E; f : E \rightarrow \mathbb{R}^{\geq 0}; h : V \rightarrow \mathbb{R}^{\geq 0})$ into a graph $G' = (V \cup \{r\}; E; f' : E \rightarrow \mathbb{R}^{\geq 0})$. It then uses an approximation algorithm for the Traveling Salesman Problem with Neighborhoods (TSPN) [10] to find a tour that visits all sensors V in G'. Finally, it splits the tour into several r-rooted tours with energy cost at most B. The number of obtained r-rooted tours corresponds to the number of UAVs that collect the data of all sensors. The pseudocode of ApproxTSPN is given in Algorithm 1.

Algorithm 1. The ApproxTSPN Algorithm

1: **Input:** A complete graph $G = (V \cup \{r\}; E; f : E \to \mathbb{R}^{\geq 0}; h : V \to \mathbb{R}^{\geq 0})$, a budget B, and the neighborhood C_i for each sensor $v_i \in V$.
2: **Output:** A set T of r-rooted tours collecting data of all sensors in V, such that the energy cost of each r-rooted tour in T is at most B.
3: Construct a graph $G' = (V \cup \{r\}; E; f' : E \to \mathbb{R}^{\geq 0})$ from G.
4: Find a tour $C : r \to p_1 \to p_2 \to \cdots \to p_n \to r$ using an approximation algorithm for the TSPN [10].
5: Set $i \leftarrow 1$, $j \leftarrow 1$, and $i \leftarrow k$;
6: **while** $j \leq n$ **do**
7:    $T_k : r \to p_i \to \cdots \to p_j \to r$;
8:    **if** $w(T_k) \leq B$ **then**
9:       **if** $j == n$ **then**
10:          $T_k : r \to p_i \to \cdots \to p_n \to r$;
11:       **else**
12:          $j \leftarrow j + 1$;
13:       **end if**
14:    **else**
15:       $j \leftarrow j - 1$;
16:       $T_k : r \to p_i \to \cdots \to p_j \to r$;
17:       $k \leftarrow k + 1$;
18:       $j \leftarrow j + 1$;
19:       $i \leftarrow j$;
20:    **end if**
21: **end while**
22: **return** the set $T = \{T_1, \cdots, T_k\}$.

Let OPT be the optimal number of r-rooted tours for the MRDPN that covers all sensors. We then get the following theorem.

Theorem 1. *The approximation ratio of algorithm* ApproxTSPN *is* $\frac{6.75 + 20.4 R_0^f}{1 - \frac{A}{B}} + 1$.

Proof. Let $T^* = \{T_1^*, T_2^*, \ldots, T_{OPT}^*\}$ be the optimal solution to the MRDPN and $|T^*| = $ OPT. We also denote with C^* the optimal shortest tour for the TSPN that covers all sensors V. Now consider any pair of consecutive tours T_i^* and T_{i+1}^* in T^*. Let e_i and e_{i+1} be edges in T_i^* and T_{i+1}^* with one endpoints being the depot r. We remove e_i and e_{i+1} and add another edge e that connects T_i^* and T_{i+1}^* through the edge e, call this new tour $C_{T_{i,i+1}^*}$. Note that based on the triangle inequality, we have $w(e) \leq w(e_i) + w(e_{i+1})$. Thus, $w(C_{T_{i,i+1}^*}) \leq$

$w(T_i^*) + w(T_{i+1}^*)$. Repeating this process for all consecutive pairs of tours T_i^* and T_{i+1}^* for $i \in \{1, \ldots, \text{OPT}\}$, where $T_{\text{OPT}+1}^* = T_1^*$, we can construct a tour C_{T^*} that visits all sensors V. We then have

$$w(C^*) \le w(C_{T^*}) \le \sum_{i=1}^{\text{OPT}} w(T_i^*) \le \text{OPT} \cdot B.$$

Therefore, we get a lower bound on OPT

$$\text{OPT} \ge \lceil \frac{w(C^*)}{B} \rceil. \tag{1}$$

Note that OPT is an integer value.

Now let T be a set of r-rooted tours obtained by Algorithm 1. We show an upper bound on the size of T. Since Algorithm 1 uses an approximation algorithm for the TSPN [10] to find a tour C that visits all sensors V, we have

$$w(C) \le 6.75w(C^*) + 20.4R_0^f.$$

Note that the cost of each r-rooted tour $\tau \in T$ obtained by Algorithm 1 is at most B, i.e., $w(\tau = r \to p_j \to p_{j+1} \to \cdots \to p_k \to r) \le B$. Now consider an r-rooted tour τ' that is obtained by adding a vertex p_{k+1} to τ, i.e., $\tau' = r \to p_j \to p_{j+1} \to \cdots \to p_k \to p_{k+1} \to r$, and $w(\tau') > B$.

Since, for any vertex $p \in C$, $w(r \to p) = w(p \to r) \le \frac{A}{2}$. Therefore, we obtain

$$w(p_j \to p_{j+1} \to \cdots \to p_k \to p_{k+1}) \ge B - A.$$

We thus get an upper bound on the size of T

$$|T| \le \lceil \frac{w(C)}{B-A} \rceil \le \lceil \frac{6.75w(C^*) + 20.4R_0^f}{B-A} \rceil \le \frac{6.75w(C^*) + 20.4R_0^f}{B-A} + 1. \tag{2}$$

Using Eqs. 1 and 2, the approximation ratio of ApproxTSPN is

$$\frac{|T|}{\text{OPT}} \le \frac{\frac{6.75w(C^*)+20.4R_0^f}{B-A}+1}{\lceil \frac{w(C^*)}{B} \rceil} \le \frac{\frac{6.75w(C^*)+20.4R_0^f}{B-A}}{\frac{w(C^*)}{B}} + 1 \le \frac{6.75 + 20.4R_0^f}{1 - \frac{A}{B}} + 1.$$

□

We finally analyze the time complexity of ApproxTSPN. Step 3 takes $O(n^2)$ time. The time complexity of Step 4 depends on computing a $(1+\eta)$-approximation of the optimal TSP tour of at most n points in $\mathbb{R}^2$, for $\eta > 0$ [2,18,20], that is used in the approximation algorithm for the TSPN. Assuming $\eta \le 0.001$, the cost of obtained tour in Step 4 is $w(C) \le 6.75w(C^*) + 20.4R_0^f$ (using the PTAS for the center points of sensors). Finally, Step 5 takes $O(n)$ time. Therefore, the time complexity of algorithm ApproxTSPN depends on Step 4 that is exponential in $\frac{1}{\eta}$. Note that by using different approximation algorithms for finding an approximate TSP tour (like the algorithm of Christofides) in Step 4, we get different approximation ratio and running time for ApproxTSPN.

4.2   The ApproxMPN Algorithm

We now present another approximation algorithm for the MRDPN, called *Approximation using the Minimum number of Paths with Neighborhoods* (ApproxMPN). Our approach is inspired by [19]. We again assume that $B \geq 2 \cdot \max_{v_i \in V} d_{v_i} = A$.

The main idea behind the proposed algorithm is to partition the sensors based on energy costs from the depot and for each partition solve a subroutine, the Minimum UAV Deployment Problem with Neighborhoods [27], this problem is the same as the MRDPN but without any depot, to get a set of paths covering all sensors in the partition. Then, turn these paths into r-rooted tours by adding two edges from the depot r to the endpoints of each path.

For any $\epsilon > 0$, let $t = \lceil \log \frac{1}{\epsilon} \rceil$ be the parameter determining the number of partitions of sensors V, according to their energy costs from the depot r. The pseudocode of ApproxMPN is given in Algorithm 2. Note that in our algorithm, we use the approximation algorithm proposed for the Minimum UAV Deployment Problem with Neighborhoods in [27]. This approximation algorithm finds a set of tours of cost at most B such that each edge in every tour is visited twice. Here, we use this algorithm to find a set of paths of cost at most B. Thus, improving the approximation factor of the proposed algorithm by a factor of 2.

We first show that the cost of r-rooted tours obtained by algorithm ApproxMPN is bounded by $(1 + \epsilon) \cdot B$.

Lemma 1. *Each r-rooted tour produced by algorithm ApproxMPN has cost at most $(1 + \epsilon) \cdot B$.*

Proof. Consider the set of sensors V_0 ($j = 0$). Since the cost of each path obtained in Step 6 of Algorithm 2 is at most $\epsilon \cdot \frac{B}{2}$ and the cost of each edge added in Step 7 is at most $\frac{B}{2}$, so the cost of each r-rooted tour is at most $\epsilon \cdot \frac{B}{2} + 2 \cdot \frac{B}{2} \leq (1 + \epsilon) \cdot B$.

Now consider any set of sensors V_j ($1 \leq j \leq t$). Each path $\sigma \in P_j$ has cost at most $2^{j-1} \epsilon B$, according to the Step 6 of Algorithm 2. Moreover, every vertex in the neighborhoods of sensors in V_j has cost at most $(1 - 2^{j-1} \epsilon) \cdot \frac{B}{2}$ from the depot r. So, the cost of each r-rooted tour is at most $2^{j-1} \epsilon B + 2 \left[(1 - 2^{j-1} \epsilon) \frac{B}{2} \right] = B$. This concludes the proof. □

Let OPT denotes the optimal number of r-rooted tours for the MRDPN. We then get the following lemma.

Lemma 2. *For each $j = 0, \ldots, t$, the optimal number of paths obtained by the Minimum UAV Deployment Problem with Neighborhoods is at most $\left(2 + \frac{8R_0^f}{\epsilon B}\right) \cdot$ OPT.*

Proof. Fix any $j \in \{0, \ldots, t\}$ and let T^* be the optimal solution to the MRDPN that covers all the sensors. Now consider any r-rooted tour $\tau \in T^*$ and let τ_j be a path in τ that visits some of the sensors in V_j (this path can be obtained easily). Note that the cost of path τ_j is at most $B - 2 \left[(1 - 2^j \epsilon) \frac{B}{2} - 2R_0^f \right] = 2^j \epsilon B + 4R_0^f$ because every vertex in the neighborhoods of sensors in V_j has cost at least $(1 - 2^j \epsilon) \frac{B}{2} - 2R_0^f$ from the depot r.

Algorithm 2. The ApproxMPN Algorithm

1: **Input:** A complete graph $G = (V \cup \{r\}; E; f : E \to \mathbb{R}^{\geq 0}; h : V \to \mathbb{R}^{\geq 0})$, a budget B, and the neighborhood C_i for each sensor $v_i \in V$.

2: **Output:** A set of r-rooted tours collecting the data of all sensors in V, such that the energy cost of each r-rooted tour is at most B.

3: Construct a graph $G' = (V \cup \{r\}; E; f' : E \to \mathbb{R}^{\geq 0})$ from G.

4: Partition V into sets $V_0, V_1, \ldots, V_t$ (where $t = \lceil \log \frac{1}{\epsilon} \rceil$) as follows:

$$
\begin{cases}
V_0 = \left\{ v : (1 - \epsilon) \cdot \frac{B}{2} < d_v \leq \frac{B}{2} \right\} & \text{if } j = 0 \\
V_j = \left\{ v : (1 - 2^j \epsilon) \cdot \frac{B}{2} < d_v \leq (1 - 2^{j-1} \epsilon) \cdot \frac{B}{2} \right\} & \text{if } 1 \leq j \leq t - 1 \\
V_t = \left\{ v : 0 \leq d_v \leq (1 - 2^{t-1} \epsilon) \cdot \frac{B}{2} \right\} & \text{if } j = t
\end{cases}
$$

5: **for** $j = 0, \ldots, t$ **do**

6:   Run the approximation algorithm for the Minimum UAV Deployment Problem with Neighborhoods [27] with budget $2^{j-1} \epsilon B$. Let P_j be the set of paths obtained.

7:   For each path in P_j, add two edges from the depot r to the endpoints of the path in order to convert the path into an r-rooted tour.

8: **end for**

9: **return** all the r-rooted obtained tours.

Now we show that τ_j can be split into at most $2 + \frac{8R_0^f}{\epsilon B}$ paths of cost at most $2^{j-1} \epsilon B$. Note that the number of distinct paths of cost at most $2^{j-1} \epsilon B$ in τ_j is

$$
\frac{2^j \epsilon B + 4R_0^f}{2^{j-1} \epsilon B} \leq 2 + \frac{8R_0^f}{\epsilon B}.
$$

Since each optimal r-rooted tour $\tau \in T^*$ can be split into at most $2 + \frac{8R_0^f}{\epsilon B}$ paths, we get a set $\mathcal{A}$ of at most $\left(2 + \frac{8R_0^f}{\epsilon B} \right) \cdot \text{OPT}$ paths with cost bound $2^{j-1} \epsilon B$ that covers all sensors in V_j. Thus, set $\mathcal{A}$ is a feasible solution to the Minimum UAV Deployment Problem with Neighborhoods [27]. □

We now prove the approximation guarantee of algorithm ApproxMPN.

Theorem 2. *Let $0 < \epsilon < 1$. Algorithm* ApproxMPN *is a* $\left((\lceil \log \frac{1}{\epsilon} \rceil + 1)\left((2 + \frac{8\gamma}{\epsilon})(13.5 + 54\gamma) \text{OPT} - (33.6\gamma + 6.25) \right), 1 + \epsilon \right)$-*bicriteria approximation algorithm, where* $\gamma = \frac{R_0^f}{B}$, *to* MRDPN.

Proof. Lemma 1 guarantees that the cost of each r-rooted tour produced by algorithm ApproxMPN is at most $(1 + \epsilon) \cdot B$. Using Lemma 2 and an approximation algorithm for the Minimum UAV Deployment Problem with Neighborhoods [27], for all $j \in 0, \ldots, t$, we get $|P_j| \leq \left(2 + \frac{8\gamma}{\epsilon} \right)(13.5 + 54\gamma) \text{OPT} - (33.6\gamma + 6.25)$, where $\gamma = \frac{R_0^f}{B}$. Since the sensors are partitioned into $t + 1$ parts, thus the proposed algorithm is an approximation algorithm that achieves a multiplicative factor of $(\lceil \log \frac{1}{\epsilon} \rceil + 1)(2 + \frac{8\gamma}{\epsilon})(13.5 + 54\gamma)$ minus a function $(\lceil \log \frac{1}{\epsilon} \rceil + 1)(33.6\gamma + 6.25)$. □

The time complexity of algorithm ApproxMPN is dominated by the running time of the approximation algorithm for the Minimum UAV Deployment Problem with Neighborhoods [27]. Since the running time of this algorithm is $O(g(\eta) \cdot n^3 \cdot \log n)$, where $g(\eta)$ grows exponentially in $\frac{1}{\eta}$ (with a similar analysis as Step 4 of Algorithm 1), thus the time complexity of algorithm ApproxMPN is $O(g(\eta) \cdot n^3 \cdot \log n)$.

Note that in the approximation guarantee of ApproxMPN, ϵ is a small value and for different values of ϵ we get different approximation guarantees. For example, let $R_0 = 50\,\mathrm{m}$ [13], $B = 5\,\mathrm{MJ}$ [25], and an average energy consumption per unit distance for flying be $200\,\mathrm{J/m}$ [14]. Then, the value of γ is $\frac{1}{500}$ and the number $|T|$ of r-rooted tours produced by algorithm ApproxMPN is

$$|T| \leq \left(\lceil \log \frac{1}{\epsilon} \rceil + 1\right)\left(13.6(2 + \frac{8}{500\epsilon})\,\mathrm{OPT} - 6.3\right).$$

For instance, for $\epsilon = 0.1$ and 0.2, we get $|T| \leq 147\,\mathrm{OPT} - 31.5$ and $|T| \leq 113.2\,\mathrm{OPT} - 25.2$, respectively.

5   Conclusion

In this paper, we formulated the minimum UAV deployments problem with neighbourhoods to collect data of all sensors using the minimum number of UAVs, subject to the constraint that the energy cost of each UAV in its flying tour is at most B. We devised two algorithms for the problem and proved guarantees on their theoretical performance. One of the proposed algorithms is a bicriteria approximation algorithm that violates the budget constraint by at most a $(1 + \epsilon)$-factor. In our future work, we will study the problem when each UAV has a storage capacity and the hovering cost of UAVs change according to their Euclidean distance from the center of sensors. Improving the approximation guarantee of the proposed algorithms and evaluating them experimentally are other future directions of work. Other possible extensions are investigating the problem by considering heterogeneous sensors and UAVs, where the communication range of sensors and the energy budget of UAVs are different.

References

1. Arkin, E.M., Hassin, R., Levin, A.: Approximations for minimum and min-max vehicle routing problems. J. Algorithms **59**(1), 1–18 (2006)
2. Arora, S.: Polynomial time approximation schemes for Euclidean traveling salesman and other geometric problems. J. ACM **45**(5), 753–782 (1998)
3. Aurambout, J.P., Gkoumas, K., Ciuffo, B.: Last mile delivery by drones: an estimation of viable market potential and access to citizens across European cities. Eur. Transp. Res. Rev. **11**(1), 1–21 (2019)
4. Calamoneri, T., Corò, F., Mancini, S.: A realistic model to support rescue operations after an earthquake via UAVs. IEEE Access **10**, 6109–6125 (2022)

5. Chen, M., Liang, W., Das, S.K.: Data collection utility maximization in wireless sensor networks via efficient determination of UAV hovering locations. In: PerCom, pp. 1–10. IEEE (2021)
6. Chen, M., Liang, W., Li, J.: Energy-efficient data collection maximization for UAV-assisted wireless sensor networks. In: Wireless Communications and Networking Conference (WCNC), pp. 1–7. IEEE (2021)
7. Curry, J., Maslanik, J., Holland, G., Pinto, J.: Applications of aerosondes in the arctic. Bull. Am. Meteorol. Soc. 85(12), 1855–1861 (2004)
8. Deng, L., et al.: Approximation algorithms for the min-max cycle cover problem with neighborhoods. IEEE/ACM Trans. Netw. 28(4), 1845–1858 (2020)
9. Dumitrescu, A., Mitchell, J.S.B.: Approximation algorithms for TSP with neighborhoods in the plane. J. Algorithms 48(1), 135–159 (2003)
10. Dumitrescu, A., Tóth, C.D.: The traveling salesman problem for lines, balls, and planes. ACM Trans. Algorithms 12(3), 43:1–43:29 (2016)
11. Frederickson, G.N., Hecht, M.S., Kim, C.E.: Approximation algorithms for some routing problems. In: 17th Annual Symposium on Foundations of Computer Science, Houston, Texas, USA, 25–27 October 1976, pp. 216–227. IEEE Computer Society (1976)
12. Guo, Q., et al.: Minimizing the longest tour time among a fleet of UAVs for disaster area surveillance. IEEE Trans. Mob. Comput. 21(7), 2451–2465 (2022)
13. Jansons, J., Dorins, T.: Analyzing IEEE 802.11 n standard: outdoor performance. In: 2012 Second International Conference on Digital Information Processing and Communications (ICDIPC), pp. 26–30. IEEE (2012)
14. Khochare, A., Simmhan, Y., Sorbelli, F.B., Das, S.K.: Heuristic algorithms for co-scheduling of edge analytics and routes for UAV fleet missions. In: 40th IEEE Conference on Computer Communications, INFOCOM 2021, Vancouver, BC, Canada, 10–13 May 2021, pp. 1–10. IEEE (2021)
15. Khuller, S., Malekian, A., Mestre, J.: To fill or not to fill: the gas station problem. ACM Trans. Algorithms (TALG) 7(3), 1–16 (2011)
16. Kim, D., Uma, R., Abay, B.H., Wu, W., Wang, W., Tokuta, A.O.: Minimum latency multiple data mule trajectory planning in wireless sensor networks. IEEE Trans. Mob. Comput. 13(4), 838–851 (2013)
17. Li, J., Zhang, P.: New approximation algorithms for the rooted budgeted cycle cover problem. Theoret. Comput. Sci. 940, 283–295 (2023)
18. Mitchell, J.S.B.: Guillotine subdivisions approximate polygonal subdivisions: a simple polynomial-time approximation scheme for geometric tsp, k-mst, and related problems. SIAM J. Comput. 28(4), 1298–1309 (1999)
19. Nagarajan, V., Ravi, R.: Approximation algorithms for distance constrained vehicle routing problems. Networks 59(2), 209–214 (2012)
20. Rao, S., Smith, W.D.: Approximating geometrical graphs via "spanners" and "banyans". In: Proceedings of the Thirtieth Annual ACM Symposium on the Theory of Computing, Dallas, Texas, USA, 23–26 May 1998, pp. 540–550. ACM (1998)
21. Silva, I.D.D., Caillouet, C.: Optimizing the trajectory of drones: trade-off between distance and energy. In: 2020 IEEE International Conference on Sensing, Communication and Networking (SECON Workshops), Como, Italy, 22–26 June 2020, pp. 1–6. IEEE (2020)
22. Silva, I.D.D., Caillouet, C., Coudert, D.: Optimizing FANET deployment for mobile sensor tracking in disaster management scenario. In: International Conference on Information and Communication Technologies for Disaster Management, ICT-DM 2021, Hangzhou, China, 3–5 December 2021, pp. 134–141. IEEE (2021)

23. Sorbelli, F.B., Corò, F., Das, S.K., Palazzetti, L., Pinotti, C.M.: On the scheduling of conflictual deliveries in a last-mile delivery scenario with truck-carried drones. Pervasive Mob. Comput. **87**, 101700 (2022)

24. Sorbelli, F.B., Navarra, A., Palazzetti, L., Pinotti, C.M., Prencipe, G.: Optimal and heuristic algorithms for data collection by using an energy- and storage-constrained drone. In: Erlebach, T., Segal, M. (eds.) ALGOSENSORS 2022. LNCS, vol. 13707, pp. 18–30. Springer, Cham (2022). https://doi.org/10.1007/978-3-031-22050-0_2

25. Stolaroff, J.K., Samaras, C., O'Neill, E.R., Lubers, A., Mitchell, A.S., Ceperley, D.: Energy use and life cycle greenhouse gas emissions of drones for commercial package delivery. Nat. Commun. **9**(1), 409 (2018)

26. Xu, W., Liang, W., Lin, X.: Approximation algorithms for min-max cycle cover problems. IEEE Trans. Comput. **64**(3), 600–613 (2015)

27. Xu, W., et al.: Minimizing the deployment cost of UAVs for delay-sensitive data collection in IoT networks. IEEE/ACM Trans. Netw. **30**(2), 812–825 (2022)

28. Xu, Z., Xu, D., Zhu, W.: Approximation results for a min-max location-routing problem. Discret. Appl. Math. **160**(3), 306–320 (2012)

29. Yu, W., Liu, Z.: Improved approximation algorithms for some min-max and minimum cycle cover problems. Theor. Comput. Sci. **654**, 45–58 (2016)

30. Yu, W., Liu, Z., Bao, X.: New approximation algorithms for the minimum cycle cover problem. Theor. Comput. Sci. **793**, 44–58 (2019)

31. Zhang, Q., Xu, W., Liang, W., Peng, J., Liu, T., Wang, T.: An improved algorithm for dispatching the minimum number of electric charging vehicles for wireless sensor networks. Wirel. Netw. **25**(3), 1371–1384 (2019)

32. Zhang, W., Song, K., Rong, X., Li, Y.: Coarse-to-fine UAV target tracking with deep reinforcement learning. IEEE Trans. Autom. Sci. Eng. **16**(4), 1522–1530 (2019)

Mutual Visibility with ASYNC Luminous Robots Having Inaccurate Movements

Subhajit Pramanick⬭, Saswata Jana⬭, Adri Bhattacharya⬭,
and Partha Sarathi Mandal$^{(\boxtimes)}$⬭

Indian Institute of Technology Guwahati, Guwahati 781039, Assam, India
psm@iitg.ac.in

Abstract. In this paper, we initiate the study of the *Mutual Visibility problem* using oblivious luminous point robots that have inaccurate movements. Robots are opaque i.e., two robots see each other only if the line segment connecting them contains no robots. Each robot operates in *Look-Compute-Move* cycles. A robot has a light attached to it. We define the inaccuracy in the movement of a robot r as a deviation from its target point T to a point T' such that $\angle TrT' < 90°$. From any initial configuration of the robots on the Euclidean plane, the aim of the problem is to arrange the robots in a configuration such that any two robots are visible to each other. We assume that the robots agree on one coordinate axis. We present a collision-free algorithm that uses 3 colors and runs in $\mathcal{O}(N)$ epoch under asynchronous setting, where N is the number of robots. An epoch is the smallest time interval in which all robots get activated and execute LCM cycle at least once. We also study the problem in presence of faulty robots, where by fault, we mean *mobility failure* in which the robots become immobile after fault. This fault does not affect the light of the robots. Any robot can encounter fault at any time. Moreover, a robot can be faulty along with exhibiting inaccuracy in its movement. We also present a fault-tolerant algorithm which aims to bring the robots in a configuration where no three non-faulty robots can collinear and no faulty robot lies between two non-faulty robot. We prove that the non-faulty robots achieve mutual visibility in $\mathcal{O}(N)$ epochs under asynchronous settings.

Keywords: Mutual visibility · Mobile robots · Inaccurate movement · Mobility failure · Luminous robots · Distributed algorithms

1 Introduction

Background and Motivation: Mobile robots with their application in different problems have gained a lot of attention from researchers around the globe.

Supported by Prime Minister's Research Fellowship (PMRF) scheme of the Govt. of India (PMRF-ID: 1902165).
Supported by CSIR, Govt. of India, Grant Number: 09/731(0178)/2020-EMR-I.

Solving complex problems using simpler and less capable robots is always the target. Classically, these robots are autonomous (no external control), anonymous (having no id), homogeneous (execute same algorithm) and disoriented (do not agree on any global coordinate system and orientation). They are used in different problems such as gathering at a point, pattern formation, dispersion over an area and many more. Mutual visibility is one such problem where the aim is to reach a configuration such that every robot can see all other robots.

A robot can either be active or inactive. When active, a robot works in *Look-Compute-Move* (LCM) cycles, which we define later in this paper. Each robot has a vision that helps them to gather data from its surrounding. The vision of a robot can be obstructed by some other robots lying on the line of sight. We call this as *obstructed visibility* and the robots are called *opaque* robots. The mutual visibility problem is investigated under both classical and luminous robot models. In the classical model, robots do not have a light on them, whereas in luminous robots, each of them has an externally visible light that flashes colors from a prefixed color set. The robots cannot remember their past actions (they are called *oblivious*) except for this persistent light. The mutual visibility problem gets challenging with obstructed visibility and oblivious robots. The problem is even more challenging when some of the robots have inaccurate movement.

In this paper, we initiate the study of the mutual visibility problem under the microscope of inaccuracy in robots' movement. Inaccuracy may occur at any time due to some technical failure in robots (for example, misalignment of the direction of motion). We assume one axis agreement which means one coordinate axis is same in direction for each robot present on the plane. The directions of the other axis may differ for different robots, which leads to no agreement on any common orientation. Robots do not have knowledge about the total number of robots and any common notion of time (asynchronous in activation).

So far, the mutual visibility problem has been investigated under different models in the literature. Most of the solutions provided heavily rely on the concept of the convex hull, where the aim is to arrange the robots at the vertices of a convex hull. Starting from a configuration, robots either expand or contract the convex hull with their movements. The property of the convex hull leads to the mutual visibility. But, when the movements of the robots are not accurate, the concept fails to solve the problem, as the inaccurate movement may distort the convex hull itself. A different type of solution is proposed by Poudel et al. [7] under the assumption of one axis agreement, where robots find a polygonal region on the plane, called *visible area*. The idea is to place a robot in its corresponding *visible area* while others are stationary, so that it does not become collinear with other robots. But, this also does not solve the problem in case of inaccurate movement of the robots, as a robot might move to a point that is not a part of its *visible area*. The same logic applies when the problem is studied under fault tolerance with inaccuracy. When we integrate inaccuracy with the fault model defined in [7], the existing solution fails to achieve the goal.

Contribution: Our contributions in this paper are listed below.

- We propose a collision-free algorithm (MV_INACC) that solves the mutual visibility problem using asynchronous robots having inaccurate movement under one axis agreement. The algorithm runs in $\mathcal{O}(N)$ epochs under an asynchronous setting, where N is the number of robots.
- To the best of our knowledge, this is the first work that approaches the mutual visibility problem with robots having *inaccurate movements*.
- We propose a fault-tolerant algorithm (FAULT_MV_INACC) that can tolerate any number of mobility faults along with the inaccurate movement of the robots under asynchronous settings. We prove that the algorithm makes the non-faulty robots mutually visible in $\mathcal{O}(N)$ epochs.

Related Work: Di Luna et al. [6] introduced the mutual visibility problem with luminous point robots under semi-synchronous setting where N, the total number of robots, is a global knowledge. Later in [5], they investigated the problem with rigid (the movement of a robot cannot be interrupted) and non-rigid robots under both semi-synchronous and asynchronous settings. Using the same model, Sharma et al. [11] presented an algorithm that improves the number of colors to 2 in both semi-synchronous and asynchronous models. Vaidyanathan et al. [15] presented a $\mathcal{O}(\log n)$ algorithm with fully synchronous luminous robots. Later, a constant time algorithm with semi-synchronous rigid luminous robots is proposed by Sharma et al. [14]. Bhagat et al. [3] investigated mutual visibility with semi-synchronous robots having 1 bit of persistent memory. Sharma et al. [13] presented a constant time algorithm with asynchronous luminous point robots. The mutual visibility is even extended to grids by Adhikary et al. [1] and Sharma et al. [12] using luminous point robots.

The problem is also studied with faults. Aljohani and Sharma [2] presented an algorithm tolerating a single mobile faulty robot under semi-synchronous setting assuming an agreement on both coordinate axes. Sharma et al. [9] solved mutual visibility for semi-synchronous luminous robots, in case of light becoming faulty, but the mobility of the robots is not affected. Using one axis agreement among the asynchronous luminous robots, Poudel et al. [7] gave an algorithm that tolerates any number of mobility faulty robots. Pramanick and Mandal [8] gave an algorithm tolerating a single fault in no axes agreement. The problem is even extended to fat robot model [4,10] where a robot is a unit disk.

Organization: We discuss the underlying model in Sect. 2. We describe and analyse the first algorithm MV_INACC in Sect. 3 and second algorithm FAULT_MV_INACC in Sect. 4 before concluding in Sect. 5. Due to space insufficiency, we exclude some of the proofs and the pseudocodes of the algorithms.

2   Model and Preliminaries

Robots: We consider a set of N autonomous and homogeneous point robots $R = \{r_1, r_2, \cdots r_N\}$ on the Euclidean plane, where r_i denotes a robot for $i = 1, 2, \cdots N$. They do not have any identifier. They are opaque, which means two robots are visible to each other only if there is no third robot lying on the line segment joining the two. A robot is visible to itself but may not see all other robots due to some robots obstructing its line of sight. Robots are oblivious, which means they cannot remember their past actions. There is no means of communication except for a persistent externally visible light on them which can determine color from a prefixed color set. The light is a form of weak communication between the robots.

None of the robots have knowledge about N. The current location of any robot r_i is assumed to be the origin of its local coordinate system. However, we assume that the robots agree on one coordinate axis (without loss of generality, we consider y-axis). The move-

Fig. 1. Illustrating inaccurate movement of r_i

ments of the robots can be inaccurate. For a robot r_i, this inaccuracy denotes a deviation from the intended target it has chosen to move. As shown in Fig. 1, if r_i decides to move to the point T, it actually moves to the point T' due to the inaccuracy in its movement. We call the angle $\angle T'r_iT$ the *inaccuracy angle* of the robot r_i and assume $T'r_iT < 90°$.

Time Cycle: A robot operates in classical *Look-Compute-Move* (LCM) cycles. Each time, after activation, a robot executes the following three phases. *Look:* It takes a snapshot of its surroundings to gather information about the positions of the other visible robots and their colors. *Compute:* It runs the algorithm using the snapshot as input and determines a target point on the plane to move or decides not to move anywhere in the current cycle. At the end of the compute phase, it changes its color if needed. *Move:* It moves to the target point, if any.

Schedulers and Run-Time: Robots are activated under ASYNC scheduler, where there is no global time. Any robot can be activated at any time, with the assumption that every robot is activated infinitely often. Time is measured by *epochs*, which is the time interval in which every robot gets activated and executes its LCM cycle at least once.

Notations:

- We denote the current position of a robot r_i by r_i itself. The y-coordinate of the location of the robot r_i is denoted by $r_i.y_{\text{coord}}$.
- For two robots r_i and r_j, $\overline{r_ir_j}$ is the line segment joining them, whereas $\overleftrightarrow{r_ir_j}$ represents the infinite line passing through r_i and r_j.
- $r_i.color$ represents the color shown by the light on the robot r_i at any time.
- At any time $t \geq 0$, C_t denotes the configuration which is the set of tuples in the form $(r_i, r_i.color)$.
- We say two robots r_i and r_j encounter a *collision* if they are collocated at one point at any time $t \geq 0$.
- For any non-perpendicular line (a line which is not parallel to the y-axis) L passing through the robot r, we call the half plane that contains the positive (and negative) y-axis of the local coordinate system of r as the *upper* (and *lower*) *half plane* and denote it by H_L^{Up} (and H_L^{Low}).

- The shortest distance between a point r_i and a line $\overleftrightarrow{AB}$ is the perpendicular distance between them and denoted by $d(r_i, \overleftrightarrow{AB})$. We use the same notation $d(r_i, r_j)$ to represent the shortest distance between the two points r_i and r_j.
- For convenience, we use the notation $\mathcal{VAR}_r^{Prev}$ to denote any variable $\mathcal{VAR}_r$ in the previous LCM cycle for any robot r.

Collinearity: For any three robots r_i, r_j and r_k, $\overline{r_i r_j r_k}$ represents that they are collinear. We denote the *line of collinearity* (we will use LOC henceforth) by $\overleftrightarrow{r_i r_j r_k}$. We classify collinearity into two types. The first one is Horizontal collinearity, where $\overleftrightarrow{r_i r_j r_k}$ is a horizontal line. The second type is Non-Horizontal collinearity in which $\overleftrightarrow{r_i r_j r_k}$ is a non-horizontal line. In the latter case, if $r_i.y_{coord} > r_j.y_{coord} > r_k.y_{coord}$, then r_i, r_j and r_k are called the *first, middle* and *last robot of collinearity*, respectively.

We define the problem formally as follows.

Problem 1 (*Mutual Visibility with Inaccurate Movement*): We are given a set of N oblivious opaque point robots on the Euclidean plane. Each robot operates in LCM cycles and has a persistent light on it that can assume a fixed number of colors. They agree on one coordinate axis. The movement of the robots can be inaccurate with an angular deviation of less than 90° from their target position. Starting from any arbitrary configuration, our aim is to reposition the robots such that no three robots are collinear.

3   Mutual Visibility with Inaccurate Movement

In this section, we present an Algorithm MV_INACC that solves the mutual visibility with robots having inaccurate movements. The algorithm is collision free and runs under ASYNC setting. We assume that the robots agree on y-axis. The algorithm is same for every robot and we describe the algorithm for a robot r. Robots use three colors: OFF (initial color), MOVE (when executing movement till termination) and FINISH (at termination).

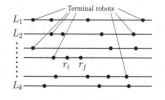

3.1   Description of the Algorithm

Initially, all robots are static and arbitrarily located at different points on the plane with color OFF. As a result of an agreement on the y-axis, we can assume that all the robots lie on k ($\leq N$) distinct horizontal lines $L_1, L_2, \cdots, L_k$. Each line passes through at least one robot on the plane. As shown in Fig. 2, these k lines covers all the robots on the plane. We call two robots r_i and r_j neighbors if they lie on same horizontal line and visible to each other. A robot r_i is called a *terminal* robot on a horizontal line L_j if either r_i is the only robot on L_j or all other robots on L_j lie on one side (either local left or right) of r_i.

Fig. 2. The horizontal lines $L_1, L_2, L_3, \cdots, L_k$ pass through at least one robots in the initial configuration. r_i and r_j are neighboring robots.

Preliminaries: We list down some of the important notations that we are going to use to describe our algorithm.

- L_r is the horizontal line passing through the robot r.
- $\mathcal{V}_r = \{r_i \in R \mid r_i \neq r$ and $\not\exists\ r_j \in R$ such that $\overline{rr_jr_i}\}$ is the set of all visible robots to r.
- $\mathcal{NB}_r = \{r_i \in \mathcal{V}_r \mid L_{r_i} = L_r\}$ is the set of neighbors of r. Note that there can be at most one neighboring robot for any terminal robot r.
- For any terminal robot r, M_r is the midpoint of $\overline{rr_i}$, where $r_i \in \mathcal{NB}_r$.
- $\mathcal{NCV}_r = \{r_i \in \mathcal{V}_r \setminus \mathcal{NB}_r \mid \not\exists\ r_j \in \mathcal{V}_r$ such that $\overline{r_irr_j}\}$ is the set of all visible robots to r such that no two robots from this set are collinear with r. For example in Fig. 3, $\mathcal{NCV}_r = \{r_k\}$.
- $\mathcal{CV}_r = \{r_i \in \mathcal{V}_r \setminus \mathcal{NB}_r \mid \exists\ r_i^c \in \mathcal{V}_r$ such that $\overline{r_irr_i^c}\}$ is the set of all visible robots to r such that for every $r_i \in \mathcal{CV}_r$, there exists a unique robot $r_i^c \in \mathcal{CV}_r$ where r is the middle robot of the collinearity $\overline{r_irr_i^c}$. In this case, we call r_i^c the *conjugate robot* of r_i for the collinearity $\overline{r_irr_i^c}$. For example, $\mathcal{CV}_r = \{r_l, r_i^c, r_j, r_j^c\}$, as illustrated in Fig. 3.

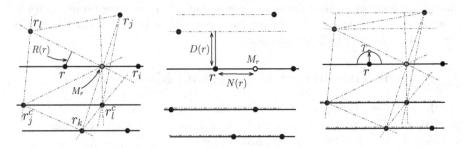

Fig. 3. Illustrating $R(r)$ by which r avoids moving to the blue lines (Color figure online)

Fig. 4. Illustrating $D(r)$ by which r avoids crossing horizontal red lines (Color figure online)

Fig. 5. r chooses T in the upward direction, where $d(r, T) = Radius_r$

Strategy S: Based on the data gathered from the snapshot taken in the Look phase of the current activation cycle, r computes three distances $R(r), D(r)$ and $N(r)$ which are defined as follows.

1. $R(r) = \min\{d(r, \overleftrightarrow{r_ir_j}) \mid r_i \neq r_j \neq r_i^c; r_i \in \mathcal{NCV}_r \cup \mathcal{CV}_r; r_j \in \mathcal{NCV}_r \cup \mathcal{CV}_r \cup \{M_r\}\}$. The robot r considers a line passing through any two non-neighbor visible robots r_i and r_j which are not collinear with r. This is to avoid the possible collinearity $\overline{r_irr_j}$, after the movement. It also avoids moving to a line that passes through r_i and M_r to prevent itself from getting collinear due to simultaneous movement of its neighboring robot. As shown in Fig. 3, $R(r)$ is the smallest of all distances from r to the blue lines.

2. $D(r) = \min\{d(r, L_{r_i}) \mid r_i \in \mathcal{V}_r \setminus \mathcal{NB}_r\}$. r avoids the horizontal lines passing through any visible robot r_i to ensure that it does not create any horizontal collinearity. Figure 4 illustrates that r takes the nearest horizontal line among all red lines to calculate the distance $D(r)$.

3. $N(r) = d(r, M_r)$ ensures that there is no collision between r and its neighbor. It is the distance of r with the midpoint M_r, as shown in Fig. 4.

Finally, r computes $Radius_r = \frac{\min}{2}\{R(r), D(r), N(r)\}$.

First Movement: After activation, a robot r first determines whether it is a terminal robot or not. This can be determined by checking whether at least one side of r on the horizontal line L_r is empty or not. If it is a non-terminal, it remains stationary and does not change its color. Otherwise, if $r.color = $ OFF and all the visible robots in the upward direction (if any) are with color FINISH, r follows the *Strategy S* and sets $r.color =$MOVE. It then starts its movement perpendicularly upward to a point T in the same activation cycle such that $d(r, T) = Radius_r$, as shown in Fig. 5. First movement of r removes any horizontal collinearity.

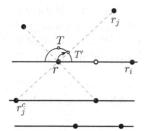 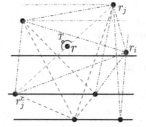 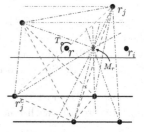

Fig. 6. r remains collinear because of inaccurate movement to T' instead of T.

Fig. 7. r_i with color MOVE, lies below r, so r chooses T for the second move

Fig. 8. r and r_i lies on same horizontal line, so r chooses T for the second move

When r gets activated with $r.color = $ MOVE, it signifies that r has already executed a movement. We illustrate r's movement to T' instead of T in Fig. 6, due to inaccuracy. Notice that r was a part of two collinearities before the first movement (shown by green lines) and it remains collinear even after the first movement. r detects the LOC only if it is a *middle robot of the collinearity*. In case, r does not detect any collinearity, which means $\mathcal{CV}_r = \emptyset$, it terminates with $r.color = $ FINISH. Otherwise, it executes a second movement.

Second Movement: Let $L = \overleftrightarrow{r_j r_j^c}$ be the LOC of r. At this point, $\mathcal{CV}_r$ contains exactly two other robots r_j and r_j^c. If r sees a robot r_i in $H_{L_r}^{Up}$ with $r_i.color = $ MOVE, it does not change its color or position. Otherwise, there can be three cases. (1) r_i lies in $H_{L_r}^{Low}$ (r_i lies below r, shown in Fig. 7) (2) r_i lies on L_r (r_i lies on the horizontal line through r, shown in Fig. 8) (3) Such r_i does not exist. In all three cases, r again computes $Radius_r$ (which is described in *Strategy S*) in the current LCM cycle and checks whether $L \perp L_r$ or not. If not, r finds a point T

in the upper half plane H_L^{Up} such that T is $Radius_r$ distance apart from r and $\overline{rT} \perp L$. If $L \perp L_r$, then r chooses the point T such that T is $Radius_r$ distance away from r in the left direction (local left with respect to the coordinate system of r) and $\overline{rT} \perp L$. In both cases, r starts moving to T with the color MOVE.

When r is activated with $r.color = $ MOVE and detects $\mathcal{CV}_r = \emptyset$ i.e., there are no two robots r_j and r_j^c such that $\overline{r_j r r_j^c}$, r sets $r.color$ to FINISH and terminates.

3.2 Analysis of the Algorithm

In this section, we prove the correctness and the time complexity of MV_INACC algorithm. To prove that mutual visibility is achieved at termination, it is sufficient to show that none of the robots becomes middle robot of some collinearity after termination.

Lemma 1. *Any two robots moving simultaneously, lie on the same horizontal line before the movement.*

Proof. If two robots r and r' lie on different horizontal lines, we assume r' lies below L_r without loss of generality. If both of them are visible to each other and $r.color \neq$ FINISH, r' cannot move. If $r.color =$FINISH, r cannot move thenceforth. If there is a robot r'' lying between r and r', $r''.color$ cannot be set to FINISH while $r.color \neq$ FINISH When r' sees r'' in upward direction with $r''.color \neq$ FINISH, r' cannot move. $\square$

Remark 1. At most two robots can move simultaneously. Also, there can be at most two robots with color MOVE at any time.

Lemma 2. *After the first movement, r cannot move to a point on L_r^{Prev} even with inaccuracy, where L_r^{Prev} is horizontal through r in the previous LCM cycle. Also, it cannot move to a point on L^{Prev}, where L^{Prev} is the LOC of r in previous LCM cycle, after the second movement.*

Proof. Due to inaccuracy in the movement, r might have moved to a point T' whereas T is its target with $\overline{rT} \perp L_r^{Prev}$. Since, the inaccuracy angle $\angle TrT' < 90°$ for any robot, T' cannot be on L_r^{Prev}.

The proof of the second part follows from the similar argument as above. $\square$

Remark 2. If r is a part of a collinearity $\overline{r_i r r_j}$, it can detect the collinearity only when it is the middle robot of that collinearity. In that case, $r_i, r_j \in \mathcal{CV}_r$.

Remark 3. Every robot r can move at most two times before termination. The second movement happens when $r.color = $ MOVE and r detects a collinearity with two other robots r_i and r_j, by Remark 2.

Lemma 3. *r cannot be collinear with any other two robots r_i and r_j after a movement, where $r_j \neq r_i^c; r_i \in \mathcal{NCV}_r \cup \mathcal{CV}_r; r_j \in \mathcal{NCV}_r \cup \mathcal{CV}_r$.*

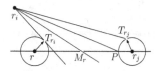

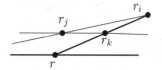

Fig. 9. Simultaneous moves of r and r_j do not create collinearity

Fig. 10. r cannot move to any point on the ine segment $\overline{r_i r_j}$ because of $\overleftrightarrow{r_k r_j}$

Proof. Since, both r_i and r_j are visible to r, r considers the line $\overleftrightarrow{r_i r_j}$ and calculates the distance $d(r, \overleftrightarrow{r_i r_j})$. r chooses a point T such that $d(r, T) = Radius_r$. By definition, $Radius_r < R(r) \leq d(r, \overleftrightarrow{r_i r_j})$. So, we have $d(T, \overleftrightarrow{r_i r_j}) > 0$, which implies T does not lie on $\overleftrightarrow{r_i r_j}$. Even if r moves inaccurately to a point T' instead of T, the above inequality holds true as $d(r, T') = Radius_r$. □

Lemma 4. *r cannot be collinear with other two robots r_i, r_j after a movement, where $r_i \in \mathcal{NCV}_r \cup \mathcal{CV}_r$; $r_j \in \mathcal{NB}_r$, even if r_j moves simultaneously with r.*

Proof. Let r_j be stationary when r is moving. Since, $d(r, M_r) = \frac{1}{2}d(r, r_j) < d(r, r_j)$ where M_r is the midpoint of the line segment $\overline{r r_j}$, the inequality $Radius_r < R(r) < d(r, \overleftrightarrow{r_i M_r}) < d(r, \overleftrightarrow{r_i r_j})$ holds. If r moves to a point T_r, it does not lie on $\overleftrightarrow{r_i r_j}$ as $d(r, T_r) = Radius_r$. In case of simultaneous movement of r and r_j, if r and r_j move to T_r and T_{r_j} respectively, as shown in Fig. 9, the inequality $d(r, \overleftrightarrow{r_i T_r}) < d(r, \overleftrightarrow{r_i M_r}) < d(r, \overleftrightarrow{r_i P}) < d(r, \overleftrightarrow{r_i T_{r_j}})$ holds. □

Lemma 5. *After a movement, r cannot be collinear with two robots r_i and r_j whom it was not collinear (as a middle robot) with, where $r_i \notin \mathcal{V}_r$ and $r_j \in R$.*

Proof. Since, $r_i \notin \mathcal{V}_r$, there is a robot $r_k \in \mathcal{V}_r$ such that $\overline{r r_k r_i}$ as shown in (Fig. 10). If $r_j \in \mathcal{V}_r$, the inequality $d(r, \overleftrightarrow{r_i r_j}) > d(r, \overleftrightarrow{r_k r_j}) > Radius_r$ holds. In case of $r_j \notin \mathcal{V}_r$, $d(r, \overleftrightarrow{r_i r_j}) > d(r, \overleftrightarrow{r_k r_l}) > Radius_r$ for some robot $r_l \in \mathcal{V}_r$ such that $\overline{r r_l r_j}$. In both account, r cannot move on the line $\overleftrightarrow{r_i r_j}$ as r moves to a point $Radius_r$ distance apart from its current location. □

Remark 4. Lemma 3, 4 and 5 ensure that r never becomes collinear (as a middle robot) with two robots after a movement, with whom it was non-collinear in previous LCM cycle.

Lemma 6. *For any robot r, $\mathcal{CV}_r \subseteq \mathcal{CV}_r^{Prev}$.*

Proof. If $\mathcal{CV}_r = \emptyset$, we are done. Otherwise, let $r_i \in \mathcal{CV}_r$. Then there is $r_i^c \in \mathcal{CV}_r$ such that $\overline{r_i r r_i^c}$. If we assume $r_i \notin \mathcal{CV}_r^{Prev}$, then we get $r_i \notin \mathcal{V}_r^{Prev}$. By Lemma 5, r cannot be collinear with r_i and r_i^c which leads to a contradiction. □

Lemma 7. *After first movement of the robot r, $\mathcal{CV}_r$ contains at most two robots.*

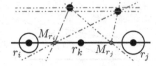
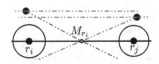

Fig. 11. The circles centered at r_i and r_j are disjoint in presence of a common neighbor r_k

Fig. 12. The circles are disjoint even if there is no common neighbor, leading to no collision

Proof. Let $r_i, r_i^c \in \mathcal{CV}_r$ such that $\overline{r_i r r_i^c}$. We will prove this lemma by contradiction. Let $r_j, r_j^c \in \mathcal{CV}_r$ be another pair of robots such that $\overline{r_j r r_j^c}$. Let r^{Prev} be the position of r in the previous LCM cycle before the movement. Note that $r \neq r^{Prev}$ even with inaccurate movement, as $Radius_r \neq 0$. By Lemma 6, $r_i, r_i^c, r_j, r_j^c \in \mathcal{CV}_r^{Prev}$. Hence, $\overline{r_i r_i^c}$ and $\overline{r_j r_j^c}$ intersect at r^{Prev} and r. This leads to a contradiction as two non-parallel lines intersect at exactly one point. $\square$

Lemma 8. *After the first movement, a robot r with color MOVE sees all other robots with color MOVE.*

Proof. By Remark 1, there can be at most two robots with color MOVE at any time. Let r_i be the other robot with $r_i.color =$MOVE, which is not visible to r. Then there is a robot $r_j \in \mathcal{V}_r$ such that $\overline{r r_j r_i}$. Clearly, $r_j \notin \mathcal{NB}_r^{Prev}$. If $r_j \in \mathcal{V}_r^{Prev}$, we have $Radius_r^{Prev} < d(r^{Prev}, L_{r_j}) < d(r^{Prev}, \overline{r r_i})$. If $r_j \notin \mathcal{V}_r^{Prev}$, there is a robot r_k such that $\overline{r^{Prev} r_k r_j}$. In that case, $Radius_r^{Prev} < d(r^{Prev}, L_{r_k}) < d(r^{Prev}, L_{r_j}) < d(r^{Prev}, \overline{r r_i})$. In both cases, we get a contradiction. $\square$

Lemma 9. *After second movement of the robot r, $\mathcal{CV}_r$ contains no robot.*

Proof. By Remark 3 and Lemma 7, $\mathcal{CV}_r^{Prev}$ contains exactly one pair of robots r_i and r_i^c. We can differentiate three cases for the second movement of r. (1) r sees no robot with color MOVE. (2) There is a robot r' with color MOVE lying on $H_{L_r}^{Low}$. (3) r' lies on L_r. Note that if r' lies on $H_{L_r}^{Up}$, r does not execute the second movement in the current LCM cycle. By Lemma 8, r' is visible to r. The above lemma follows from Lemma 2 and Remark 4 in case of (1) and (2). By Lemma 4, if $L_{r'} = L_r$ and r' moves simultaneously with r, it is not possible for r to be the middle robot of the collinearity $\overline{r' r r''}$ for some robot r''. $\square$

Corollary 1. *For a robot r with r.color = FINISH, $\mathcal{CV}_r$ remains empty.*

Corollary 2. *A robot r sees all the robots with color FINISH in the current LCM cycle, before it moves.*

Theorem 1. *The movements of the robots are free from collision.*

Proof. Let r_i and r_j be any two robots in R lying on two different horizontal lines. Without loss of generality, r_j lies below r_i i.e., $L_{r_i} \neq L_{r_j}$. r_j does not move until all the robots above it are with color FINISH. Consequently, r_i and r_j

cannot meet a collision with each other. If r_i and r_j lie on the same horizontal line $L_{r_i} = L_{r_j} = L$, then they move simultaneously only if they both are terminal robots on L. If there is a robot r_k lying between them on L, as shown in Fig 11, then r_i and r_j move to two points T_{r_i} and T_{r_j} such that $Radius_{r_i} = d(r_i, T_{r_i}) < d(r_i, M_{r_i})$ and $Radius_{r_j} = d(r_j, T_{r_j}) < d(r_j, M_{r_j})$, where M_{r_i} and M_{r_j} are the midpoints of $\overline{r_i r_k}$ and $\overline{r_k r_j}$ respectively. If no such robot r_k exists, it means r_i and r_j are neighbors on L, illustrated in Fig. 12. Then, $M_{r_i} = M_{r_j}$. Even if both of them move simultaneously, the above inequalities hold. Since, the circles of radius $Radius_{r_i}$ and $Radius_{r_j}$ are disjoint, both the robots cannot collide.   □

Theorem 2. *At termination, all robots achieve mutual visibility in $\mathcal{O}(N)$ epochs.*

Proof. Let us assume that after termination, there are three robots r_i, r_j and r_k such that $\overline{r_i r_k r_j}$. At termination, all robots are with color FINISH. Then, $r_k.color =$ FINISH. As $\overline{r_i r_k r_j}$, we have $\mathcal{CV}_{r_k} \neq \emptyset$, contradicting Corollary 1.

Any robot r moves at most twice before setting its color to FINISH. Under ASYNC setting, r takes one epoch to set $r.color =$ MOVE and execute the first move. Afterwards, if r detects a collinearity, it takes another epoch to move for the second time with $r.color =$ MOVE. Finally, it takes one epoch to change $r.color$ to FINISH and terminate. So, it takes at most 3 epochs for a robot to change its color from OFF to FINISH. In the worst case, each of N robots lies on a vertical line in the initial configuration. In that case, we get n horizontal lines $L_1, L_2, \cdots L_N$ each of which is passing through a robot. Robots on L_2 to L_n cannot move till the robot on L_1 is with color FINISH. Then, the robot on L_2 gets the chance to move and ends up with FINISH color. Proceeding this way, robots execute and reach to FINISH color one by one. Hence, it takes at most $3N$ epochs for all robots to reach to FINISH color.   □

4   Fault-Tolerant Mutual Visibility with Inaccuracy

This section presents an algorithm (FAULT_MV_INACC) that tolerates *mobility failure* of the robots along with *inaccuracy* in their movements. This algorithm uses 8 colors: OFF (initial color), MOVE1 (during first move), HALT (after the first move is complete), MOVE2 (during second move), FAULT (if collinearity persists after second move), COLLINEAR (if collinear with a HALT-colored robot), NON-COLLINEAR (if non-collinear with every HALT-colored robot), FINISH (at termination). When fault occurs, a robot does not move thenceforth. However, it can change the color of its light without any trouble. A robot can become faulty at any point of time. All other elements of the previous model in Sect. 2 remain unchanged. We revise the problem definition as follows.

Problem 2 (*Fault-Tolerant Mutual Visibility with Inaccurate Movement*): N oblivious, opaque, luminous point robots, each of which operates in LCM cycles, are situated at distinct points on the plane. They agree on one coordinate axis. The movements of the robots can be inaccurate with an angular deviation of less than 90° from their target position. By fault, we mean that the robots remain stationary after becoming faulty. The light of a robot remains functional even if it experiences fault. From any initial configuration, our aim is to rearrange the robots such that no three non-faulty robots are collinear and no faulty robot lies between two non-faulty robots, even if f $(\leq N)$ robots become faulty.

4.1   Description of the Algorithm

As described in the previous algorithm MV_INACC, we consider distinct horizontal lines, shown in Fig 2. In that algorithm, the criteria of a robot for executing its first movement is when it becomes a terminal robot. But, in this case, the terminal robots on a horizontal line can be faulty, because of which a non-terminal robot keeps on waiting forever, even if it is non-faulty. So, we revise the criteria for a robot to execute its first movement. A robot r is called an *eligible robot* if both the following conditions are satisfied. (I) All the visible robots above r are either with color FINISH or FAULT. (II) At least one side of r on L_r is either empty or has robots with color FAULT. Note that any robot showing color FAULT is faulty. The set of all non-neighbor visible faulty robots of r whose current color is FAULT, COLLINEAR or NON-COLLINEAR is represented by $\mathcal{FV}_r$ and defined as $\mathcal{FV}_r = \{r_i \in \mathcal{V}_r \setminus \mathcal{NB}_r | \ r_i.color = \text{FAULT}, \text{COLLINEAR or NON-COLLINEAR}\}$. We modify the *Strategy S* as follows. However, the definition of L_r, M_r, $\mathcal{V}_r$, $\mathcal{NB}_r$, $\mathcal{NCV}_r$ and $\mathcal{CV}_r$ remains same.

Strategy S_{Mod}: r computes four distance $R(r), D(r)$, $N(r)$ and $P(r)$, out of which $R(r), D(r)$ and $N(r)$ are calculated as described in *Strategy S*. If $\mathcal{FV}_r$ has exactly one element, r does not need to calculate $P(r)$. Otherwise,

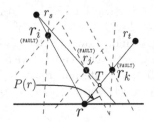

Fig. 13. Calculating $P(r)$ prevents r moving to T

- $P(r) = \min\{d(r, L)|\ L \parallel \overleftrightarrow{rr_i} \text{ and } L \text{ goes through } r_j; \forall r_i, r_j \in \mathcal{FV}_r; r_i \neq r_j\}$. If r sees any two robots r_i and r_j with color FAULT, it considers a line L which is passing through r_j and parallel to the line $\overleftrightarrow{rr_i}$. It then calculates the distance from its current position to the line L. The minimum of all such distances is represented by $P(r)$. Figure 13 illustrates the significance of calculating $P(r)$. Here, $r_i, r_j, r_k \in \mathcal{FV}_r$. Since, $r_s \notin \mathcal{V}_r$, r might move to T which makes r collinear not only with r_t and r_k, but with r_s and r_j whereas we want at most one collinearity after every movement.

Finally, r calculates $Radius_r = \frac{1}{2} \min\{R(r), D(r), N(r), P(r)\}$.

First Movement: When r gets activated. it first checks whether it is an *eligible robot* with $r.color = $ OFF or not. If not, r does not move or change its color. Otherwise, it uses the *Strategy* S_{Mod} to calculate a distance $Radius_r$ and chooses a point T perpendicularly upward from its current position such that $d(r, T) = Radius_r$. Finally, r start moving towards T after setting $r.color = $ MOVE1. Note that before first movement, $\mathcal{FV}_r$ consists of all robots having color FAULT. At this moment, there is no robot with color COLLINEAR or NON-COLLINEAR.

When r gets activated with $r.color = \texttt{MOVE1}$, it recognizes this as an indication of completing its initial movement. If, within the same LCM cycle, r observes that there are no other robots in $H_{L_r}^{Up}$ with the colors $\texttt{MOVE1}$ or $\texttt{HALT}$, it changes its own color to $\texttt{HALT}$. Until this condition is met, r maintains its current color and position without any change. r now waits till all the visible robots with color $\texttt{FAULT}$ in $H_{L_r}^{Up}$ set their color either to $\texttt{COLLINEAR}$ or $\texttt{NON-COLLINEAR}$. When that happens, r needs to determine whether it is still collinear with the other two robots or not.

Detection of LOC: When r is with color $\texttt{HALT}$, it is possible that another robot r' moved and changed its color to $\texttt{HALT}$ in sync with r. In this situation, $L_r = L_{r'}$, as otherwise the robot with lower y-coordinate would not change its color to $\texttt{HALT}$ from $\texttt{MOVE1}$. They might execute the process to determine their respective LOCs and second move together. We have two cases for the robot r. **Case 1 (r is a middle robot of a collinearity):** As a middle robot, r sees two robots r_j and r_j^c such that $\overline{r_j r r_j^c}$. So, $r_j, r_j^c \in \mathcal{CV}_r$. In this case, $\overline{r_j r r_j^c}$ is considered as the LOC, as shown in Fig. 7, 8.

Case 2 (r is not a middle robot of a collinearity): In this case, r itself cannot understand whether it is a part of any collinearity or not, as $\mathcal{CV}_r = \emptyset$. So, the robots with color $\texttt{FAULT}$ act as guiding robots in determining the LOC by setting their color either to $\texttt{COLLINEAR}$ or $\texttt{NON-COLLINEAR}$. Depending on the number of robots with color $\texttt{COLLINEAR}$, r decides its LOC. We explain this process by considering following three sub-cases with proper examples.

- **Case 2.1 (r sees r' with color $\texttt{HALT}$ and two other robots with color $\texttt{COLLINEAR}$):** Before the first movement, let us assume that r is a part of two collinearities $\overline{r_i' r_i r}$ and $\overline{r_j' r_j r}$ while r' is on $\overline{r_k' r_k r'}$, as shown in Fig. 14. All of r_i, r_j and r_k have color $\texttt{FAULT}$. Due to inaccuracy, r and r' move to the points on $\overleftrightarrow{r_i' r_i}$ and $\overleftrightarrow{r_k' r_k}$ respectively after the first movement. This makes r and r' retain their collinearity $\overline{r_i' r_i r}$ and $\overline{r_k' r_k r'}$. When r and r' change their color to $\texttt{HALT}$ simultaneously, both r_i and r_k are able to detect the collinearities as middle robots, because of which both of them change their color to $\texttt{COLLINEAR}$. r_j changes its color to $\texttt{NON-COLLINEAR}$ as it is not a part of any collinearity either with r or r'. At this point, r sees two robots with color $\texttt{COLLINEAR}$ and hence it has to distinguish that out of $\overleftrightarrow{r r_i}$ and $\overleftrightarrow{r r_k}$, which one is actually its own LOC. If r sees a third robot on $\overleftrightarrow{r' r_k}$ (or $\overleftrightarrow{r' r_i}$), it recognizes that the color $\texttt{COLLINEAR}$ on r_k (or r_i) is the indication for r', not for its own. Therefore, it chooses $\overleftrightarrow{r r_i}$ (or $\overleftrightarrow{r r_k}$) as its LOC. If r does not see any third robot on $\overleftrightarrow{r' r_k}$ and $\overleftrightarrow{r' r_i}$, it understands that the third robot must be either on the intersection of $\overleftrightarrow{r r_i}$ and $\overleftrightarrow{r' r_k}$ or on the intersection of $\overleftrightarrow{r r_k}$ and $\overleftrightarrow{r' r_i}$. As shown in Fig. 15, r sees the intersection of $\overleftrightarrow{r r_k}$ and $\overleftrightarrow{r' r_i}$. So the third robot must be on on the intersection of $\overleftrightarrow{r r_i}$ and $\overleftrightarrow{r' r_k}$. In this case, r takes $\overleftrightarrow{r r_i}$ as its LOC.
- **Case 2.2 (r sees r' with color $\texttt{HALT}$ and exactly one other robot with color $\texttt{COLLINEAR}$):** Let us consider a configuration where r and r' are part of

the collinearities $\overline{r_i'r_ir}$ and $\overline{r_i''r_ir'}$, as depicted in Fig. 16. Here, both r and r' are with color HALT while r_i is with color COLLINEAR, indicating both of the collinearities $\overline{r_i'r_ir}$ and $\overline{r_i''r_ir'}$. In this case, r and r' respectively consider $\overleftrightarrow{rr_i}$ and $\overleftrightarrow{r'r_i}$ as the LOC.

- **Case 2.3** (r **sees no such** r', **but a robot with color COLLINEAR**): If r_i is with color COLLINEAR, r considers $\overleftrightarrow{rr_i}$ as its LOC, as shown in Fig. 17.

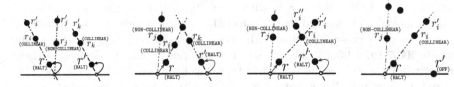

Fig. 14. Two robots with color HALT and two with COLLINEAR   **Fig. 15.** Two robots with color HALT and two with COLLINEAR   **Fig. 16.** Two robots with color HALT and one with COLLINEAR   **Fig. 17.** One robot with color HALT and one with COLLINEAR

After the LOC is detected, r starts executing its second movement.

Second Movement: Let L be the LOC. At this point, $\mathcal{FV}_r$ consists of all robots with color COLLINEAR and NON-COLLINEAR. r calculates $Radius_r$ by following *Strategy* S_{Mod}. If $L \perp L_r$, r chooses a point T in locally left direction such that $d(r,T) = Radius_r$ and $\overline{rT} \perp L$. If L is not perpendicular to L_r, T is a point in H_L^{Up} with $d(r,T) = Radius_r$ and $\overline{rT} \perp L$. In both cases, r changes its color to MOVE2 and starts its movement to T. r might reach to T' inaccurately instead of T, but $d(r,T) = d(r,T')$. When this movement is complete and r gets activated again in the next LCM cycle, the color MOVE2 indicates that r has moved twice.

Detection of Fault: If r has color MOVE2, but $\mathcal{CV}_r \neq \emptyset$, it changes its color to FAULT. This is necessary because if r is a middle robot of some collinearity $\overline{r_jrr_j^c}$ and it is faulty, the last robot of the collinearity is unable to detect the LOC $\overleftrightarrow{r_jrr_j^c}$. In this case, r acts as a guiding robot for non-faulty robots. When a robot r_j shows the color HALT and $\overline{r_j^crr_j}$ is a collinearity, r changes its color to COLLINEAR from FAULT. If all the robots with color HALT are not part of its own collinearity, r changes its color to NON-COLLINEAR. In case of r having either color COLLINEAR or NON-COLLINEAR and no visible robot with color HALT, it changes its color to FAULT again.

Termination: r changes its color to FINISH and terminates if one of the following situations occurs. (1) $r.color = $ HALT with $\mathcal{CV}_r = \emptyset$ and all robots in $H_{L_r}^{Up}$ are either with color FINISH or NON-COLLINEAR. (2) $r.color = $ HALT with $\mathcal{CV}_r = \emptyset$ and r sees no other robots with color HALT, but multiple robots with color COLLINEAR. (3) $r.color = $ MOVE2 and $\mathcal{CV}_r = \emptyset$. (4) $r.color = $ FAULT and $\forall r' \in \mathcal{CV}_r$ with color either FINISH or FAULT.

4.2   Analysis of the Algorithm

Here we discuss the correctness and time complexity of FAULT_MV_INACC. This algorithm is also collision-free by a similar argument as Theorem 1. Due to space requirement, we could not include some of the proofs in this paper.

Lemma 10. *Two robots with color* HALT *lie in the same horizontal line and can see each other.*

Lemma 11. *A non-faulty robot r can be a part of at most one collinearity, either as a middle robot or the last robot of that collinearity, after its first movement.*

Corollary 3. *If there exists exactly one robot r with color* HALT *at any time, there can be at most one other robot with color* COLLINEAR. *If there are two robots with color* HALT, *there can be at most two other robots with color* COLLINEAR.

Lemma 12. *A non-faulty robot r cannot be a middle robot or the last robot of a collinearity after its second movement.*

Lemma 13. *For any two non-faulty robots r, r' and a faulty robot r'', $\overline{rr''r'}$ cannot be a collinearity, at termination.*

Proof. If r and r' lie on different horizontal lines in the initial configuration, they cannot lie on a horizontal line thereafter, as if r lies below r', $Radius_r < D(r) \leq d(r, L_{r'})$. If r and r' lie on same horizontal line in the initial configuration and r'' lie on a different horizontal line, $L_r \neq L_{r''}$ after the movement, as $Radius_r < D(r) \leq d(r, L_{r''})$. If all three robots lie on a same horizontal line in the initial configuration, all of them cannot be eligible robots at the same time, because of which r'' cannot move simultaneously with r and r''. So, after the movement of r and r', $L_r \neq L_{r''}$, which means the robots become non-collinear. Even after any future movement of either robots, they remains non-collinear by Remark 4. □

Theorem 3. *At termination, all non-faulty robots achieve mutual visibility in $\mathcal{O}(N)$ epochs.*

Proof. By Lemma 13 and Theorem 2, we can conclude that all the non-faulty robots achieve mutual visibility at termination.

A non-faulty robot r can take at most 9 epochs to reach to termination. It takes one epoch to set $r.color$ to MOVE1 from OFF while executing its first movement. If there a robot r' moving simultaneously with r and $r' \in H_{L_r}^{Up}$ after the first move, r has to wait till $r'.color =$ FINISH. r' takes one epoch to change its color to HALT from MOVE1. All the faulty robots with color FAULT in $H_{L_{r'}}^{Up}$ need one epoch to set their color to either COLLINEAR or NON-COLLINEAR from FAULT. r' then takes one epoch to change its color to MOVE2 and executes the second movement, and finally takes one more epoch to set its color to FINISH. So, r needs total 5 epochs to change its color to HALT from MOVE1. Similar to r', r needs 3 epochs to change the color from HALT to FINISH. So, in total, FAULT_MV_INACC runs in $\mathcal{O}(9N) \approx \mathcal{O}(N)$ epochs. □

5   Conclusion

To the best of our knowledge, this paper is the first work that studies the problem of mutual visibility with robots that may exhibit inaccuracies in their movements. Inaccuracy may occur due to multiple reasons such as hardware or software malfunction, geomagnetic hazard etc. If the movements of the robots are not carefully designed, the mutual visibility may never be achieved. We consider luminous opaque robots that neither have any knowledge about the total number of robots nor agree on any global orientation. However, they agree on only one coordinate axes. We present two algorithms. MV_INACC solves the problem under ASYNC setting using 3 colors, when the robots has inaccuracy in movement. FAULT_MV_INACC solves the problem when the robots can be faulty as well as exhibiting inaccuracy in movement. This paper opens many interesting future works. It will be interesting to study the problem with no agreement on any coordinate axis. The problem can also be studied with a different model of robots where they do not have any light on them or the lights become faulty.

References

1. Adhikary, R., Bose, K., Kundu, M.K., Sau, B.: Mutual visibility by asynchronous robots on infinite grid. In: Gilbert, S., Hughes, D., Krishnamachari, B. (eds.) ALGOSENSORS 2018. LNCS, vol. 11410, pp. 83–101. Springer, Cham (2019). https://doi.org/10.1007/978-3-030-14094-6_6
2. Aljohani, A., Sharma, G.: Complete visibility for mobile agents with lights tolerating a faulty agent. In: 2017 IEEE International Parallel and Distributed Processing Symposium Workshops (IPDPSW), pp. 834–843. IEEE (2017)
3. Bhagat, S., Mukhopadhyaya, K.: Mutual visibility by robots with persistent memory. In: Chen, Y., Deng, X., Lu, M. (eds.) FAW 2019. LNCS, vol. 11458, pp. 144–155. Springer, Cham (2019). https://doi.org/10.1007/978-3-030-18126-0_13
4. Bose, K., Chakraborty, A., Mukhopadhyaya, K.: Mutual visibility by fat robots with slim omnidirectional camera. J. Parallel Distrib. Comput. **180**, 104716 (2023)
5. Di Luna, G.A., Flocchini, P., Chaudhuri, S.G., Poloni, F., Santoro, N., Viglietta, G.: Mutual visibility by luminous robots without collisions. Inf. Comput. **254**, 392–418 (2017)
6. Di Luna, G.A., Flocchini, P., Poloni, F., Santoro, N., Viglietta, G.: The mutual visibility problem for oblivious robots. In: CCCG (2014)
7. Poudel, P., Aljohani, A., Sharma, G.: Fault-tolerant complete visibility for asynchronous robots with lights under one-axis agreement. Theor. Comput. Sci. **850**, 116–134 (2021)
8. Pramanick, S., Mandal, P.S.: Fault-tolerant mutual visibility for ASYNC mobile robots with local coordinate. In: 2023 IEEE Guwahati Subsection Conference (GCON). pp. 1–6 (2023). https://doi.org/10.1109/GCON58516.2023.10183479
9. Sharma, G.: Mutual visibility for robots with lights tolerating light faults. In: 2018 IEEE International Parallel and Distributed Processing Symposium Workshops (IPDPSW), pp. 829–836. IEEE (2018)
10. Sharma, G., Alsaedi, R., Busch, C., Mukhopadhyay, S.: The complete visibility problem for fat robots with lights. In: Proceedings of the 19th International Conference on Distributed Computing and Networking. ICDCN 2018, Association for Computing Machinery, New York, NY, USA (2018)

11. Sharma, G., Busch, C., Mukhopadhyay, S.: Mutual visibility with an optimal number of colors. In: Bose, P., Gąsieniec, L.A., Römer, K., Wattenhofer, R. (eds.) ALGOSENSORS 2015. LNCS, vol. 9536, pp. 196–210. Springer, Cham (2015). https://doi.org/10.1007/978-3-319-28472-9_15
12. Sharma, G., Vaidyanathan, R., Trahan, J.: Optimal randomized complete visibility on a grid for asynchronous robots with lights. Int. J. Networking Comput. **11**(1), 50–77 (2021)
13. Sharma, G., Vaidyanathan, R., Trahan, J.L.: Constant-time complete visibility for robots with lights: the asynchronous case. Algorithms **14**(2), 56 (2021)
14. Sharma, G., Vaidyanathan, R., Trahan, J.L., Busch, C., Rai, S.: Complete visibility for robots with lights in $O(1)$ time. In: Bonakdarpour, B., Petit, F. (eds.) SSS 2016. LNCS, vol. 10083, pp. 327–345. Springer, Cham (2016). https://doi.org/10.1007/978-3-319-49259-9_26
15. Vaidyanathan, R., Busch, C., Trahan, J.L., Sharma, G., Rai, S.: Logarithmic-time complete visibility for robots with lights. In: 2015 IEEE International Parallel and Distributed Processing Symposium, pp. 375–384. IEEE (2015)

Minimum Degree and Connectivity in 1-Dimensional Line-of-Sight Networks

Hankang Gu and Michele Zito[✉]

Department of Computer Science, University of Liverpool, Liverpool, UK
H.Gu10@liverpool.ac.uk, michele@liverpool.ac.uk

Abstract. We study the relationship between the smallest positive vertex degrees and the (vertex) connectivity in 1-dimensional line-of-sight (LoS) networks. We show that these networks differ from their higher dimensional counterparts. While a strong relationship exists between the presence of certain low degree vertices and the connectivity of d-dimensional line-of-sight networks, for $d > 1$, the relationship is much weaker in the 1-dimensional case. In particular, the absence of isolated vertices is not sufficient to guarantee connectivity.

1 Introduction and Motivations

Geometric graphs are a popular tool for modelling wireless networks. Typically, wireless devices positioned in some physical space can be seen as a collection of vertices. Communication between physical devices is usually only possible of they are close to each other. A graph can then be constructed on the abstract vertices by representing communication between pairs of devices as edges. Frieze et al. [FKRD09] introduced the notion of (random) 2-dimensional Line-of-Sight (LoS) networks as a model that incorporates visibility as well as distance constraints. A 2-dimensional n by n square lattice is given. A graph vertex is placed at each of the $n \times n$ intersections randomly and independently with probability p. The distance between two vertices lying on a same horizontal or vertical line is the minimum number of intersections one needs to traverse to move from one vertex to the other (with the convention that the lattice is in fact "wrapped around" in a torus). The edges of the network are obtained by connecting pairs of collinear vertices at distance is at most ω. Clearly the larger p the denser the resulting network. And it turns out that, as p grows, the vertex connectivity and the minimum vertex degree of such networks vary fairly regularly in a way that is reminiscent of the evolution of the analogue quantities in Gilbert's binomial random graphs [Gil59]. The model and (to some extent) a study of its connectivity was later extended to higher dimensions and more general visibility patterns by Devroye and Farczadi [DF13].

While the picture is fairly clear for LoS networks in dimension $d \geq 2$, the 1-dimensional networks seem to have received less attention. A 1-dimensional toroidal lattice of size n is just a collection of n points (rather than intersections) which can be thought of as sitting on the circumference of a circle (an example is given on the left

---

Mr. Gu worked on this project during his final year as an undergraduate at the University of Liverpool and, later, in the months leading to the start of his PhD. M. Gu is currently a PhD student in Liverpool.

K. Georgiou and E. Kranakis (Eds.): ALGOWIN 2023, LNCS 14061, pp. 58–73, 2023.
https://doi.org/10.1007/978-3-031-48882-5_5

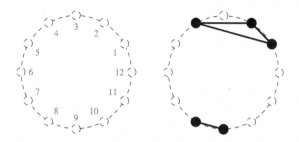

Fig. 1. A 1-dimensional lattice on $n = 12$ points (left) and a LoS network on 5 vertices with $\omega = 3$ (right). Vertex at point 4 and vertex at point 8 are not joined by an edge as their distance is 4, which is larger than ω.

hand side of Fig. 1). Each of these points contains a single vertex of the LoS network G with probability p, and two vertices are adjacent if the minimum number of points one needs to traverse to move from one to the other is at most ω. In this setting we say that G is a 1-dimensional LoS network of size n, range ω and vertex probability p (or an (n, ω, p)-LoS network). A small example of 1-dimensional LoS network is given on the right hand side of Fig. 1. Clearly if $\omega \leq 1$ connectivity is only guaranteed if $p = 1$, and on the other hand if $\omega \geq n$ the resulting network will be connected for any $p > 0$. In what follows, to avoid similar trivialities, we assume that $\omega \gg \log n$, and $\omega = n^{\beta}$, for some β sufficiently small that will be determined in the forthcoming analysis. Topologies of this type have applications in communication problems [HPD07]. Full 1-dimensional LoS networks (i.e. networks built using $p = 1$) are examples of *circulant graphs* [BH90]. Watts and Strogatz [WS98] pointed out that these graphs have interesting clustering features and used them as a basis for their small world networks (obtained from full 1-dimensional LoS networks by randomly rewiring the edges with a small probability q). Figure 2 gives an example. An appropriate choice of q guarantees that the resulting networks will tipically have large clustering coefficients and fairly small vertex to vertex distances. Their model however has hard density constraints: the number of edges in the network is $2\omega n$ and it is not affected by the rewiring. Arbitrary, connected, 1-dimensional LoS networks could be used as an alternative, more general,

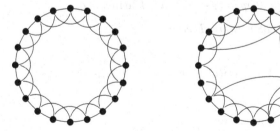

Fig. 2. An example of Watts and Strogatz *small world network*. Starting from a full 1-dimensional LoS network on 20 nodes, with $\omega = 2$ (left), the small world network is the structure resulting from that by rewiring its edges with a fixed, small probability (right). The overall tendency to connect locally is preserved, but the few shortcuts significantly reduce the distances between vertices.

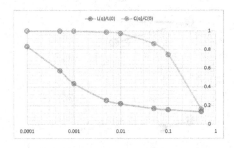
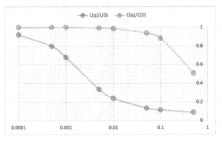

Fig. 3. The plots of the average clustering coefficient $C(q)$, and the average distance $L(q)$ (as defined in [WS98]), relative to their values in the networks with no rewiring, for various values of q, 100 graphs in each case. We used Watts and Strogatz networks on 10,000 nodes and $\omega = O((\log n)^2)$ (left) and small world networks of the same order and visibility range defined starting from 1-dimensional LoS network (right).

starting point. In such case the network density would also be controlled by the vertex probability p rather than just the visibility range ω. Figure 3 shows the results of a very small experiment comparing the clustering and distance properties of the two models. In both cases, values of q around 1% seem to lead to networks with high clustering and small distances.

Here we complement the results in [DF13,FKRD09] and study the smallest non-zero vertex degrees and the connectivity of 1-dimensional LoS networks. We argue that the picture is quite interesting. Similar to line-of-sight networks in higher dimensions, and other random graph models, the most likely value of the minimum degree shifts (in the sense of Theorem 1 below) in a very regular, predictable way as we increase the vertex probability p, but the connectedness seems to follow a different dynamics. We denote by $\delta(G)$ the minimum vertex degree in G. Our first result describes a sequence of phase-transitions of the likely value of $\delta(G)$. In the theorem below, and in the rest of the paper, $\ln x$ denotes the natural logarithm of x, and we use $\log x$ to denote a generic, arbitrary base, logarithm.

Theorem 1. *Let k be a fixed positive integer, assume n and ω are integers, and that n, ω, and p satisfy:*

$$2\omega p = (1 - \beta) \ln n + k \ln \ln n + c_n. \tag{1}$$

Let G be an (n, ω, p)-LoS network. Then

$$\lim_{n \to \infty} \Pr[\delta(G) \geq k] = \begin{cases} 0 & c_n \to -\infty \\ e^{-\lambda_k} & c_n \to c \\ 1 & c_n \to \infty. \end{cases}$$

where

$$\lambda_k = \frac{(1 - \beta)^k e^{-c}}{2(k - 1)!}.$$

and c is a finite real value.

The picture depicted by Theorem 1 is consistent with what happens in higher dimensions. For instance, in the 2-dimensional case, the change from "$\delta(G) \geq k - 1$" to

"$\delta(G) \geq k$" occurs when p satisfies $2\omega p = \left(1 - \frac{\beta}{2}\right)\ln n + \frac{x}{2}\ln\ln n + c$, and x moves from $k - 1$ to k. In particular, if $x = k$, and c is a fixed constant, $\delta(G) \geq k$ with probability approaching $\exp\left\{-\frac{(2-\beta)^k e^{-2c}}{2^2(k-1)!}\right\}$.

Moving on to connectivity, our main result goes as follows:

Theorem 2. *Let n is an integer, and assume that n, ω, and p satisfy:*

$$\omega p = (1 - \beta)\ln n + \ln\ln n + c_n \tag{2}$$

Let G be an (n, ω, p)-LoS network. Then

$$\lim_{n\to\infty}\Pr[G \text{ is connected}] = \begin{cases} 0 & c_n \to -\infty \\ (1 + \lambda)e^{-\lambda} & c_n \to c \\ 1 & c_n \to \infty \end{cases}$$

where

$$\lambda = (1 - \beta)e^{-c}.$$

and c is a finite real value.

The theorem does not rely on the complicated argument used in d-dimensional networks, for $d > 1$, involving a two stage vertex exposure process. In fact we conjecture that the more restricted topology of the 1-dimensional networks makes that argument fail. Instead we use a characterization of the vertex k-connectivity (as defined, say, in [Die00, sect. 1.4]) in 1-dimensional LoS networks in terms of particular configurations of vertices and unoccupied points that we call *holes*. Also, Theorem 2 implies that there is a way to set p so that the resulting graph G has $\delta(G) = 1$ but is not connected, asymptotically almost surely.

The rest of the paper is organized as follows. In Sect. 2 we provide details of our analysis of vertex degrees. Section 3.1 describes our characterization of the connectivity of 1-dimensional LoS network. The rest of Sect. 3 is devoted to the proof of Theorem 2. Following common practice, from here on we will say that an event describing a property of a random structure which depends on a parameter n holds *asymptotically almost surely* (or a.a.s. in short) if the probability of the event tends to one as n tends to infinity.

2 Low Degree Vertices

Let p satisfy (1) for some fixed positive integer k. Define $X_l = X_l(n, \omega, p)$ as the number of vertices of degree l in an (n, ω, p)-LoS network G, for $0 \leq l < k$. Each vertex v, if present, may have as many as 2ω neighbours. The probability that it will have exactly l neighbours is $p\binom{2\omega}{l}p^l(1 - p)^{2\omega-l}$. Therefore, the expected value of X_l, satisfies:

$$\mathbf{E}X_l = np\binom{2\omega}{l}p^l(1 - p)^{2\omega-l}.$$

Here and in the rest of the paper expressions of the form $f(n) \sim g(n)$ are shorthands for the statement

$$\lim_{n \to \infty} \frac{f(n)}{g(n)} = 1.$$

If $2\omega p$ satisfies (1) and $\omega = n^\beta$

$$\mathbf{E}X_l \sim np^{l+1} \frac{2^l \omega^l}{l!} e^{-2\omega p}$$

$$= np^{l+1} \frac{2^l \omega^l}{l!} \frac{e^{(\beta-1)\ln n} e^{-c_n}}{(\ln n)^k}$$

$$= \frac{(2\omega p)^{l+1}}{2\, l!} \frac{e^{-c_n}}{(\ln n)^k}$$

$$= \frac{((1-\beta)\ln n + k \ln\ln n + c_n)^{l+1}}{(\ln n)^k} \frac{e^{-c_n}}{2\, l!}.$$

To prove Theorem 1 we split the analysis depending on how large c_n is. If $c_n \to \infty$ the first of the two fractions is $O((\ln n + c_n)^{l+1}/(\ln n)^k)$, and the whole expression, for $l < k$, is dominated by the factor e^{-c_n}. Therefore $\mathbf{E}X_l \to 0$, for any fixed $l < k$. Hence Markov inequality implies that $X_l = 0$ a.a.s. for $l < k$ and therefore $\delta(G) \geq k$ a.a.s.

Lower Region. At the other extreme, if $c_n \to -\infty$ then e^{-c_n} diverges, $\mathbf{E}X_{k-1} \to \infty$, and we apply the so called second moment method. We use Chebyshev's inequality to show that $X_{k-1} > 0$ and therefore $\delta(G) < k$, a.a.s. In symbols

$$\Pr[X_{k-1} = 0] \leq \Pr[|X_{k-1} - \mathbf{E}X_{k-1}| \geq \mathbf{E}X_{k-1}] \leq \frac{\mathbf{E}(X_{k-1})^2 - (\mathbf{E}X_{k-1})^2}{(\mathbf{E}X_{k-1})^2}.$$

Here and in the forthcoming study of the minimum degree in what we call the central region crucial to our argument is the analysis of the expected number of pairs of vertices of given degree. In particular we will exploit the limited dependence between such objects. The phenomenon, described informally in Fig. 4, will enable us to prove that $\mathbf{E}(X_{k-1})^2 \sim (\mathbf{E}X_{k-1})^2$.

In what follows if B is a boolean condition then $\delta_B = 1$ (resp. 0) if B is true (false). Also, the terms in the sums exist only if the binomial coefficients within them are non-zero, and, similarly, the sums are non-zero only if the top limit for their index is not smaller than the lower one.

Lemma 1. *The expected number of pairs of vertices of degree l, in an (n, ω, p)-LoS network, $\mathbf{E}(X_l)^2$, is the sum of three parts:*

– *the contribution for each vertex, squared,*

$$n \binom{2\omega}{l}^2 p^{2l+2}(1-p)^{4\omega-2l},$$

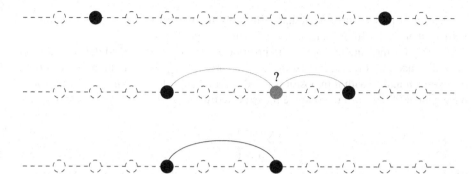

Fig. 4. Assume $\omega = 3$. The degrees of two vertices at distance more than 2ω are independent (top drawing). If the distance between the two is at most 2ω they are dependent (mid drawing): the presence of a vertex between them will affect their degrees. Finally (bottom drawing) two vertices at distance at most ω cannot have degree zero.

– *the contribution from all pairs of distinct vertices at distance $i \leq 2\omega$:*

$$2np^2 \sum_{i=1}^{2\omega} \sum_{d=\max(0,l-(2\omega-i-1+2\delta_{i>\omega}))}^{\min(i,l-1+\delta_{i>\omega})} \binom{i-\delta_{i>\omega}}{d}^2 \binom{2\omega-i-1+2\delta_{i>\omega}}{l-1+\delta_{i>\omega}-d}$$
$$\times p^{l-1+\delta_{i>\omega}+d}(1-p)^{2\omega+i-l-\delta_{i>\omega}-d},$$

– *and the contribution from all pairs of vertices at distance greater than 2ω:*

$$(n(n-1)-2\omega n)\binom{2\omega}{l}^2 p^{2l+2}(1-p)^{4\omega-2l}.$$

Proof. For each $l \geq 0$, the random variable X_l is the sum of n random indicators, one for each position in the ring, witnessing the event

$l(x) \equiv$ position x is occupied by a vertex and the degree of such vertex is l.

Hence $(X_l)^2$ has the form

$$\sum_x (\mathbb{I}_{l(x)})^2 + 2 \sum_{x,x'} \mathbb{I}_{l(x)} \mathbb{I}_{l(x')},$$

the second sum being over all unordered pairs of positions. By linearity of expectation:

$$\mathbf{E}(X_l)^2 = \sum_x \mathbf{E}(\mathbb{I}_{l(x)})^2 + 2 \sum_{x,x'} \mathbf{E}\mathbb{I}_{l(x)} \mathbb{I}_{l(x')},$$

and the first part of the statement follows as

$$\sum_x \mathbf{E}(\mathbb{I}_{l(x)})^2 = n \binom{2\omega}{l}^2 p^{2l+2}(1-p)^{4\omega-2l}.$$

The third part follows from analyzing only the part of the second sum involving vertices that are far from each other (and using independence).

Finally for the middle one fix u in position $x \in \{1, \dots, n\}$ around the circle, v can be at distance $i \in \{1, \dots, 2\omega\}$ from u. Therefore, if $\mathbb{I}_{(x,i)}$ is the random indicator for the event "u and v, with u in position x and v at distance i to the right (clockwise) of u, have degree l", we need to compute the expected value of

$$2 \sum_{x=1}^{n} \sum_{i=1}^{2\omega} \mathbb{I}_{(x,i)}.$$

The indicators are not independent, however their distribution only depends on i, the distance between u and v. For each choice of x and i,

$$\Pr[\mathbb{I}_{(x,i)} = 1] = p^2 \times$$
$$\sum_{d_1=0}^{l-1+\delta_{i>\omega}} \sum_{d_2=0}^{l-1+\delta_{i>\omega}} \binom{i - \delta_{i>\omega}}{d_1} \binom{i - \delta_{i>\omega}}{d_2} \binom{2\omega - i - 1 + 2\delta_{i>\omega}}{s} \times$$
$$p^{d_1+d_2+s}(1-p)^{2\omega+i-1-d_1-d_2-s}.$$

In this expression p^2 is the probability that u and v are present. If u and v are at distance i there are exactly $2\omega - i - 1 + 2\delta_{i>\omega}$ positions that, if occupied, lead to an increase in the degree of both u and v. Parameter s counts the number of such *shared* neighbours. The remaining $l - 1 - s$ neighbours of u and v will be among the other $i - \delta_{i>\omega}$ vertices around. Note that the probability does not depend on u. Therefore the expected number of pairs of degree l at distance at most 2ω is

$$2n \sum_{i=1}^{2\omega} \Pr[\mathbb{I}_{(x,i)} = 1].$$

Finally note that s, d_1 and d_2 are dependent as $2s + d_1 + d_2 = 2(l - 1 + \delta_{i>\omega})$. In fact if the two vertices have s common neighbours, and they both have degree l, then they must also have the same number of individual additional neighbours. In other words, $d_1 = d_2 = d$, $s = l - 1 + \delta_{i>\omega} - d$, and the expression above reduces to the one in the theorem statement (if the two vertices have degree l then they have a total of $l - 1 + \delta_{i>\omega} + d$ distinct neighbours). ∎

Clearly for any positive integer l

$$n \binom{2\omega}{l}^2 p^{2l+2}(1-p)^{4\omega-2l} + (n(n-1) - 2\omega n) \binom{2\omega}{l}^2 p^{2l+2}(1-p)^{4\omega-2l}$$

equals $\left(1 - \frac{2\omega}{n}\right)(\mathbf{E}X_l)^2$. So to conclude our argument we need to show that the contribution to $\mathbf{E}(X_{k-1})^2$ due to pairs of distinct vertices at distance at most 2ω is asymptotically a lot smaller than $(\mathbf{E}X_{k-1})^2$. We split the analysis in few cases depending on the distances between pairs of vertices and, when the distance is at least $k - 1$ and at most $2\omega - k + 1$, we use the tight relationship between hypergeometric and multinomial probabilities to obtain bounds of sufficient accuracy.

For given positive integers N and $m \leq N$, integers $b > 1$ and $k_1, \ldots, k_b$ adding up to m, and discrete probability distribution $p_1, \ldots, p_b$, the hypergeometric probabilities are defined as

$$P_{N,m,\mathbf{p}}(\mathbf{k}) = \binom{N}{m}^{-1} \prod_{j=1}^{b} \binom{Np_j}{k_j}$$

(in our treatment we assume that Np_j are positive integers, for all j) while the "corresponding" multinomial ratios are:

$$Q_{m,\mathbf{p}}(\mathbf{k}) = \frac{m}{\prod_{j=1}^{b} k_j!} \prod_{j=1}^{b} p_j^{k_j}.$$

Lemma 2. *Let γ be a positive real number. If $m \leq \gamma N$, and $\max_{1 \leq j \leq b}(k_j/p_j) \leq \gamma N$, we have*

$$\log \left(\frac{P_{N,n,\mathbf{p}}(\mathbf{k})}{Q_{n,\mathbf{p}}(\mathbf{k})} \right) \leq \frac{1}{N} \left[\binom{m}{2} - \sum_{j=1}^{b} \frac{1}{p_j} \left(k_j^2 - \frac{k_j}{2} \right) \right] +$$

$$- \sum_{j=1}^{b} \frac{k_j}{2(Np_j)^2} \left[\frac{k_j^2 - k_j/2}{1 - k_j/Np_j} + \frac{2}{(12 - (k_j - 1)/Np_j)} \right] +$$

$$+ \frac{n^3}{2N^2} + \frac{n^2}{4N^2} + \frac{n^3}{4N^3} + \frac{12n}{12(N - n)(12N + 1)}.$$

Proof. Clearly we can write $\log \left(\frac{P_{N,m,\mathbf{p}}(\mathbf{k})}{Q_{m,\mathbf{p}}(\mathbf{k})} \right)$ as:

$$\sum_{j=1}^{b} \log(Np_j)! - \sum_{j=1}^{b} \log(Np_j - k_j)! + \log(N - m)! - \log N! - \sum_{j=1}^{b} k_j \log p_j.$$

Then, using

$$\frac{1}{2} \log \pi + (m + \frac{1}{2}) \log m - m + \frac{1}{12m + 1} \leq \log m! \leq \frac{1}{2} \log \pi + (m + \frac{1}{2}) \log m - m + \frac{1}{12m}. \tag{3}$$

we can bound $\log \left(\frac{P_{N,m,\mathbf{p}}(\mathbf{k})}{Q_{m,\mathbf{p}}(\mathbf{k})} \right)$ by

$$- \sum_{j=1}^{b} \left[Np_j \left(1 - \frac{k_j}{Np_j} \right) \log \left(1 - \frac{k_j}{Np_j} \right) + \frac{1}{2} \log \left(1 - \frac{k_j}{Np_j} \right) \right]$$

$$+ N \left(1 - \frac{m}{N} \right) \log \left(1 - \frac{m}{N} \right)$$

$$+ \frac{1}{2} \log \left(1 - \frac{m}{N} \right) + \frac{12\,m}{12(N - m)(12N + 1)} - \sum_{j=1}^{b} \frac{12k_j}{12Np_j(12(Np_j - k_j) + 1)}.$$

We can then get rid of the logarithms using

$$-x - \frac{x^2}{2(1-x)} \leq \log(1-x) \leq -x - \frac{x^2}{2},$$

which are valid for any real number x with $|x| < 1$ (Also note that $\sum k_j = m$).   ∎

We now come to the main result.

Theorem 3. *Let k be a fixed positive integer, assume n and ω are integers with $\omega = n^\beta$ for some $\beta > 0$, and that n, ω, and p satisfy:*

$$2\omega p = (1 - \beta) \ln n + k \ln \ln n + c_n$$

for some $c_n \to -\infty$. Let G be an (n, ω, p)-LoS network. Then

$$\mathbf{E}(X_{k-1})^2 = (1 + o(1))(\mathbf{E}X_{k-1})^2.$$

Proof. Clearly for any positive integer l

$$n\binom{2\omega}{l}^2 p^{2l+2}(1-p)^{4\omega-2l} + (n(n-1) - 2\omega n)\binom{2\omega}{l}^2 p^{2l+2}(1-p)^{4\omega-2l}$$

equals $\left(1 - \frac{2\omega}{n}\right)(\mathbf{E}X_l)^2$. Therefore Theorem 3 will follow if we can show that the contribution to $\mathbf{E}(X_l)^2$ from pairs at distance at most 2ω is small compared to $(\mathbf{E}X_l)^2 = n^2\binom{2\omega}{l}^2 p^{2l+2}(1-p)^{4\omega-2l}$. when

$$2\omega p = (1 - \beta) \ln n + (l+1) \ln \ln n + c_n$$

with $c_n \to -\infty$. To keep the presentation tidy we only give details for the case $i \leq \omega$. The case $i \in \{\omega+1, \dots, 2\omega\}$ can be handled similarly.

If $i \leq \omega$ we distinguish two further cases (if $l > 0$). When $i \leq l-1$ we have $\binom{i}{d} \leq 2^i \leq 2^{l-1}$ and $\binom{2\omega-i-1}{l-1-d} \leq \binom{2\omega}{l}$, for large n, since l is a fixed constant. Hence

$$\sum_{i=1}^{l-1} \sum_{d=0}^{i} \binom{i}{d}^2 \binom{2\omega-i-1}{l-1-d} p^{l-1+d}(1-p)^{2\omega+i-l-d} \leq$$

$$\leq \binom{2\omega}{l}(2p)^{l-1}(1-p)^{2\omega-l} \sum_{i=1}^{l-1} \sum_{d=0}^{i} \binom{i}{d} p^d(1-p)^{i-d}$$

$$= \binom{2\omega}{l}(2p)^{l-1}(1-p)^{2\omega-l}(l-1).$$

Also

$$\frac{2np^2}{n^2\binom{2\omega}{l}^2 p^{2l+2}(1-p)^{4\omega-2l}} = \frac{2(1-p)^{2l}}{n\binom{2\omega}{l}^2 p^{2l}(1-p)^{4\omega}}$$

Therefore the contribution to $\mathbf{E}(X_l)^2$ from pairs at distance at most $l-1$, for large n, relative to $(\mathbf{E}X_l)^2$, is at most

$$(l-1) \times \frac{(2l)^l(1-p)^l}{n(2\omega)^l p^{l+1}(1-p)^{2\omega}}.$$

(using $\binom{2\omega}{l} \geq (2\omega/l)^l$). For any fixed $l > 0$, $(l-1)(2l)^l(1-p)^l$ is a bounded quantity. Also $np \sim (1-\beta)\ln n$, $(2\omega p)^l \sim ((1-\beta)\ln n)^l$, and $(1-p)^{-2\omega} \sim e^{2\omega p} = n^{1-\beta}(\ln n)^{l+1}e^{c_n}$. Hence

$$\frac{1}{np(2\omega p)^l(1-p)^{2\omega}} \sim \frac{n^{1-\beta}(\ln n)^{l+1}e^{c_n}}{n^{1-\beta}(1-\beta)^{l+1}(\ln n)^{l+1}} \sim \frac{e^{c_n}}{(1-\beta)^{l+1}} \to 0.$$

We now focus on larger distances. The contribution from all pairs of distinct vertices at distance $l \leq i \leq \omega$ (divided by $(\mathbf{E}X_l)^2$) is

$$\frac{2np^2}{n^2\binom{2\omega}{l}^2 p^{2l+2}(1-p)^{4\omega-2l}} \sum_{i=l}^{\omega}\sum_{d=0}^{l-1} \binom{i}{d}^2\binom{2\omega-i-1}{l-1-d}p^{l-1+d}(1-p)^{2\omega+i-l-d}. \quad (4)$$

Multiplying and dividing by $\binom{2\omega+i-1}{l-1+d}$ we get

$$\frac{2np^2}{n^2\binom{2\omega}{l}^2 p^{2l+2}(1-p)^{4\omega-2l}} \sum_{i=l}^{\omega}\sum_{d=0}^{l-1} \frac{\binom{i}{d}^2\binom{2\omega-i-1}{l-1-d}}{\binom{2\omega+i-1}{l-1+d}}\binom{2\omega+i-1}{l-1+d}p^{l-1+d}(1-p)^{2\omega+i-l-d}.$$

Using Lemma 2 with $b = 3$, $(k_1, k_2, k_3) = (d, d, l-d-1)$, $N = 2\omega+i-1$ and $Np_1 = Np_2 = i$, and $Np_3 = 2\omega-i-1$ we have

$$\frac{\binom{i}{d}^2\binom{2\omega-i-1}{l-1-d}}{\binom{2\omega+i-1}{l-1+d}} \leq (1+o(1))\frac{(l+d-1)!}{d!\,d!\,(l-d-1)!}\left(\frac{i}{2\omega+i-1}\right)^{2d}\left(\frac{2\omega-i-1}{2\omega+i-1}\right)^{l-d-1}.$$

If $l \leq i \leq \omega$, the double sum is at most a constant times

$$\sum_{i=l}^{\omega}\sum_{d=0}^{l-1} \frac{(l+d-1)!}{d!\,d!\,(l-d-1)!}\left(\frac{i}{2\omega+i-1}\right)^{2d}\left(\frac{2\omega-i-1}{2\omega+i-1}\right)^{l-d-1}\binom{2\omega+i-1}{l-1+d}p^{l-1+d}(1-p)^{2\omega+i-l-d}.$$

Combining the factorials and the binomial coefficient, and re-arranging the exponential factors gives

$$\sum_{i=l}^{\omega}\sum_{d=0}^{l-1} \binom{2\omega+i-1}{d,d,l-d-1}\left(\frac{ip}{2\omega+i-1}\right)^{2d}\left(\frac{(2\omega-i-1)p}{2\omega+i-1}\right)^{l-d-1}(1-p)^{2\omega+i-l-d}.$$

We work on the term in the sums.

$$\binom{2\omega+i-1}{d,d,l-d-1}\left(\frac{ip}{2\omega+i-1}\right)^{2d}\left(\frac{(2\omega-i-1)p}{2\omega+i-1}\right)^{l-d-1}(1-p)^{2\omega+i-l-d} \leq$$

$$\leq e^{-\frac{2i(l-1)}{2\omega+i-1}}p^{l-1}(1-p)^{2\omega+i-l}\binom{2\omega+i-1}{d,d,l-d-1}\left(\frac{i^2p}{((2\omega-1)^2-i^2)(1-p)}\right)^{d}.$$

The first sum is bounded above by the following geometric sum

$$\sum_{i=l}^{\omega}\left[e^{-\frac{2(l-1)}{3\omega-1}}(1-p)\right]^{i}.$$

The second one is a multinomial quantity, we claim that there is a value $\mathbf{B}_l$ independent of n such that

$$\sum_{d=0}^{l-1} \binom{2\omega+i-1}{d,d,l-d-1} \left(\frac{i^2 p}{((2\omega-1)^2-i^2)(1-p)}\right)^d \le \mathbf{B}_l \left(\frac{3\omega^3 p}{\omega-1}\right)^{l-1}$$

(This can be proved by bounding each term in the sum using textbook bounds on the binomial coefficients). Hence (4) is at most (omitting multiplicative constants)

$$\frac{n^{1-2\delta}e^{2c}}{(\ln n)^{l-1}} p^{l-1}(1-p)^{2\omega-l}\left(\frac{3\omega^3 p}{\omega-1}\right)^{l-1}\sum_{i=l}^{\omega} e^{-\frac{2i(l-1)}{2\omega+i-1}}(1-p)^i \le$$

$$\le \frac{n^{1-2\delta}e^{2c}}{(\ln n)^{l-1}}(1-p)^{2\omega-l}\left(\frac{3\omega^3 p^2}{\omega-1}\right)^{l-1}\sum_{i=l}^{\omega}\left[e^{-\frac{2(l-1)}{3\omega-1}}(1-p)\right]^i$$

$$= \frac{n^{1-2\delta}e^{2c}}{(\ln n)^{l-1}}(1-p)^{2\omega-l}\left(\frac{3\omega^3 p^2}{\omega-1}\right)^{l-1}\left\{\frac{\left[e^{-\frac{2(l-1)}{3\omega-1}}(1-p)\right]^l-\left[e^{-\frac{2(l-1)}{3\omega-1}}(1-p)\right]^{\omega+1}}{1-e^{-\frac{2(l-1)}{3\omega-1}}(1-p)}\right\}$$

using the geometric sum. Now the right-most factor converges to $1/p$. So we have

$$\frac{n^{1-2\delta}e^{2c}}{(\ln n)^{l-1}}p^{l-1}(1-p)^{2\omega-l}\left(\frac{3\omega^3 p}{\omega-1}\right)^{l-1}\sum_{i=l}^{\omega}e^{-\frac{2i(l-1)}{2\omega+i-1}}(1-p)^i \le \frac{n^{1-2\delta}e^{2c}}{(\ln n)^{l-1}}(1-p)^{2\omega-l}\left(\frac{3\omega^3 p^2}{\omega-1}\right)^{l-1}\times\frac{2\omega}{\ln n}$$

For large n, $\left(\frac{3\omega^3 p^2}{\omega-1}\right)^{l-1}$ approaches $(3\omega^2 p^2)^{l-1}$ and $(1-p)^{2\omega-l}$ is no different from $(1-p)^{2\omega}$. So the main parts of the bound above are:

$$\frac{n^{1-2\delta}e^{2c}}{(\ln n)^{l-1}}(1-p)^{2\omega}(\omega^2 p^2)^{l-1}\times\frac{\omega}{\ln n}\le\frac{n^{1-2\delta}e^{2c}}{(\ln n)^{l-1}}e^{-2\omega p}(\omega^2 p^2)^{l-1}\times\frac{\omega}{\ln n}$$

$$\le\frac{n^{1-2\delta}e^{2c}}{(\ln n)^{l-1}}\times\frac{n^{-(1-\delta)}e^{-c}}{(\ln n)^{l+1}}\times(\ln n)^{2(l-1)}\times\frac{n^\delta}{\ln n}$$

$$=\frac{e^c}{(\ln n)^3}$$

as $1-2\delta-1+\delta+\delta=0$ (the exponent of n) and $2(l-1)-2l-1=-3$ (the exponent of $\ln n$).   ∎

Central Region. If $c_n = c$, a fixed constant, then $\mathbf{E}X_l$ goes to zero if $l < k-1$, converges to

$$\lambda_k = \frac{(1-\beta)^k e^{-c}}{2(k-1)!}$$

if $l = k-1$, and diverges for larger[1] values of l. We will use an argument similar to that of Frieze *et al.* (see [FKRD09, Section 2.1]), however our analysis of the expected

---

[1] Obviously $\mathbf{E}X_l = 0$ for $l > 2\omega$, and it may well be that $\mathbf{E}X_l \to 0$ for $l < 2\omega$ but $l = l(n) \to \infty$. We do not investigate that region of values, related to the maximum degree of the LoS network, in this report.

number of pairs of low degree vertices that are not too far from each other will need to be more accurate.

Let's denote by X the number of vertices of degree less than k ($X = \sum_{l<k} X_l$). The random variable X is the sum of all contributions from vertices that are at distance greater than 2ω, which is denoted by X', and those from all other vertices, X''. Arguing as we did in the lower region one can show that the expectation of X'' is:

$$np^2 \sum_{i=1}^{2\omega} \sum_{s=0}^{k-2+\delta_i>\omega} \binom{2\omega - i - 1 + 2\delta_{i>\omega}}{s} p^s(1-p)^{2\omega-i-1+2\delta_{i>\omega}-s} \times$$

$$\left(\sum_{d=0}^{k-2+\delta_{i>\omega}-s} \binom{i - \delta_{i>\omega}}{d} p^d(1-p)^{i-\delta_{i>\omega}-d} \right)^2 \quad (5)$$

and then show that $\mathbf{E}X''$ tends to zero as n grows to infinity. This implies that we get accurate information about X by just working with X' as

$$\Pr[X - X' > 0] = \Pr[X'' > 0] \le \mathbf{E}X'' \to 0.$$

Finally we prove that X' converges in distribution to a Poisson random variable with parameter λ_k. To do this we use the so called method of moments, a classical result in probability (see [Chu74, Theorem 4.5.5]) which gives information about the asymptotic distribution of a sequence of random variables $Z_0, Z_1, \ldots, Z_n, \ldots$ based on the values of their factorial moments $\mathbf{E}(Z_n)_r = \mathbf{E}(Z_n(Z_n - 1)(Z_n - 2) \ldots (Z_n - r + 1))$. The following formulation, is a special case of [Bol01, Theorem 1.22]:

Theorem 4. *Let λ be a non-negative bounded real number. Let $Z_0, Z_1, \ldots$ be non-negative integer valued random variables, such that*

$$\lim_{n\to\infty} \mathbf{E}(Z_n)_r = \lambda^r$$

for each positive integer r. Then the sequence $(Z_n)_{n\in\mathbb{N}}$ converges in distribution to a Poisson random variable with parameter λ.

In our setting

$$\mathbf{E}X' = np \sum_{i=0}^{k-1} p^i(1-p)^{2\omega-i}$$

and the expected value of $(X')_r$ can be found using repeatedly the fact that $\mathbf{E}X'^2 = (\mathbf{E}X')^2$, which is valid because of the independence of the degree of the vertices that are far from each other. We obtain

$$\mathbf{E}(X')_r \sim \left(np \sum_{i=0}^{k-1} p^i(1-p)^{2\omega-i} \right)^r \sim \left(\frac{(1-\beta)^k e^{-c}}{2(k-1)!} \right)^r .$$

3 Connectivity

In the higher dimensional case one argues that LoS networks can be generated by producing the vertices in two stages. Most vertices are generated in the first stage, the second one is there to allow the creation of few more vertices that are likely to patch up into a connected whole all components created during stage one. A probabilistic argument is needed to show that most vertex neighbours are quite well-populated at the end of stage one and this implies that adding few more vertices in stage two is likely to result in a connected network. Here there is only one direction for the edges, and the argument above does not seem to work. We find, however, that connectivity depends on the presence of large sequences of unoccupied points in the 1-dimensional toroidal lattice.

3.1 Holes

A *hole starting at vertex* v in a 1-dimensional LoS network G is a sequence of consecutive lattice points starting with the one occupied by v, followed by a collection of empty points up to, but not including, the next occupied one, in a circular way, counterclockwise. We call the vertex in the hole and that immediately following the hole the *(hole) border*. The *width* of a hole is the number of empty points it contains. The network on the right-hand side of Fig. 1 has four holes, two of width one, one of width two, and one of width three. Clearly the two vertices in the border of a hole are connected by an edge if and only if the hole has width less than ω. Hence the following statement characterizes vertex connectivity in 1-dimensional LoS networks.

Theorem 5. *Let $k \geq 0$ be a fixed integer, and G be an arbitrary 1-dimensional LoS network. Then G is (vertex) k-connected if and only if for any set U of at most $k - 1$ vertices $G - U$ contains at most one hole of width at least ω.*

For $k = 1$ the condition applies to G itself. Note that the result has a simple algorithmic consequence: the connectivity problem in 1-dimensional LoS networks can be reduced to checking the existence of two wide holes.

3.2 Connectivity Phase Transition

A key property of holes is that pairs of holes can't intersect. Therefore the presence of a hole of width at least ω starting at v is uniquely determined by the presence of a hole of width exactly ω starting at v. Let H be the random variable counting holes of width at least ω in an (n, ω, p)-LoS network. If $\mathbb{I}_v$ is a random indicator equal to one (resp. 0) if vertex v and the subsequent ω points in the lattice form a hole, then we can write

$$H = \mathbb{I}_0 + \sum_v \mathbb{I}_v,$$

where $\mathbb{I}_0$ is the random indicator for the occurrence of the empty network. The following will be crucial in our analysis.

Lemma 3.
$$\mathbf{E}H = (1-p)^n + np(1-p)^\omega. \tag{6}$$

Also
$$\mathbf{Var}H = \mathbf{E}H - (\mathbf{E}H)^2 + (n - 2\omega - 1)np^2(1-p)^{2\omega}. \tag{7}$$

Proof. We have $\Pr[\mathbb{I}_0 = 1] = (1-p)^n$ (no vertex is present) and $\Pr[\mathbb{I}_v = 1] = p(1-p)^\omega$ (all that matters is that v is present and the following ω points are unoccupied). Equation (6) is immediate. To believe (7) notice that

$$\mathbf{Var}H = \sum_{v=0}^{n} \mathbf{Var}\mathbb{I}_v + 2 \sum_{\{u,v\}\in\{0,\dots,n\}} \mathbf{Cov}\mathbb{I}_u\mathbb{I}_v$$

and observe that two holes cannot intersect so

$$\mathbf{Cov}\mathbb{I}_u\mathbb{I}_v = -\Pr[\mathbb{I}_u = 1]\Pr[\mathbb{I}_v = 1]$$

if u and v are close to each other, and $\mathbf{Cov}\mathbb{I}_u\mathbb{I}_v = 0$ otherwise. ∎

In this section we prove Theorem 2. Similarly to what we did in the analysis of the minimum degree, we split the presentation in three parts. First notice that $\mathbf{E}H \to 0$ if p satisfies

$$\omega p = (1-\beta)\ln n + \ln\ln n + c_n$$

and $c_n \to \infty$. To see this observe that as long as p is asymptotically larger than $1/n$ the first term in $\mathbf{E}H$ is $o(1)$. The second term is at most $npe^{-p\omega}$. Remembering that $n^\beta = \omega$ and replacing $p\omega$ gives

$$np\frac{n^{-(1-\beta)}e^{-c_n}}{\ln n} = \frac{pn^\beta e^{-c_n}}{\ln n}.$$

Using (2) and the assumption about ω again gives

$$\frac{[(1-\beta)\ln n + \ln\ln n + c_n]\,e^{-c_n}}{\ln n} \to (1-\beta)(1+o(1))\,e^{-c_n},$$

and the result follows.

Corollary 1. $\Pr[(n,\omega,p)\text{-LoS network is NOT connected}] \to 0$ *if p satisfies*

$$\omega p = (1-\beta)\ln n + \ln\ln n + c_n$$

and $c_n \to \infty$.

Proof. A 1-dimensional LoS network is NOT connected if and only if it contains at least two large holes. By Markov's inequality

$$\Pr[H \geq 2] \leq \frac{\mathbf{E}H}{2}$$

and the result follows from the calculations above.

Lower Region. We need a simple second moment analysis to show that 1-dimensional LoS networks are a.a.s. NOT connected if $c_n \to -\infty$.

Theorem 6. $\Pr[(n, \omega, p)\text{-LoS network is connected}] \to 0$ *if p satisfies*

$$\omega p = (1 - \beta) \ln n + \ln \ln n + c_n$$

and $c_n \to -\infty$.

Proof. Notice that the event "$H < 2$" is equivalent to "$H - \mathbf{E}H < 2 - \mathbf{E}H$". Hence

$$\Pr[H < 2] \le \Pr[|H - \mathbf{E}H| > \mathbf{E}H - 2] \le \frac{\mathrm{Var}H}{(\mathbf{E}H - 2)^2}$$

where the first inequality is simply a union bound, the second one is Chebyshev's (see, for instance, [Bol01, p. 2]). It is easy to see that for sufficiently large n

$$\mathbf{E}H \ge n^{-\frac{p}{1-p}(1-\beta)} \frac{((1 - \beta) \ln n + \ln \ln n + c_n)e^{-\frac{c_n}{1-p}}}{(\ln n)^{1/(1-p)}}.$$

Hence, if $c_n \to -\infty$ then $\mathbf{E}H \to \infty$. The result now follows since $\mathrm{Var}H \le \mathbf{E}H$. ■

Central Region. Finally, if $c_n = c$ and c is a constant then $\mathbf{E}H \to (1 - \beta)e^{-c}$. We can prove that H converges in distribution to a Poisson random variable with parameter $(1 - \beta)e^{-c}$. We use Theorem 4 again, on H. We have already argued about $\mathbf{E}H$.

Claim. $\mathbf{E}(H)_2 \to (1 - \beta)^2 e^{-2c}$.

To believe this notice that for any r.v. X, $\mathbf{E}(X)_2 = \mathbf{E}(X(X - 1)) = \mathbf{E}X^2 - \mathbf{E}X$, and $\mathbf{E}X^2 = \mathrm{Var}X + (\mathbf{E}X)^2$. Hence:

$$\mathbf{E}(X)_2 = \mathrm{Var}X + (\mathbf{E}X)^2 - \mathbf{E}X.$$

Equality (7) gives an expression for $\mathrm{Var}H$. Therefore we have

$$\mathbf{E}(H)_2 = (n - 2\omega - 1)np^2(1 - p)^{2\omega}$$

which converges to $(np)^2(1 - p)^{2\omega}$, and the claim follows substituting the asymptotic expression for $\mathbf{E}H$.

Claim. In general

$$\mathbf{E}(H)_k = \sum \mathbf{E}\mathbb{I}_{j_1} \cdot \ldots \cdot \mathbb{I}_{j_k}$$

where the sum is over all ordered k-tuples of distinct indicators.

Note that

$$\mathbf{E}\mathbb{I}_{j_1} \cdot \ldots \cdot \mathbb{I}_{j_k} \sim p^k(1 - p)^{k\omega}$$

as it is simply the joint probability that all indicators are one, and that expression only has contributions from k-tuples of indicators referring to disjoint runs. There are $O(n^k)$ terms in the sum (the number of ways to choose the k disjoint sequences).

Applying Theorem 4 we conclude that the distribution of H converges to a Poisson law with parameter $(1 - \beta)e^{-c}$. Hence,

$$\Pr[\text{1-dimensional LoS network is connected}] = \Pr[H < 2] \to \frac{1 + (1 - \beta)e^{-c}}{e^{(1-\beta)e^{-c}}}$$

which completes the proof of Theorem 2.

3.3 Conclusions

We presented tight results on the minimum degree and connectivity of 1-dimensional line-of-sight networks. The approach can be extended to study k-connectivity for $k > 1$. One can define a random variable $H^{(k)}$ which is positive if and only if G is not k-connected:

$$H^{(k)} = \mathbb{I}_{H_\omega > 1} + \sum_{j=1}^{n} \mathbb{I}^{-\{j\}} + \sum_{\{i,j\}} \mathbb{I}^{-\{i,j\}} + \dots$$

where, if U is a set of at most $k - 1$ positions, $\mathbb{I}^{-U}$ is one (resp. zero) if G is $|U|$-connected, all positions in U are occupied and $G - U$ is NOT connected (i.e. it has at least two wide holes). However, for $k > 2$ the distribution of $\mathbb{I}^{-U}$ becomes quite difficult to analyze. We preferred to present the key results on degrees and connectivity here, and leave the study of higher connectivity to a follow up to this work.

References

[BH90]   Buckley, F., Harary, F.: Distance in Graphs. Addison-Wesley, Boston (1990)

[Bol01] Bollobás, B.: Random Graphs. Cambridge Studies in Advanced Mathematics, vol. 73, 2nd edn. Cambridge University Press, Cambridge (2001)

[Chu74] Chung, K.L.: A Course in Probability Theory. Academic Press, Cambridge (1974)

[DF13]   Devroye, L., Farczadi, L.: Connectivity for line-of-sight networks in higher dimensions. Discret. Math. Theor. Comput. Sci. **15**(2), 71–86 (2013)

[Die00] Diestel, R.: Graph Theory. Graduate Texts in Mathematics, vol. 173. Springer, Heidelberg (2000)

[FKRD09] Frieze, A., Kleinberg, J., Ravi, R., Debany, W.: Line-of-sight networks. Comb. Probab. Comput. **18**(1–2), 145–163 (2009)

[Gil59] Gilbert, E.N.: Random graphs. Ann. Math. Stat. **30**, 1141–1144 (1959)

[HPD07] Hall, B., Paulitsch, M., Driscoll, K.: FlexRay BRAIN fusion a FlexRay-based braided ring availability integrity network. SAE Trans. **116**, 460–473 (2007)

[WS98]   Watts, D.J., Strogatz, S.H.: Collective dynamics of "small-world" networks. Nature **393**(4), 440–442 (1998)

WUBBLE: Energy Efficient BLE Neighborhood Discovery Leveraging Wake-Up Radio

Nour El Hoda Djidi[1][iD], Damien Wohwe Sambo[2][✉][iD], Matthieu Gautier[1][iD],
Olivier Berder[1][iD], and Nathalie Mitton[2][iD]

[1] Univ Rennes, CNRS, IRISA, Lannion, France
{nour-el-hoda.djidi,matthieu.gautier,olivier.berder}@irisa.fr
[2] FUN Team, INRIA, Lille, France
{damien.wohwe-sambo,nathalie.mitton}@inria.fr

Abstract. In wireless sensor networks, much energy is wasted during connecting and control processes. This is particularly true for the neighborhood discovery process carried out in Bluetooth Low Energy (BLE) before the communications between devices. However, the fixed duration of this process has a critical energy cost when the number of neighbors is low or when only a few neighbors are required by the application. In order to address this issue, a novel protocol called WUBBLE is proposed to leverage wake-up radio technology to start and end the discovery process. Wake-up radio enables additional communications between devices with an ultra-low energy overhead. WUBBLE is validated by combining analytical analysis and experimental measurements, and results show that half of the energy could be gained to discover 90% of the neighbors.

Keywords: BLE · Wake-up radio · MAC protocols · Wireless Sensor Networks

1 Introduction

Wireless connected devices are strongly energy-constrained as most use batteries for powering. Recent studies reveal that the Bluetooth Low Energy (BLE) [1,2] gives a good trade-off between energy efficiency and Quality of Service (QoS) for applications that do not especially need long-range communications [9]. However, before establishing a BLE connection between two devices, an initial contact must be initiated between them. The find-out process between devices is known as Neighbor Discovery Process (NDP) and needs additional energy before the beginning of a transmission. The NDP is the primary operation before any operation (data transmission). Indeed, in a usual way, the BLE communications occur in a master/slave manner. A successful neighbor discovery happens when at least two BLE devices discover each other during the discovery phase. The device which sends data during the NDP is the advertiser, whereas the node that receives the advertisements is the scanner.

K. Georgiou and E. Kranakis (Eds.): ALGOWIN 2023, LNCS 14061, pp. 74–86, 2023.
https://doi.org/10.1007/978-3-031-48882-5_6

Two kinds of advertising are possible. Direct advertising occurs only for already known devices (a successful NDP has already occurred before), whereas undirected advertising is related to unknown devices which want to discover each other. For the latter, the NDP can either be through a connectable or a non-connectable mode. For a connectable discovery, a master/slave connection is established between the two devices so that the scanner can reply to the advertiser after the reception of an advertisement. However, in a non-connectable discovery, the advertiser does not introduce a connection request during the advertising. Thus, the scanner will only receive advertisements without being able to interact with the advertiser [12,17]. Meanwhile, using a battery as a power supply involves a limited lifetime for the BLE device. To extend their lifespan, sensor nodes need to use their energy efficiently. Thus, recent techniques that aim to reduce the energy consumption during NDP of the BLE are widely used in the literature [8,18].

In order to allow synchronization between the advertisers and the scanner, the proposed approach leverages ultra-low power radio receivers called Wake-up Receivers (WuRs) [13]. The use of a secondary WuR allows to let the primary BLE transceiver into sleep mode most of the time as it continuously listens to the wireless channel while consuming a few microwatts. Thanks to our previous works, the wake-up latency can be greatly reduced with negligible energy consumption [3,4]. The Protocol overhead is then reduced since the main BLE transceiver wakes up only when the WuR receives a specific signal called Wake-Up Beacon (WUB).

This paper proposes a novel approach called WUBBLE to reduce the NDP energy cost by using two different kinds of Wake-Up Beacons (WUB). The proposed approach helps to reduce the energy consumption to the number of neighbors to discover during this process and is suitable for non-connectable undirected advertising. The scanner sends the first WUB to initialize the NDP while the second WUB is sent to stop the transmission of advertisements. Furthermore, to reduce collisions, a random backoff delay is added before the transmission of an advertisement by the advertiser. For evaluating and validating our approach, we propose an energy model based on real measurements, and we extend the results with intensive simulations.

The rest of the paper is organized as follows: related works are discussed in Sect. 2 while Sect. 3 gives more details on our proposed discovery solution. The experiments and the validation of the proposal are given in Sect. 4. The conclusion and future directions are provided in Sect. 5.

2   Background and Related Works

Several researchers proposed techniques and solutions that aim to reduce the energy consumed during NDP.

Wei et al. [19] proposed a novel deterministic and one-way NDP. To reduce the discovery delay, the authors assumed that there are only a few active slots in each period, and the remaining time is for the sleep slot. Thus, according to a duty cycle, the proposal can find the best periods to achieve the NDP. In [7], the authors proposed a mathematical analysis of a few NDP parameters to reduce NDP delay. However, they assumed in their analysis that an advertising event and a scan window have the same length, which cannot be confirmed in real life. In the same way, Shan et al. [17] focused on minimizing the advertisement interval. They show that it should be a multiple of 0.625 ms and be taken from 20 ms to 10.24 s for an advertisement delay taken in [0–10] ms. An advanced study of optimizing the NDP parameters according to IoT application is conducted by Luo et al. [11]. Contrary to previous probabilistic solutions, the proposed solution is based on the Chinese remainder theorem to find the optimal NDP delay and the related average energy consumption. More recent works aim to evaluate and improve the advanced NDP introduced in Bluetooth 5 by finding the trade-off between reducing collisions and minimizing energy consumption [15,16,18].

Many works proposed to couple a low-power WuR with BLE to explore its benefits. Giovanelli et al. proposed in [6] to integrate the WuR in the BLE protocol stack. They defined two scenarios, connection-oriented and broadcast oriented. In connection-oriented, the trigger from the WuR is used to change from non-connectable to connectable advertising when nodes need to be connected. With broadcast oriented, the scanner uses WuR to wake up the nodes before sending a broadcast packet. The authors claim their protocol obtains better latency and energy consumption than the regular BLE. However, no experimental evaluation was performed. Sanchez [10] demonstrated that WuR-based BLE outperforms the classic BLE solution for low packet rate. However, they considered only two nodes. Mikhaylov et al. [14] also evaluated that the WuR-based BLE performs better than the traditional BLE solution if the maximum data delivery tolerable by the application does not exceed 21 s. The authors did not consider scalability and collisions between nodes. Furthermore, the advertisement could be repeated many times, and no process to stop advertising was proposed.

Contrary to the previous works and to the best of our knowledge, there are no works that combine WuR and BLE to dynamically adapt the advertising duration, while being energy efficient. Thus, the solution we propose and which is described in Sect. 3 constitutes a novel contribution.

3   WUBBLE Protocol

3.1   Problem Statement

Reducing the energy of NDP is very challenging because it has to find the best trade-off between energy consumption and QoS. Knowing that devices must be in sleep mode most of the time to save their energy, the additional WuR allows synchronization before the beginning of the NDP as proposed in [14]. However, the duration of NDP is fixed, and NDP remains active even if all or at least the desired number of nodes have been discovered. In the next part, the WUBBLE approach is introduced. It minimizes the duration of the NDP according to the desired number of nodes to discover.

3.2 Network Scenario and Protocol Concept

The scenario in which a new node arrives in a network of N nodes and wants to discover its neighbors is considered. It may need to discover K nodes ($K \leq N$) in its BLE and WuR communication ranges. Hence, each node embeds a BLE module and a WuR.

Figure 1 shows the timeline of the proposed protocol. The new node (the scanner) starts by sending a WUB that is called *Wubb* (WUB begin) that requests neighbors to begin advertising. Upon the reception of the *Wubb* by the advertisers, the WuR of each advertiser sends an interrupt to wake up the main node in order to start advertising with the BLE. Each node waits for a random backoff between 0 and 30 ms before starting advertising to limit collisions.

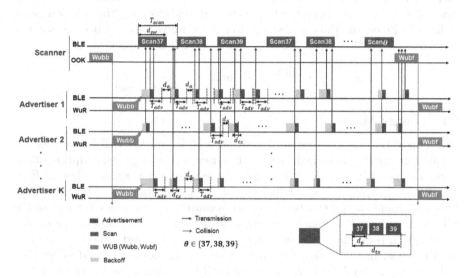

Fig. 1. WUBBLE: Neighborhood discovery protocol based on WUB (*Wubb* and *Wubf*).

Among the 40 BLE channels (numbered from 0 to 39), only 3 channels (37, 38 and 39) are used for NDP. Each advertiser broadcasts messages repeatedly (every advertisement interval T_{adv} plus random advertisement delay d_a) over these three advertisement channels. As well as in [17], the advertisement interval is set between 20 ms and 10.24 s; the advertisement delay is a random value in the range of 0 to 10 ms. During the discovery process, the scanner node periodically scans each of the three advertisement channels at every scan interval T_{scan} and listens for advertisements during the scan windows d_{sw}.

Traditionally, in connectionless BLE, the advertisers periodically send advertisements many times even if the scanner has discovered the K required nodes because no acknowledgment process that will waste energy is used. To overcome this issue, the WUBBLE protocol is proposed. When the scanner receives the K

required node advertisements, it stops scanning and sends a WUB called *Wubf* (WUB finish) to inform advertisers to stop advertising. The *Wubf* has a different format than *Wubb*; thus, the WuR can make the difference between them. When an advertiser receives *Wubf*, its WuR sends an interruption to the main node to stop advertising. Thus, WUBBLE minimizes the time required for advertising in order to save energy by reducing the discovery delay. Furthermore, WUBBLE does not change the basic parameters of the NDP; thus, it can perfectly work with any existing version of the BLE [1,2].

3.3 Collisions Probability Model

Within a network with several advertisers and at least one scanner, some advertisers likely attempt to simultaneously communicate with a scanner in the same channel. In such cases, packet collisions are unavoidable, and the collision probability will follow the Poisson distribution. This probability has been previously approximated in [5] by (1). λ denotes the packet transmission rate.

$$p_c = 1 - e^{-2N\lambda d_p}, \qquad \text{with } \lambda = \frac{1}{(T_{adv} + d_a)} \tag{1}$$

3.4 Energy Model

To evaluate the energy consumption of both BLE and WUBBLE, we consider the average energy consumed by the advertiser. The energy consumption of the scanner is not considered, as it is about the same when using either BLE or WUBBLE, except for a slight increase of energy to transmit the two WUBs. This additional energy can be neglected because the transmission times of the WUBs are minimal compared to the scan duration. Thus, the average energy consumption is evaluated for N_f time slots, and each advertisement occurs in a one-time slot. In the basic BLE protocol, when the node starts advertising, it will periodically send the advertisements until the end of a fixed number of time slots N_s. The energy consumed by the advertiser node while using BLE is E_{ble}:

$$\begin{aligned} E_{ble} &= \tau_s(T_{adv} + d_a)P_{idl} + \tau_s d_{tx}P_{tx} \\ &+ (\tau_f - \tau_s)(T_{adv} + d_a)P_s + E_{in}, \end{aligned} \tag{2}$$

with P_{idl}, P_{tx} and P_s the idle, transmission, and sleep power consumption, respectively. d_{tx} is the transmission duration and E_{in} gives the energy consumption during BLE initialisation. It corresponds to the energy consumed when the node wakes up from deep sleep end initializes its BLE module.

Using WUBBLE, the node keeps advertising until it receives a *Wubf* from the scanner. Therefore, it will send advertisements for N_s^o time slots ($N_s^o \leq N_s$) that is the minimal number of time slots that meets the requirements of discovering K needed nodes. The energy consumption E_{wubble} of the advertiser node when using WUBBLE is expressed as:

$$\begin{aligned} E_{wubble} &= \tau_s^o(T_{adv} + d_a)P_{idl} + \tau_s^o d_{tx}P_{tx} + 2d_w P_{rx}^{wur} + E_{in} \\ &+ (\tau_f - \tau_s^o)(T_{adv} + d_a)P_s + [\tau_f(T_{adv} + d_a) - 2d_w]P_{idl}^{wur}, \end{aligned} \tag{3}$$

where P_{idl}^{wur} and P_{rx}^{wur} are respectively the power consumed by the WuR while monitoring and processing the signal in a channel. d_w denotes the WUB duration.

4 Evaluation

4.1 Experimental Measurements

WUBBLE protocol has been implemented on real platforms in order to measure both the power consumption and the duration of each step of the protocol. The measured parameters are, for a second time, included in the energy models presented in Sect. 3.2.

Testbed. Figure 2 shows the experimental testbed. Only two nodes are considered, one as a scanner and the other as an advertiser. These two nodes are sufficient since we are interested in feeding the energy model with the experimental power consumption measurements. A Firebeetle from DFRobot is used for the BLE module, which contains the microcontroller ESP32. At the advertiser side, the WuR from [13] is used and is connected to the Firebeetle node to send an interrupt to either wake up the node or ask the node to stop advertising. On the scanner side, the b-L0722 LRWAN1 development board from STMicroelectronics is used to send the WUB with OOK modulation. It is connected to the Firebeetle that sends to it a command to send either *Wubb* or *Wubf*. *Wubb* contains the address 0x52 and *Wubf* contains the address 0x53. Once the WuR receives *Wubb*, it sends an interruption signal to the Firebeetle to wake up from its sleep state and start advertising. When the WuR receives a *Wubf*, it sends a different interrupt to the Firebeetle to stop advertising and return to sleep mode.

Micro-Benchmark. Figure 3 presents the microbenchmark of the WUBBLE protocol. A N6705A DC power analyzer measured the current consumption of each node. All the steps of the protocol can be seen. The scanner starts by sending *Wubb* to wake up the advertiser and then starts scanning (BLE-Rx). Before opening the scan windows, there is a step of BLE initialization. At the advertiser side, the node wakes up after receiving the *Wubb* and starts advertising (BLE-Tx). When the scanner receives ten advertisements, it stops scanning and sends *Wubf* to ask the advertiser to stop advertising. The measured parameters are summarized in Table 1.

4.2 Simulation Results

Simulation Setup. An NDP simulator at the medium access level has been implemented for both BLE and WUBBLE. The simulator instantiates N advertising nodes and assigns them the desired parameters, such as advertising interval and duration. Each node has a random initial backoff in the range [0–30] ms,

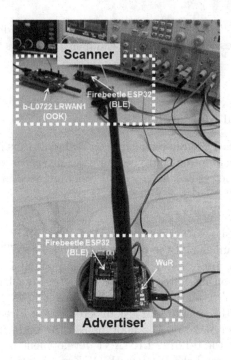

Fig. 2. Experimental testbed.

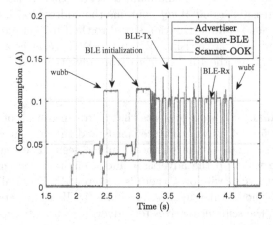

Fig. 3. Micro-benchmark of WUBBLE protocol.

after which it starts broadcasting its advertising packet. Each packet is sent after $T_{adv} + d_a$. At the beginning of the simulation, the scanner starts the node discovery. A random delay in the range of [0–10] ms is added before each scan window to avoid desynchronization between the scanner and the advertiser. When the scanner receives a non-colliding packet from the advertiser, it marks that node as discovered. If any advertised packets are overlapped, a collision occurs, and

Table 1. Measured power consumption and duration.

Param.	Value	Param.	Value	Param.	Value
d_{sw}	60 ms	P_{rx}^{wur}	284 µW	P_s	0.39 mW
d_p	376 µs	d_w	16 ms	τ_f	1000
d_{tx}	5.1 ms	T_{scan}	100 ms	P_{idl}^{wur}	1.83 µW
P_{tx}	390 mW	T_{adv}	110 ms	E_{in}	145.26 mJ
P_{idl}	90 mW	d_a	$[0-10]$ ms		

the scanner discards the packet. The simulation lasts for 1000 time slots and is repeated 1000 times. For the first time, to validate the simulator, the collision probability obtained by the simulator is compared with the analytical expression of (1).

Collision Probability. Figure 4 summarizes the simulation and analytical results of the collision probability as a function of the number of nodes in the network w.r.t three values of the packet transmission rate. It can be seen that the simulation results fit the theoretical ones, which validates our simulation.

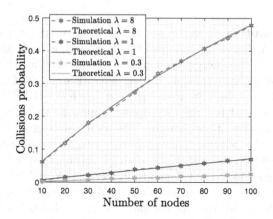

Fig. 4. Collision probability as a function of the number of nodes.

Time Slot. Figure 5 shows the average time slot per node as a function of the number of nodes found w.r.t the number of nodes in the network. Three network sizes ($N = 50, 70, 100$) are considered. This average time slot represents the number of advertising per node required to discover K nodes by the scanner (N_s^o in (3)). Obviously, the more the scanner needs to discover nodes, the higher the time slot is. It can be seen that to discover all the nodes available (100%), fewer time slots are needed with a small network of $N = 50$ compared to a big network with $N = 100$. Furthermore, if $N_s = 150$, the scanner is not able to discover all the N nodes available when $N \geq 70$.

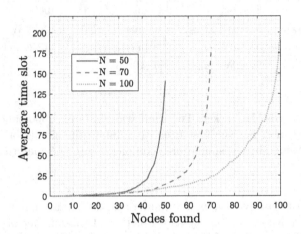

Fig. 5. Average time slots as a function of number of nodes found w.r.t number of nodes in the network.

Energy Consumption. Figure 6 shows the average energy consumption per advertiser as a function of the number of nodes found, w.r.t BLE and WUBBLE protocols. For BLE, the energy consumption is estimated for three values of N_s (i.e. the fixed number of time slots to stop advertising) and, for each N_s, three network sizes ($N = 50, 70, 100$) are considered. With WUBBLE, the exact three network sizes are considered. In our proposed approach, the energy consumption depends on the number of nodes found. The more the scanner needs to discover nodes, the more the advertiser keeps advertising for many time slots, which consumes more energy. With BLE, the energy consumption does not depend on the number of nodes found but depends only on the N_s value.

We observe that to discover the same maximum number of nodes per time slot, the advertiser could consume the same energy with BLE and WUBBLE. If, for example, N_s is fixed to 25 time slots with BLE, with a network of 50 nodes, the scanner could discover up to 42 nodes. However, 42 nodes are discovered in the average time slot of 20.99, so the advertising is stopped earlier with WUBBLE, which will compensate for the overhead of the continuous listening of the WuR inducing the same energy consumption with BLE and WUBBLE.

It can also be seen that with WUBBLE, the advertiser could consume more energy than when using BLE. However, in this case, fewer nodes are discovered with BLE than with WUBBLE because N_s is underestimated, and the advertising process finishes earlier. For example, with a network of 50 nodes, if N_s is fixed to 25, WUBBLE could consume up to 45% more energy than BLE while 45 nodes are found against 42 with BLE.

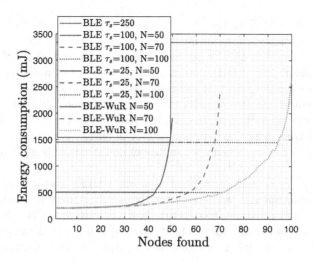

Fig. 6. Energy consumption as a function of number of nodes found w.r.t number of nodes in the network.

It is shown that, if $N_s = 250$, all nodes are discovered in all the different network scenarios. The advertiser consumes more energy with BLE than with WUBBLE. With a network of 50 nodes, 45% of the energy is saved with WUBBLE to discover all nodes compared to BLE due to the stop mechanism.

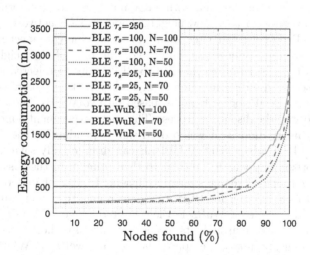

Fig. 7. Energy consumption as a function of the percentage of nodes found from the nodes available in the network.

Figure 7 presents the average energy consumption as the percentage of nodes found in BLE and WUBBLE protocols. We observe that the energy can be saved compared to BLE to discover a portion number of nodes with WUBBLE. For example, to discover 50% of nodes, more than 40% of energy is saved with WUBBLE compared to BLE when N_s is fixed to 25-time slots. Moreover, we can also see that if N_s is fixed to 25-time slots, only 84% of nodes are discovered within a network of 50 nodes. If the required portion of nodes to be discovered is 90%, BLE could not discover all of them and consumes 30% less energy than WUBBLE, while with our proposal, all the required nodes are discovered. If N_s is fixed to 100-time slots, 54%, 46%, and 21% of energy is saved with WUBBLE to discover 90% of nodes when the number of nodes available is 50, 70, and 100, respectively.

In short, if N_s is underestimated in normal BLE, nodes stop advertising while the scanner has not yet discovered the required number of nodes. In this case, the advertiser consumes less energy than when using WUBBLE, while with WUBBLE, the number of nodes to be discovered is reached. Meanwhile, if N_s is overestimated, the advertiser consumes more energy than when using WUBBLE. Finally, if N_s is fixed and close to the optimum, the advertiser consumes about the same energy as BLE and WUBBLE. It is difficult to fix the optimal time slot to stop advertising with BLE since it could change depending on the network size and channel conditions not considered in this work. Nevertheless, WUBBLE allows having a good stopping of advertising while being energy efficient.

5   Conclusions

Wireless nodes entering an unknown area must exchange information with present nodes to discover their new neighborhood. In BLE networks, this Neighbor Discovery Protocol (NDP) represents an energy-hungry mechanism, while for many discovering applications, only a specific part of the neighborhood is necessary. Adding a wake-up mechanism to BLE nodes can decrease the energy needed to discover a sufficient number of nodes. In this paper, we proposed WUBBLE, a new NDP for BLE nodes based on two WUBs, one to begin and another one to stop the discovery process. Thanks to experimental measurements and accurate energy models, it was proved that depending on the time horizon of the classical BLE advertising, WUBBLE can dramatically save energy. Even if the time horizon happens to be close to the optimum in the case of the classical NDP, our proposal remains energy efficient. In case of underestimated or overestimated time horizon for BLE, the gain in energy saving can add a unit after 10. The drawback of WuRs is their limited range so WUBBLE will be efficient only for dense environments. Emerging wake-up schemes try to increase this radio range using duty-cycle approaches. Future works on WUBBLE are to explore the capacity of our NDP to adapt to this intermittent approach.

Acknowledgment. This work is part of the project *GoodFloow* funded by the ADEME. The authors would like to thank the anonymous reviewers for their insightful comments.

References

1. Core specification 4.0 - bluetooth® technology website (2010). https://www. bluetooth.com/specifications/specs/core-specification-4-0/
2. Core specification 5.0 - bluetooth® technology website (2016). https://www. bluetooth.com/specifications/specs/core-specification-5-0/
3. Djidi, N.E.H., Gautier, M., Courtay, A., Berder, O., Magno, M.: How can wake-up radio reduce LoRa downlink latency for energy harvesting sensor nodes? Sensors **21**(3), 733 (2021)
4. Djidi, N.E.H., et al.: The revenge of asynchronous protocols: wake-up radio-based multi-hop multi-channel MAC protocol for WSN. In: IEEE Wireless Communications and Networking Conference (WCNC), Austin, United States (2022)
5. Ghamari, M., et al.: Detailed examination of a packet collision model for bluetooth low energy advertising mode. IEEE Access **6**, 46066–46073 (2018). https://doi.org/ 10.1109/ACCESS.2018.2866323
6. Giovanelli, D., Milosevic, B., Brunelli, D., Farella, E.: Enhancing bluetooth low energy with wake-up radios for IoT applications. In: International Wireless Communications and Mobile Computing Conference (IWCMC), pp. 1622–1627 (2017). https://doi.org/10.1109/IWCMC.2017.7986527
7. Jeon, W.S., Dwijaksara, M.H., Jeong, D.G.: Performance analysis of neighbor discovery process in bluetooth low-energy networks. IEEE Trans. Veh. Technol. **66**, 1865–1871 (2017). https://doi.org/10.1109/TVT.2016.2558194
8. Kindt, P.H., Narayanaswamy, S., Saur, M., Chakraborty, S.: Optimizing BLE-like neighbor discovery. IEEE Trans. Mob. Comput. **21**(5), 1779–1797 (2022). https:// doi.org/10.1109/TMC.2020.3028270
9. Kindt, P.H., Saur, M., Balszun, M., Chakraborty, S.: Neighbor discovery latency in BLE-like protocols. IEEE Trans. Mob. Comput. **17**(3), 617–631 (2018). https:// doi.org/10.1109/TMC.2017.2737008
10. Liendo Sanchez, A.: Study of adaptation mechanisms of the wireless sensor nodes to the context for ultra-low power consumption. Theses, Université Grenoble Alpes (2018)
11. Luo, B., Xiang, F., Sun, Z., Yao, Y.: BLE neighbor discovery parameter configuration for IoT applications. IEEE Access **7**, 54097–54105 (2019). https://doi.org/ 10.1109/ACCESS.2019.2912493
12. Luo, B., Yao, Y., Sun, Z.: Performance analysis models of BLE neighbor discovery: a survey. IEEE Internet Things J. **8**, 8734–8746 (2021). https://doi.org/10.1109/ JIOT.2020.3046263
13. Magno, M., Jelicic, V., Srbinovski, B., Bilas, V., Popovici, E., Benini, L.: Design, implementation, and performance evaluation of a flexible low-latency nanowatt wake-up radio receiver. IEEE Trans. Industr. Inf. **12**(2), 633–644 (2016). https:// doi.org/10.1109/TII.2016.2524982
14. Mikhaylov, K., Karvonen, H.: Wake-up radio enabled BLE wearables: empirical and analytical evaluation of energy efficiency. In: International Symposium on Medical Information Communication Technology (ISMICT), pp. 1–5 (2020). https://doi. org/10.1109/ISMICT48699.2020.9152699
15. Shan, G., Choi, G., Roh, B.h., Kang, J.: An improved neighbor discovery process in BLE 5.0. In: 2019 IEEE 10th Annual Information Technology, Electronics and Mobile Communication Conference (IEMCON), pp. 0809–0812. IEEE (2019). https://doi.org/10.1109/IEMCON.2019.8936200

16. Shan, G., Roh, B.H.: Maximized effective transmission rate model for advanced neighbor discovery process in bluetooth low energy 5.0. IEEE Internet Things J. **4662**, 1–13 (2022). https://doi.org/10.1109/JIOT.2022.3152513

17. Shan, G., Roh, B.H.: Advertisement interval to minimize discovery time of whole BLE advertisers. IEEE Access **6**, 17817–17825 (2018). https://doi.org/10.1109/ACCESS.2018.2817343

18. Shan, G., Roh, B.H.: Performance model for advanced neighbor discovery process in bluetooth low energy 5.0-enabled internet of things networks. IEEE Trans. Ind. Electron. **67**, 10965–10974 (2020). https://doi.org/10.1109/TIE.2019.2962401

19. Wei, L., et al.: Lightning: a high-efficient neighbor discovery protocol for low duty cycle WSNs. IEEE Commun. Lett. **20**, 966–969 (2016). https://doi.org/10.1109/LCOMM.2016.2536018

Byzantine Fault-Tolerant Protocols for (n, f)-Evacuation from a Circle

Pourandokht Behrouz, Orestis Konstantinidis, Nikos Leonardos,
Aris Pagourtzis, Ioannis Papaioannou$^{(\boxtimes)}$, and Marianna Spyrakou

School of Electrical and Computer Engineering, National Technical University of
Athens, Zografou, Greece
{pbehrouz,orestkonstantinidis,mspyrakou}@mail.ntua.gr,
{nleon,pagour}@cs.ntua.gr, ipapaioannou@corelab.ntua.gr

Abstract. In this work, we address the problem of (n, f)-evacuation on
a circle, which involves evacuating n robots, with f of them being faulty,
from a hidden exit located on the perimeter of a unit radius circle. The
robots commence at the center of the circle and possess a speed of 1.

We introduce an algorithm for the Wireless communication model
under any number of Byzantine faults. We analyze the time requirements of our proposed algorithm and we establish an upper bound on
its performance.

1 Introduction

Evacuation problems play a pivotal role in various branches of mathematics and
theoretical computer science, and they have significant and diverse applications,
including the field of robotics. One particularly well-studied problem in mobile
agent computing is the search for targets in unknown territory by a group of
robots. Over the past few decades, numerous algorithms and hardness results
have been developed in response to this problem.

In this context, a specific case of great interest arises when the target represents an exit, and the objective of the robots is either to discover the exit
(referred to as the *search problem*) or to evacuate the territory swiftly (referred
to as the *evacuation problem*). This work aims to address both of these scenarios under minimal assumptions. Specifically, the objective is to search for an
unknown exit location on the perimeter of a unit radius disk and to evacuate all
honest robots in an adversarial environment where f of them can exhibit Byzantine behavior. It is worth noting that Byzantine behavior places additional strain
on the remaining agents, thereby further complicating the task at hand.

1.1 Model and Preliminaries

The objective of this paper is to introduce an algorithm specifically designed for
the general case of the (n, f)-evacuation problem on a circle with unit radius.
We aim to analyze the time requirements associated with this algorithm and

© The Author(s), under exclusive license to Springer Nature Switzerland AG 2023
K. Georgiou and E. Kranakis (Eds.): ALGOWIN 2023, LNCS 14061, pp. 87–100, 2023.
https://doi.org/10.1007/978-3-031-48882-5_7

evaluate its performance. In this section, we provide an overview of the setting in which our study is conducted. We outline the main parameters of the model that govern the behavior of the robots, including aspects such as communication, movement, faults, as well as the extent of the adversary's power.

Location and Movement (Robot Trajectories). The movement of the robots begins from the center of a disk with a radius of 1 unit. All robots move at the same speed, at a rate of 1 unit per time step. Robots possess the capability to perceive the perimeter of the disk and detect the exit if they happen to be in close proximity to it. They can navigate along the perimeter of the disk, but they are also allowed to take shortcuts by moving within the interior of the disk.

Communication Model. In this work we explore the wireless model.

The robots can communicate wirelessly and instantaneously (with no delay) at any time and regardless of their distance from each other, operating under a synchronous model. Messages exchanged among robots can contain various types of information, such as their respective locations, whether they have discovered the exit, the distance they have traversed from their initial positions, and more. Each message carries a unique identifier attributed to the sender, which remains unaltered throughout the communication process. By analyzing these messages, all robots can deduce their relative positions in relation to one another. Additionally, the robots are equipped with pedometers to accurately measure distances covered during their movement. In the wireless communication model, robots can communicate instantly regardless of distance. Messages exchanged between robots carry various information such as locations, exit discovery, distances traveled, and more.

Fault Types. In our study, we take into account two types of faulty behaviors exhibited by the robots: crash faults and Byzantine faults.

- **Crash fault** behavior refers to a robot suddenly ceasing to function, stop moving and becoming unresponsive, resulting in a complete breakdown of message communication.
- **Byzantine fault** behavior involves a robot exhibiting malicious behaviour. This includes deliberately altering its trajectory and manipulating information to confuse the honest (non-faulty) robots. Additionally, a Byzantine robot can mimic the behavior of a crash-faulty robot.

Adversary. For the worst-case analysis of our algorithm, we consider an adversary who selects the location of the exit and the behaviour of the malicious robots (their trajectories as well as the messages they will broadcast) to maximize the resulting search and evacuation completion time. The adversary also chooses which robots are faulty, adding to the challenge.

Search Problem. In the case of a total of n robots, with f of them being faulty, we introduce the notation $S(n, f)$ to denote the time required to successfully solve the search problem. This represents the duration it takes for the non-faulty robots to reach the exit and ensure that all honest robots possess undeniable knowledge of the location of the exit. This collaborative effort of the robots to locate and establish the precise position of the exit is commonly referred to as group search.

Evacuation Problem. The Evacuation Problem denoted as $E(n, f)$ involves n robots, including f faulty ones, and aims to determine the time required for a successful evacuation. In a complete evacuation, a non-faulty robot discovers the exit, and all non-faulty robots must safely reach the exit location. It is important to note that the evacuation time $E(n, f)$ is inherently greater than or equal to the time required to find the exit $S(n, f)$, as finding the exit is a prerequisite for a successful evacuation.

1.2 Related Work

The line search problem, focused on a single mobile agent searching for an unknown exit on an infinite line, has been extensively studied in the literature. Pioneering papers by Beck and Bellman [1,2], Baeza-Yates et al. [3], have laid the groundwork for this research line, exploring both stochastic and deterministic settings. Building upon these works, notable contributions by Ahlswede and Wegener [4], Alpern and Gal [5], Stone [6], have resulted in significant publications and books. Further investigations have explored various line search algorithms, including randomized approaches [7] and considerations of turn cost [8]. Additionally, the line search problem has been extended to consider the presence of faulty robots, leading to intriguing research on crash-faulty [9] and Byzantine-faulty robots [10]. These studies shed light on the challenges and strategies involved in solving the line search problem when robot faults are present.

It is worth noticing that the evacuation problem shares a close relationship with the search problem, with both problems overlapping when only a single robot is involved. The study of evacuation in circular topologies began with the seminal work, where researchers explored both the wireless and face-to-face communication models [11]. This work laid the foundation for subsequent research on circle evacuation, encompassing various scenarios such as the face-to-face model [12], equilateral triangles [13], l_p unit disk [14], and robots with asymmetric communication capabilities [15]. For a comprehensive overview of the field, we recommend referring to [16]. In the study of the search problem in circular topologies and considering f crash or one Byzantine failure, a tight bound was introduced for locating the exit [17].

A closely related work to this paper in the context of fault-tolerant evacuation in circular topologies is [18]. In their study, the authors focused on the problem involving three robots, one of which is faulty. They provided upper and lower bounds for both crash-faulty and Byzantine-faulty robot scenarios. Building upon their findings, [19] further investigated both the wireless and face-to-face communication models in scenarios involving one and two faulty robots. The present work draws upon the results presented there.

For a summary of the known results in the unit disk topology, please refer to Table 1.

1.3 Results of the Paper

In Sect. 2 we consider the evacuation problem for n robots f of which are Byzantine faulty in the wireless communication model, and we propose an algorithm for that case, proving the following upper bound

$$E(n, f) \leq 1 + (f+1) \cdot \frac{2\pi}{n} + \max\{G_e(k^*), H_e(k^*)\}$$

where $G_e(k^*)$ and $H_e(k^*)$ is the time needed to evacuate two crucial groups of robots, during the execution of our algorithm. For a more detailed analysis please refer to Theorem 1.

Table 1. Summary of known results for the unit disk topology

Work	Problem	Adversary	Model	Bound	$n = 2$	$n = 3$	$n \geq 4$
[11]	Evacuation	None	F2F	Upper	~ 5.740	~ 5.090	$3 + 2\frac{\pi}{n}$
				Lower	~ 5.199	~ 4.519	$3 + 2\frac{\pi}{n} - O(n^{-2})$
			Wireless	Upper	~ 4.830	~ 4.220	$3 + \frac{\pi}{n} + O(n^{-4/3})$
				Lower	~ 4.830	~ 4.159	$3 + \frac{\pi}{n}$
[12]	Evacuation	None	F2F	Upper	~ 5.628		
				Lower	~ 5.255		
[18]	Evacuation	1 crash	Wireless	Upper		~ 6.309	
				Lower		~ 5.188	
		1 Byzantine		Upper		~ 6.921	
				Lower		~ 5.948	
[17]	Search	f crash	Wireless	Upper		$1 + (f+1)\frac{2\pi}{3}$	$1 + (f+1)\frac{2\pi}{n}$
				Lower		$1 + (f+1)\frac{2\pi}{3}$	$1 + (f+1)\frac{2\pi}{n}$
		1 Byzantine		Upper		~ 5.188	$1 + \frac{4\pi}{n}$
				Lower		~ 5.188	$1 + \frac{4\pi}{n}$
[19]	Evacuation	1 Byzantine	Wireless	Upper		~ 7.188	$3 + \frac{4\pi}{n}$
				Lower		~ 6.188	$1 + \frac{4\pi}{n} + 2\sin(\frac{\pi}{2} - \frac{\pi}{n})$
			F2F	Upper		~ 8.055	$3 + \frac{4\pi}{n} + \sin\frac{\pi}{n}$
		2 Byzantines	Wireless	Upper			$3 + \frac{6\pi}{n} + \delta(n)$
			F2F	Upper			$3 + \frac{6\pi}{n} + 2\sin\frac{2\pi}{n}$

2 Evacuating Under Wireless Communication

We define (n, f)-evacuation, to mean evacuation of $n > 1$ robots, $f < \frac{n}{2}$ of which are faulty. In this work, we study Byzantine faults.

We consider n robots $a_0, a_1, \ldots, a_{n-1}$ with a starting position at the center of a unit circle and set $\theta := 2\pi/n$. Each robot a_i moves along a radius to the point $i\theta$ of the perimeter of the unit circle.[1] We call the arc $[i\theta, (i+1)\theta)$ sector

---

[1] Note that in fact we represent the circle points in polar coordinates; as the radius is always equal to 1 we give only their angle, for the sake of simplicity.

s_i. After one time unit, robot a_i will be located at the beginning of sector s_i and will have searched sector s_i in time $1 + \theta$, moving counterclockwise (ccw). Each sector search counts as a round. Each robot is tasked to search $(f+1)$ consecutive sectors. Robots make announcements if they find the exit and approve/disprove the announcements of other robots accordingly.

In our analysis, it is important to know the announcements' distance because in that way we can eliminate the number of unsettled announcements.

Definition 1 (Sector distance). *We define $d(s_i, s_j) = \min\{(i-j) \bmod n, (j-i) \bmod n\}$ to be the* distance *between sectors s_i, s_j. Let the distance of a set of announcements X be the length of the shortest arc containing all announcements in X; let this arc be called $arc(X)$. Finally, let the* sector distance *of X be the distance between the sectors where the two endpoints of $arc(X)$ fall.*

According to this definition, when the announcements are made in the same sector their sector distance is 0, whereas when announcements are in adjacent sectors their sector distance is 1.

Since faulty robots are present, it is difficult for honest robots to differentiate between these announcements. To help our analysis, we will next define disputable announcements and the group of robots responsible for resolving them:

Definition 2 (Disputable announcement). *An announcement is* disputable *when neither its validity nor its invalidity is deducible from the available information. An announcement that is not disputable is* settled.

For example, if an announcement has neither $f + 1$ approvals nor $f + 1$ disproofs it is disputable. Note that in cases where the honesty of a robot can be deduced, its approvals and/or disproofs result in the corresponding announcements being settled and, therefore not disputable. Note also that, if only one announcement is made during the first $f + 1$ rounds, then this announcement is also settled, as it must have come from an honest robot. If there are k disputable announcements we will denote them as $X_1, \ldots X_k$, where X_j is before X_{j+1} in counterclockwise order (ccw), $j \in \{1, \ldots, k-1\}$ and X_1 is the announcement with the maximum sector distance from its previous announcement ccw.

In case consensus is not reached after $f+1$ rounds (i.e. disputable announcements are present), we need more robots to visit and settle them. We will call these robots *inspector robots* and define them as follows.

Definition 3 (Inspector robots).
Assume that there are k disputable announcements, $X_1, \ldots X_k$. Let the first X_1 be in sector s_j. Then the i-th inspector is the robot that is located at the beginning of sector $s_{j-i+1 \pmod n}$ at time $1 + (f + 1)\theta$.

Based on the number of disputable announcements and their maximum distance, we will determine the number of inspector robots that are sufficient to settle the disputable announcements.

Lemma 1. *Assume that after executing $f + 1$ rounds of the algorithm there are $k = 2$ disputable announcements with sector distance $d \leq f - 1$. Then $f - d$ inspectors are sufficient for all the honest robots to learn where the exit is.*

Proof. At the $f + 1$ rounds of the algorithm in total $f + 1 + d$ different robots searched the area of the 2 disputable announcements. Assume that among them there are exactly h honest robots, $1 \leq h \leq f + 1 + d - (k - 1)$.

Therefore each false announcement has at least $k - 2 + h$ disproofs, since each announcement is a disproof of any other announcement and all of the h robots have visited at least one of the two announcements. Since there are $f - d$ inspectors, there are at most $f - (f + 1 + d - h) = h - d - 1$ faulty robots and at least $f - d - (h - d - 1) = f + 1 - h$ honest robots among them.

Hence each false announcement will have at least $k - 2 + h + f + 1 - h = f + 1$ disproofs. □

As a result of Lemma 1, when we have $k = 2$ announcements made with sector distance d, the number of inspectors needed is $f - d$. Because inspectors should be robots that have not previously visited any of the announcements, $n \geq f + 1 + d + f - d = 2f + 1$.

Lemma 2. *Assume that after executing $f + 1$ rounds of the algorithm there are k disputable announcements with sector distance d. Then $f + 2 - k$ inspectors are sufficient for all the honest robots to learn where the exit is.*

Proof. At the $f + 1$ rounds of the algorithm in total $f + 1 + d$ different robots searched the area of the k announcements. We assume that the robots that searched the sector containing the first announcement, after the end of the $f + 1$ rounds, will visit the rest of the announcements.

Therefore, $f + 1$ robots know the location of the correct exit. Let $f_1, 0 \leq f_1 \leq f$ of them be faulty and $f + 1 - f_1$ be honest. From the rest $f + 1 + d - (f + 1) = d$ robots that searched the area of the k announcements, let $f_2, 0 \leq f_2 \leq d$, $f_1 + f_2 \leq f$ be faulty and $d - f_2$ be honest.

Since each announcement is a disproof for any other announcement, each false announcement has $k - 2$ disproofs from the other $k - 2$ false announcements, plus $f + 1 - f_1$ disproofs from the honest robots that search all the sectors with announcements.

Since there are $f + 2 - k$ inspectors then at most $f - (f_1 + f_2)$ are faulty and at least $f + 2 - k - (f - (f_1 + f_2)) = 2 - k + f_1 + f_2$ are honest.

Therefore the number of disproofs that each false announcement has is at least:

$$k - 2 + f + 1 - f_1 + 2 - k + f_1 + f_2 = f + 1 + f_2 \geq f + 1$$

and hence each false announcement is settled. □

We now present Algorithm 1, for the problem of Evacuating n robots, $f < \frac{n}{2}$ of which are Byzantine faulty, in the wireless communication model and then analyze its time requirements. Figures 1, 2, 3 and 4 helps visualizing the steps of Algorithm 1.

Algorithm 1. (n, f)-evacuation

1: Set $\theta = 2\pi/n$.
2: Robot a_i moves along a radius of the circle to the point $i\theta$ of the unit circle.
3: Until time $1 + (f+1)\theta$, robot a_i searches ccw and makes an announcement if it finds the exit. It also disproves faulty announcements made at sectors it visits (Staying silent when passing over an announcement's location, counts as disproof). Every search of a sector θ counts as a round.
4: At time $1 + (f+1)\theta$:
5: **if** there is a consensus regarding the position of the exit (no disputable announcements are present) **then** all honest robots move via a chord to the exit in order to evacuate.
6: **else if** there are $k \geq 2$ disputable announcements and their distance is d **then**
7:     *Inspector(s):*
8:     The $f + 2 - k$ inspectors move via a chord to the location of the nearest announcement (X_1). If the exit is not there, they move via a chord to the location of the next nearest announcement (X_2). They continue until they find the exit and they evacuate.
9:     *Honest (non-inspector) robots:*
10:     The honest robots gather to the center of the circle. By the time they arrive, c announcements have been approved or disproved by the inspectors. Then they move towards the middle M_{c+1} of the chord that connects the announcements X_{c+1}, X_k, and wait until X_{c+1} is approved or disproved by the inspectors, then move to the middle M_{c+2} of the chord that connects the announcements X_{c+2}, X_k, and continue this process iteratively. If, at any point, the exit is discovered, the robots head toward it to evacuate.

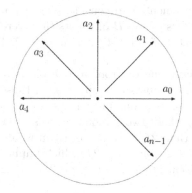

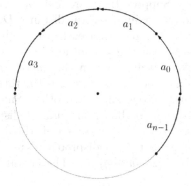

Fig. 1. Each robot a_i moves from their starting position (center of the circle) to point $i\theta$ of the circle ($t < 1$)

Fig. 2. Robots search the unit circle counter-clockwise ($t < 1 + (f + 1)\theta$)

After executing Algorithm 1 for $f + 1$ rounds, it is expected that a range of 1 to $f + 1$ robots will have made announcements. Some of these announcements

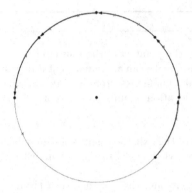

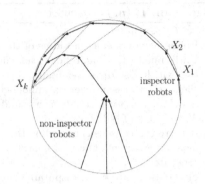

Fig. 3. After f+1 rounds of search, announcements are present ($t = 1 + (f+1)\theta$)

Fig. 4. Evacuation paths of inspector robots and non-inspector robots, ($t > 1 + (f+1)\theta$)

will be settled, and some of them will be disputable. Regarding the distance of disputable announcements, we get the following lemmas:

Lemma 3. *If* $2 \leq k \leq f+1$ *announcements are made, the maximum sector distance of any two of them, in order for all k of them to remain disputable is* $f+1-k$.

Proof. Suppose there are k disputable announcements and consider the two of them at maximum sector distance D. For the sets A and B of robots that were supposed to pass over each one, we have $|A \cup B| = f+1+d$ where $d = f+1$ if $D > f+1$ and $d = D$ otherwise.

Any silent robot in this union casts at least one disproof to one of these announcements. Suppose z is the total number of robots that spoke, w of those confirming one and y the other. Since the $z - w - y$ announcements count as a disproof for both, the sum of disproofs for these two announcements is at least $f+1+d+z-w-y$. If this is greater than $2f$, then one of them would have at least $f+1$ disproofs. Thus, $f+1+d+z-w-y \leq 2f$, which implies $d \leq f - (z-w-y) - 1$. The bound follows because $z - w - y \geq k - 2$.   □

In order to calculate the worst placement of disputable announcements by the Adversary, we prove the following lemma.

Lemma 4 (Maximum Robot Trajectory). *Assume that we have $k+1$ points on the circle that can lie in an arc of angle $a < 2\pi$. The maximum distance that a robot will traverse in order to visit all $k+1$ points is if the points are placed in equal distances in the arc of angle a.*

Proof. Assume that $\theta_1, \theta_2, \ldots, \theta_k$ are the interior angles that are formed with the placement of the points. Then we must have that $\theta_1 + \theta_2 + \cdots + \theta_k = a$ and that $\theta_i < \pi$, $i = 1, \ldots, n$ (Fig. 5).

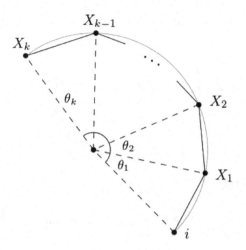

Fig. 5. Maximum distance scenario

Then the distance that a robot will traverse in order to visit all points is:

$$D(\theta_1, \theta_2, \ldots, \theta_k) = \sum_{i=1}^{k} x_i$$

$$= \sum_{i=1}^{k} 2 \cdot sin\left(\frac{\theta_i}{2}\right)$$

Let $f(\theta) = sin\left(\frac{\theta}{2}\right)$, $\quad f'(\theta) = \frac{1}{2} \cdot cos\left(\frac{\theta}{2}\right)$, $\quad f''(\theta) = -\frac{1}{4} sin\left(\frac{\theta}{2}\right) < 0$ when $\theta \in (0, 2\pi)$. Hence f is concave. We wish to find the angles θ_i such that D is maximized. We will work on the maximization of the quantity

$$\frac{D(\theta_1, \theta_2, \ldots, \theta_k)}{2k} = \sum_{i=1}^{k} \frac{1}{k} sin\left(\frac{\theta_i}{2}\right), \quad w.r.t. \ \theta_1, \theta_2, \ldots, \theta_k$$

Now by Jensen's inequality, since f is concave, we have that:

$$\sum_{i=1}^{k} \frac{1}{k} \cdot sin\left(\frac{\theta_i}{2}\right) \leq f\left(\frac{\sum_{i=1}^{k} \theta_i}{k}\right)$$

$$= sin\left(\frac{\sum_{i=1}^{k} \theta_i}{2k}\right)$$

$$= sin\left(\frac{a}{2k}\right)$$

We note that the equality holds ($\frac{D(\theta_1,\theta_2,...,\theta_k)}{2k}$ is maximised) if $\theta_i = \frac{a}{k}$, $i = 1,\ldots,k$, since

$$\sum_{i=1}^{k} \frac{1}{k} \cdot sin\left(\frac{\theta_i}{2}\right) = \sum_{i=1}^{k} \frac{1}{k} \cdot sin\left(\frac{a}{2k}\right)$$

$$= \frac{k}{k} \cdot sin\left(\frac{a}{2k}\right)$$

$$= sin\left(\frac{a}{2k}\right)$$

Therefore, we have that:

$$\max_{\theta_1,\theta_2,...,\theta_k} D(\theta_1,\theta_2,\ldots,\theta_k) = 2 \cdot k \cdot sin\left(\frac{a}{2 \cdot k}\right)$$

□

Next, we will calculate the chord between two consecutive disputable announcements, in their maximum distance.

Lemma 5. *Let n be the total number of robots, f be the total number of faulty robots and $2 \le k \le f + 1$ be the number of disputable announcements of Algorithm 1. Then the worst case maximum distance of two consecutive disputable announcements X_j, X_{j+1} is:*

$$\chi = 2 \cdot sin\left(\frac{d+1}{k-1} \cdot \frac{\pi}{n}\right)$$

where d is the sector distance of X_1, X_k.

Proof. By Lemma 4, the worst placement of the announcements by the Adversary is when all the consecutive announcements are equidistant ($d(X_j, X_{j+1}) = d(X_j, X_{j-1}), j \in [2, k-1]$).
The arc distance of X_1, X_k is $(d+1) \cdot \frac{2\pi}{n}$. Therefore the chord that connects X_j, X_{j+1} has length $\chi = 2 \cdot sin\left(\frac{d+1}{k-1} \cdot \frac{\pi}{n}\right)$ □

Corollary 1 (Inspector Search Time). *Inspectors need to check $k - 1$ announcements in order to know the location of the exit, in the worst case. The time that inspectors need to search is*

$$G_s(k) = 2(k - 1) \cdot sin\left(\frac{f - k + d + 2}{k} \cdot \frac{\pi}{n}\right)$$

Proof. By Lemma 4, the worst placement of the announcements by the Adversary is when the last inspector and the disputable announcements are equidistant. In that way, the Adversary maximizes the total required search time (and as a result the required evacuation time). By Lemma 2 the arc distance of the last inspector and X_k is $(d + (f - k + 2)) \cdot \frac{2\pi}{n} = (f - k + d + 2)\frac{2\pi}{n}$ □

We immediately gain the following corollary:

Corollary 2 (Inspector Evacuation Time). *The time that inspectors need to evacuate is*

$$G_e(k) = 2k \cdot \sin\left(\frac{f - k + d + 2}{k} \cdot \frac{\pi}{n}\right)$$

Theorem 1 $((n, f)$- Evacuation with Byzantine faults (Wireless)).
The worst-case time of Algorithm 1 for (n, f) - Evacuation with $n > 2f$ robots and f Byzantine faults in the Wireless model, satisfies:

$$E(n, f) \leq 1 + (f + 1) \cdot \frac{2\pi}{n} + \max\{G_e(k^*), H_e(k^*)\}$$

where,

$$H_e(k^*) = 1 + \sqrt{1 - \sin^2\left((k^* - c - 1)\frac{f - k^* + d + 2}{k^*} \cdot \frac{\pi}{n}\right)} + (k^* - c - 1) \cdot \sin\left(\frac{k^* - f + d + 2}{k^*} \cdot \frac{\pi}{n}\right),$$

$$k^* = \underset{k \in \{2, f+1\}}{\arg\max} \left(2(k - 1) \sin\left(\frac{f - k + d + 2}{k} \cdot \frac{\pi}{n}\right)\right)$$

Proof. First we prove the correctness of Algorithm 1, and then its time complexity:

Correctness: For the correctness of Algorithm 1 it suffices to prove that all non-faulty robots will eventually evacuate. Since every sector of the circle is searched by $(f + 1)$ different robots, by the end of round $(f + 1)$, the exit is among the disputable announcements. By Lemma 2, $f + 2 - k$ inspectors are sufficient to settle all the disputable announcements, hence all non-faulty robots will learn the location of the exit and evacuate.

Time Complexity: The worst case time of Algorithm 1 is analyzed as follows:
All robots move from the center to the perimeter of the circle in 1 time unit and conduct search for $(f+1) \cdot \theta$ time units. Then the inspector robots search for the exit among the disputable announcements and at the same time the honest robots move closer to the candidate exits in order to evacuate. The *inspector* robots by Corollary 2 need $G_e(k^*)$ time to evacuate.
The *honest* robots need at worst case H_e time which is analysed as:

- One time unit to get to the middle of the circle. By the time the robot arrives at the center $c = \left\lfloor \frac{1}{2 \cdot \sin \frac{f - k + d + 2}{k} \cdot \frac{\pi}{n}} \right\rfloor$ announcements have been approved or disproved.
- The robot moves to the middle point M_{c+1} of the line segment between X_{c+1}, X_k which has distance $\overline{OM_{c+1}} = \sqrt{1 - \sin^2\left((k^* - c - 1)\frac{f - k + d + 2}{k} \cdot \frac{\pi}{n}\right)}$ (see Fig. 6).

- The time needed to move through the middle point M_j of the line segments of $X_j, X_k, j \in \{c+2, k\}$ is $(k^* - c - 1) \cdot \sin\left(\frac{k^* - f + d + 2}{k^*} \cdot \frac{\pi}{n}\right)$.

We note that the triangles $X_k \overset{\triangle}{X_c} X_{c+1}$ and $X_k \overset{\triangle}{M_c} M_{c+1}$ are similar, since $X_{c+1} \widehat{X_k} X_{c+2} = M_{c+1} \widehat{X_k} M_{c+2}$ and $\frac{X_k X_{c+1}}{X_k M_{c+1}} = \frac{X_k X_{c+2}}{X_k M_{c+2}}$ (see Fig. 7). Therefore, by the similarity of the triangles, it holds that:

$$\frac{\overline{M_{c+1} M_{c+2}}}{\overline{X_{c+1} X_{c+2}}} = \frac{\overline{X_k X_{c+2}}}{\overline{X_k M_{c+2}}} \Rightarrow \overline{M_{c+1} M_{c+2}} = \frac{1}{2} \overline{X_{c+1} X_{c+2}} = \sin\left(\frac{k^* - f + d + 2}{k^*} \cdot \frac{\pi}{n}\right)$$

Similarly, in order to move through the middle points $M_j, j \in \{c+2, k\}$ (Fig. 7) the time required is:

$$\overline{M_{c+1} M_{c+2} \dots M_k X_k} = \frac{1}{2} \overline{X_{c+1} X_{c+2} \dots X_k} = (k^* - c - 1) \cdot \sin\left(\frac{k^* - f + d + 2}{k^*} \cdot \frac{\pi}{n}\right)$$

$\square$

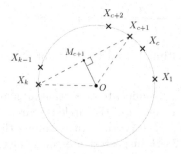

Fig. 6. Honest robots move from the center of the circle to the first middle point M_{c+1}

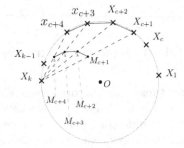

Fig. 7. Final evacuation trajectory of the honest robots, moving through the middle points.

2.1 Simulation Results for the Wireless Model

To complement our analysis about the performance of Algorithm 1 we simulated the running time as illustrated in Fig. 8. Its effectiveness is showcased under varying ratios of n and f.

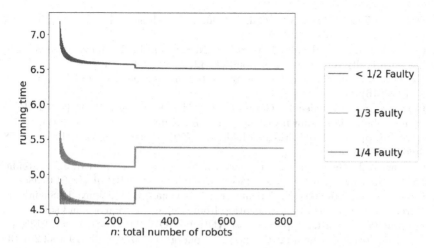

Fig. 8. Total evacuation time using Algorithm 1, in different values of n and f

Notably, our algorithm demonstrates its best performance as the percentage of faulty robots f decreases.

3   Conclusion

The study presented in this paper enhances our understanding of evacuation problems on circular topology and highlights the significance of addressing faulty robots in evacuation algorithms. We introduce an algorithm that caters to the general case of having f Byzantine faults among the n robots. The algorithm is designed for the wireless communication model, considering the movement capabilities of the robots, which allows them to move anywhere on the platform with a speed of 1. Our proposed algorithm contributes to the field by providing an upper bound in this communication model. Finding a lower bound and tightening the gap between them is a challenging open question.

References

1. Beck, A.: On the linear search problem. Israel J. Math. **2**(4), 221–228 (1964)
2. Bellman, R.: An optimal search. SIAM Rev. **5**(3), 274–274 (1963)
3. Baeza Yates, R., Culberson, J., Rawlins, G.: Searching in the plane. Inf. Comput. **106**(2), 234–252 (1993)
4. Ahlswede, R., Wegener, I.: Search Problems. Wiley-Interscience (1987)
5. Alpern, S., Gal, S.: The Theory of Search Games and Rendezvous, vol. 55. Springer, New York (2003). https://doi.org/10.1007/b100809
6. Stone, L.: Theory of Optimal Search. Academic Press, New York (1975)
7. Kao, M.-Y., Reif, J.H., Tate, S.R.: Searching in an unknown environment: an optimal randomized algorithm for the cow-path problem. Inf. Comput. **131**(1), 63–79 (1996)

8. Demaine, E.D., Fekete, S.P., Gal, S.: Online searching with turn cost. Theoret. Comput. Sci. **361**(2), 342–355 (2006)
9. Czyzowicz, J., Kranakis, E., Krizanc, D., Narayanan, L., Opatrny, J.: Search on a line with faulty robots. Distrib. Comput. **32**(6), 493–504 (2019)
10. Czyzowicz, J., et al.: Search on a line by byzantine robots. In: ISAAC, pp. 27:1–27:12 (2016)
11. Czyzowicz, J., Gąsieniec, L., Gorry, T., Kranakis, E., Martin, R., Pajak, D.: Evacuating robots via unknown exit in a disk. In: Kuhn, F. (ed.) DISC 2014. LNCS, vol. 8784, pp. 122–136. Springer, Heidelberg (2014). https://doi.org/10.1007/978-3-662-45174-8_9
12. Czyzowicz, J., Georgiou, K., Kranakis, E., Narayanan, L., Opatrny, J., Vogtenhuber, B.: Evacuating using face-to-face communication, CoRR abs/1501.04985
13. Czyzowicz, J., Kranakis, E., Krizanc, D., Narayanan, L., Opatrny, J., Shende, S.: Wireless autonomous robot evacuation from equilateral triangles and squares. In: Papavassiliou, S., Ruehrup, S. (eds.) ADHOC-NOW 2015. LNCS, vol. 9143, pp. 181–194. Springer, Cham (2015). https://doi.org/10.1007/978-3-319-19662-6_13
14. Georgiou, K., Leizerovich, S., Lucier, J., Kundu, S.: Evacuating from l_p unit disks in the wireless model. Theor. Comput. Sci. **944**, 113675 (2023)
15. Georgiou, K., Giachoudis, N., Kranakis, E.: Evacuation from a disk for robots with asymmetric communication. In: 33rd International Symposium on Algorithms and Computation (ISAAC 2022). Leibniz International Proceedings in Informatics (LIPIcs), Schloss Dagstuhl - Leibniz-Zentrum für Informatik, Dagstuhl, Germany, vol. 248, pp. 19:1–19:16 (2022)
16. Czyzowicz, J., Georgiou, K., Kranakis, E.: Group search and evacuation. In: Flocchini, P., Prencipe, G., Santoro, N. (eds.) Distributed Computing by Mobile Entities. LNCS, vol. 11340, pp. 335–370. Springer, Cham (2019). https://doi.org/10.1007/978-3-030-11072-7_14
17. Georgiou, K., Kranakis, E., Leonardos, N., Pagourtzis, A., Papaioannou, I.: Optimal circle search despite the presence of faulty robots. Inf. Process. Lett. **182**, 106391 (2023)
18. Czyzowicz, J., et al.: Evacuation from a disc in the presence of a faulty robot. In: Das, S., Tixeuil, S. (eds.) SIROCCO 2017. LNCS, vol. 10641, pp. 158–173. Springer, Cham (2017). https://doi.org/10.1007/978-3-319-72050-0_10
19. Leonardos, N., Pagourtzis, A., Papaioannou, I.: Byzantine fault tolerant symmetric-persistent circle evacuation. Theoret. Comput. Sci. **956**, 113839 (2023)

Temporal Reachability Dominating Sets: Contagion in Temporal Graphs

David C. Kutner[1]([⊠]) [iD] and Laura Larios-Jones[2] [iD]

[1] Durham University, Durham, England, UK
david.c.kutner@durham.ac.uk
[2] University of Glasgow, Glasgow, Scotland, UK
laura.larios-jones@glasgow.ac.uk

Abstract. SARS-CoV-2 was independently introduced to the UK at least 1300 times by June 2020. Given a population with dynamic pairwise connections, we ask if the entire population could be (indirectly) infected by a small group of k initially infected individuals. We formalise this problem as the TEMPORAL REACHABILITY DOMINATING SET (TARDIS) problem on temporal graphs. We provide positive and negative parameterized complexity results in four different parameters: the number k of initially infected, the lifetime τ of the graph, the number of locally earliest edges in the graph, and the treewidth of the footprint graph $\mathcal{G}_\downarrow$. We additionally introduce and study the MAXMINTARDIS problem, which can be naturally expressed as scheduling connections between individuals so that a population needs to be infected by at least k individuals to become fully infected. Interestingly, we find a restriction of this problem to correspond exactly to the well-studied DISTANCE-3 INDEPENDENT SET problem on static graphs.

Keywords: Temporal Graphs · Temporal Reachability · Treewidth · Polynomial Hierarchy

1 Introduction

Information and disease spread in real-world systems is often modeled using graphs. The time-sensitive nature of interactions between individuals is highlighted in *temporal graphs*, in which the set of vertices remains constant but the edge-set changes over time. These have been formalised in various ways; in Kempe, Kleinberg and Kumar's seminal work [29], a static graph G is extended with a *time-labeling function* $\lambda : E(G) \to \mathbb{N}^+$ assigning to each edge e a positive integer $\lambda(e)$ corresponding to the time at which it is active. A *temporal path* is then a static path where the edges are available in the order in which they are traversed. A vertex u is said to *reach* another vertex v if there is a temporal path from u to v.

Reachability and connectivity problems on temporal graphs have drawn significant interest in recent years. These have been studied in the context of net-

K. Georgiou and E. Kranakis (Eds.): ALGOWIN 2023, LNCS 14061, pp. 101–116, 2023.
https://doi.org/10.1007/978-3-031-48882-5_8

work design [3,7,14] and transport logistics [24] (where maximizing connectivity and reachability at minimum cost is desired), and the study of epidemics [10,19,20,37] and malware spread [35] (where it is not).

One metric closely related to a temporal graph's vulnerability to infection is its *maximum reachability*. That is, the largest number k of vertices which can be temporally reached by any vertex in the graph. In Enright et al.'s works [19,20], the problems of deleting and reordering edges in order to minimize k is shown to be NP-complete.

This framing of reachability asks what the worst-case spread is from a single source in the temporal graph. In reality, studied populations are often infected by several individuals. For example, SARS-CoV-2 had been independently introduced to the UK at least 1300 times by June 2020 [34]. We investigate how many sources are needed for the entire population to become infected - the TEMPORAL REACHABILITY DOMINATING SET (TARDIS) problem. Later, we ask: if we can choose when connections between individuals occur and know k individuals will be initially infected (but not which ones) can we guarantee that the entire population will not be infected?

The answers to both of these questions will depend heavily on our model definition. In particular, the instantaneous transmission of infection through a large swath of the population, while realistic in some computer networks, is inconsistent with the spread of biological phenomena. Further, should multiple interactions between the same pair of individuals be allowed? Lastly, should it be possible for a single individual to simultaneously interact with several others?

These three definitional choices are dubbed *strictness*, *simpleness*, and *properness* respectively, by Casteigts et al. [12]. In that work, the authors identify the class of so-called *happy* temporal graphs (in which our last two questions are answered in the negative). As they note, hardness results on *happy* temporal graphs generalise to the other restrictions, in particular to the strict and nonstrict settings.

1.1   Problem Setting

We begin with defining temporal graphs and related concepts. A *temporal graph* $\mathcal{G} = (V, E, \lambda)$ consists of a set of vertices V, a set of edges E and a function $\lambda : E \rightarrow [\tau]$[1]. We refer to λ as the *temporal assignment* of $\mathcal{G}$. The *lifetime* τ of a temporal graph is the value of the latest timestep. We abuse notation and write $\lambda(u, v)$ to mean $\lambda((u, v))$. For a static graph $G = (V, E)$, we denote the temporal graph (V, E, λ) by (G, λ). We also use $V(\mathcal{G})$, $E(\mathcal{G})$ to refer to the vertex and edge set of $\mathcal{G}$, respectively, and use $E_t(\mathcal{G})$ to refer to the set of edges active at time t. We say $\mathcal{G}$ and λ are *happy* if every vertex u is incident to at most 1 edge at a time[2]. The static graph $\mathcal{G}_{\downarrow} = (V, E)$ is called the *footprint* of $\mathcal{G}$.

---

[1] For a given $n \in \mathbb{N}^{>0}$ we denote by $[n]$ the set $\{1, 2, \ldots, n\}$.

[2] In Casteigts et al.'s work [12], a temporal graph is happy if it is both simple (only one time per edge) and proper (every vertex incident to at most 1 edge at a time); under our definition, all temporal graphs are simple.

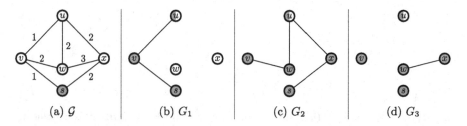

(a) $\mathcal{G}$ (b) G_1 (c) G_2 (d) G_3

Fig. 1. Reachability and spread in a temporal graph from source s through snapshots. Vertices are shaded (half-shaded) when reached from s by a strict (non-strict) temporal path. u is only reachable from s by a nonstrict path.

A *strict* (respectively *nonstrict*) *temporal path* from a vertex u to a vertex v is a static path from u to v consisting of edges $e_1, \ldots, e_l$ such that $\lambda(e_i) < \lambda(e_{i+1})$ (resp. $\lambda(e_i) \le \lambda(e_{i+1})$) for $i \in [1, l-1]$. A vertex u *temporally reaches* a vertex v (we sometimes say "reaches" for conciseness) if there is a temporal path from u to v. The *reachability set* $R_u(\mathcal{G})$ of a vertex u is the set of vertices reachable from u. We say a vertex u is reachable from a set S if for some $v \in S$, $u \in R_v$. A set of vertices T is *temporal reachability dominated* (or just *dominated*) by another set of vertices S if every vertex in T is reachable from S. Domination of and by single vertices is defined analogously. Strict and nonstrict spread are illustrated in Fig. 1. We differentiate between strict and nonstrict reachability by introducing a superscript $<$ or $\le$ to the appropriate operators. For example, in Fig. 2a, d is in $R_a^{\le}$ and not $R_a^{<}$. We can now introduce our protagonist.

Definition 1 (TaRDiS). *In a temporal graph $\mathcal{G}$, a (strict) temporal reachability dominating set (TaRDiS) is a set of vertices S such that every vertex $v \in V(\mathcal{G})$ is temporally reachable from a vertex in S by a (strict) temporal path.*

Definition 2 (Sole Reachability Set). *We define the* sole reachability set *of a vertex v in a TaRDiS T as the set $SR(\mathcal{G}, T, v) = R_v(\mathcal{G}) \setminus (\cup_{u \in T \setminus \{v\}} R_u(\mathcal{G}))$. Equivalently, it is the set of vertices reachable from v and not from other vertices in T[3].*

A minimum TaRDiS is a TaRDiS of fewest vertices in $\mathcal{G}$. Note that in a minimum TaRDiS, every vertex has a non-empty sole reachability set.

We now formally define our problems.

(Strict/Nonstrict) TaRDiS

Input: A temporal graph $\mathcal{G} = (V, E, \lambda)$ and an integer k.
Question: Does $\mathcal{G}$ admit a (strict/nonstrict) TaRDiS of size at most k?

The restriction to *happy* inputs $\mathcal{G}$ is referred to as Happy TaRDiS and is a subproblem of both Strict TaRDiS and Nonstrict TaRDiS.

---
[3] When $\mathcal{G}$ is clear from context, we write R_u for $R_u(\mathcal{G})$ and $SR(T, v)$ for $SR(T, \mathcal{G}, v)$.

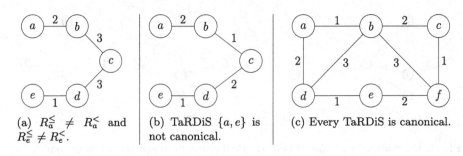

(a) $R_a^{\leq} \neq R_a^{<}$ and $R_e^{\leq} \neq R_e^{<}$.

(b) TaRDiS $\{a, e\}$ is not canonical.

(c) Every TaRDiS is canonical.

Fig. 2. Three temporal graphs, all admitting $\{a, e\}$ as a minimum TaRDiS.

(Strict/Nonstrict) MaxMinTaRDiS

Input: A static graph $H = (V, E)$ and integers k and τ.

Question: Does there exists a temporal assignment $\lambda : E \to [\tau]$ such that every strict/nonstrict TaRDiS admitted by (H, λ) is of size at least k?

Likewise, the variant of this problem in which the temporal assignment λ is required to be happy is referred to as Happy MaxMinTaRDiS. Note this is not a subproblem of Strict MaxMinTaRDiS or Nonstrict MaxMinTaRDiS.

Definition 3 (Locally earliest, Canonical TaRDiS). *In a temporal graph $\mathcal{G}$, an edge (u, v) is* locally earliest *if every other edge incident[4] to either u or v is at a time $t > \lambda(u, v)$. A* canonical TaRDiS *consists exclusively of vertices which are incident to a locally earliest edge.*

In Fig. 2b, each of $\{b, d\}$ and $\{a, c, e\}$ is a TaRDiS, but only the former is canonical.

1.2   Our Contribution

At a high level, our work identifies the minimum lifetime τ for which each problem is computationally hard. This justifies the need for parameters other than τ in tractability results. We show existence of such algorithms when the parameters τ, k and $\text{tw}(\mathcal{G}_{\downarrow})$ are all bounded.

Our main results are highlighted in Table 1. For the case of happy temporal graphs, we exactly characterize the complexity of both TaRDiS and MaxMinTaRDiS with lifetime $\tau \leq 3$. Both problems are trivially solvable in linear time for $\tau \leq 2$. We show NP-completeness of Happy TaRDiS and Σ_2^P-completeness of Happy MaxMinTaRDiS when $\tau = 3$ - even when restricted to planar inputs[5].

---

[4] If $e = (u, v)$ is an edge, u is said to be incident to vertex v and to edge e. Also, u is incident to a set S of vertices or edges if and only if it is incident to some element of S.

[5] In this work, we say a temporal graph is planar if and only if its footprint is planar.

Table 1. A summary of results.

Problem variant	TARDiS			MaxMinTARDiS		
	Strict	Nonstrict	Happy	Strict	Nonstrict	Happy
$\tau = 1$	NP-c, W[2]-c (Lemma 6)	Linear (Lemma 5)	Linear (Lemma 5)	coNP-c (Lemma 7)	Linear (Lemma 5)	Linear (Lemma 5)
$\tau = 2$	NP-c (Lemma 6)	NP-c, W[1]-h (Theorem 3)			NP-c, W[1]-c (Theorem 4)	
$\tau = 3$			NP-c (Theorem 1)		$\in \Sigma_2^P$ (Lemma 1)	Σ_2^P-c Theorem 2
$\tau \geq 4$						NP-h and $\in \Sigma_2^P$ (Corollary 1 and Lemma 1)

For MaxMinTARDiS, membership of NP is nontrivial; even the existence of a polynomial-time verifiable certificate is uncertain. Interestingly, we show equivalence[6] of Nonstrict MaxMinTARDiS restricted to inputs where $\tau = 2$ and Distance-3 Independent Set, which is NP-complete [22], in Sect. 4.

Having shown τ and planarity alone are insufficient for tractability, we show existence of an algorithm which is fixed-parameter tractable with respect to lifetime, k, and treewidth of the footprint of the input graph[7] combined. This is achieved in Sect. 5 by applying Courcelle's theorem [16]. In the full version of the paper, we also give an exact algorithm for TARDiS on trees where the input graph can have unbounded lifetime.

1.3 Related Work

For a static graph $G = (V, E)$, a dominating set is a set of vertices S such that $\forall u \in G \setminus S \; \exists v \in S : (u, v) \in E$. The decision problem Dominating Set (given G and k, is there a dominating set in G of size k?) is $W[2]$-complete when parameterized by k [18]. That is, even if k is fixed it is unlikely there exists an algorithm solving the problem with running time $f(k) \cdot n^{O(1)}$. However, Dominating Set can be solved in polynomial time on graphs of bounded treewidth [8,17].

TARDiS is exactly the problem of solving the directed variant of Dominating Set on a Reachability Graph [6]. This graph is also referred to as the transitive closure of journeys in a temporal graph and is shown to be efficiently computable by Whitbeck et al. [39]. Temporal versions of dominating set and other classical covering problems have been well studied [3,11,38], however these interpretations do not allow a chosen vertex to dominate beyond its neighbours. Furthermore, many other problems looking to optimally assign times to the edges

---

[6] We say that two problems X and Y are *equivalent* if they have the same language - that is, an instance I is a yes-instance of X if and only if the same instance I is a yes-instance of Y. Where X has a language consisting of triples (G, k, τ) and Y has a language of tuples (G, k), we may say that Y is equivalent to X with τ fixed to some value.

[7] Intuitively, the treewidth $tw(G)$ of a graph G represents how "treelike" G is. We refer the interested reader to Chap. 7 in [17].

of a static graph have been studied [2, 20, 30]. TaRDiS also generalises TEMPO-RAL SOURCE, which asks whether a single vertex can infect every other vertex in the graph. This is equivalent to the graph being a member of the class $\mathcal{J}^{1\forall}$ in the temporal graph classification given by Casteigts [11].

In research on networks, broadcasting refers to transmission to every device. In a typical model, there is a single source (which is input rather than chosen) in a graph which does not vary with time, in a setting where communication rather than computation is at a premium [33]. Broadcasting-based questions deviating from this standard have been studied as well. Namely, the NP-hardness of computing optimal broadcasting schedules for one or several sources [21, 28], broadcasting in ad-hoc networks or time-varying graphs [13], and the choice of multiple sources (originators) for broadcasting in minimum time in a static graph [15, 25]. To our knowledge, ours is the first work to focus on the hardness of choosing multiple sources in a temporal graph to minimize the number of sources, in an offline setting.

2 Preliminary Results

Proofs of the following results can be found in the full version of the paper on arXiv.

Lemma 1. *Each variant*[8] *of* TaRDiS *is contained in NP, and each variant of* MaxMinTaRDiS *is contained in* Σ_2^P.

We now explore some properties of HAPPY TaRDiS and HAPPY MaxMinTaRDiS.

Lemma 2. *In a happy temporal graph, there always exists a minimum TaRDiS which is also canonical. It follows that the number of locally earliest edges upper-bounds the size of the minimum TaRDiS*[9].

Note that a temporal graph which has no locally earliest edges is necessarily not happy, and cannot admit any canonical TaRDiS. The converse does not hold; in Fig. 2c, $\mathcal{G}$ is not canonical (b is incident to two edges at time 3), but every TaRDiS is canonical, since every node is incident to a locally earliest edge.

Lemma 3. HAPPY TaRDiS *is FPT (Fixed-Parameter Tractable) in the number of locally earliest edges.*

We now note the relationship between the proper edge colourings of a static graph and the happy temporal assignments it admits.

Lemma 4. *A static graph H admits a happy time-labeling function $\lambda : E(G) \to [\tau]$ if and only if H is τ-edge colourable.*

---

[8] In this work, by "each variant" we refer to the Strict, Nonstrict and Happy variants of the problems introduced in Sect. 1.1.

[9] This mirrors Lemma 54 from [5].

Corollary 1. HAPPY MAXMINTARDIS *restricted to instances with* $k = 0$ *asks only if there exists a happy labeling* λ *with lifetime* τ *for the input graph* G. *This is equivalent to the* EDGE COLOURING *problem with* τ *colours.* EDGE COLOURING *is NP-complete for 3 or more colours [27], so* HAPPY MAXMINTARDIS *is NP-hard for any* $\tau \geq 3$.

The following two lemmas consider the case where the lifetime of the graph is 1. We stress the contrast between the strict and nonstrict settings under this restriction.

Lemma 5. *When* $\tau = 1$, *the size of a minimum nonstrict TaRDiS depends only on the number of connected components in* $\mathcal{G}_\downarrow$. *Hence,* NONSTRICT TARDIS *and* NONSTRICT MAXMINTARDIS *can be computed in linear time in this case.*

Further, when $\tau \leq 2$ *the problems* HAPPY TARDIS *and* HAPPY MAXMINTARDIS *are solvable in linear time.*

Lemma 6. DOMINATING SET *is a special case of* STRICT TARDIS, *namely when* $\tau = 1$.

Given that the classical problem DOMINATING SET is a special case of TARDIS, our problem STRICT MAXMINTARDIS inherits the following hardness result.

Lemma 7. *For any static graph* H *and* $k \in \mathbb{N}^+$, (H, k) *is a yes-instance of* STRICT MAXMINTARDIS *if and only if* $(H, k - 1)$ *is a no-instance of* DOMINATING SET. *Hence* STRICT MAXMINTARDIS *is coNP-complete.*

The intuition follows from the idea that, for STRICT MAXMINTARDIS, it is always optimal to assign every edge the same time.

3   Hardness

STRICT TARDIS and STRICT MAXMINTARDIS are computationally hard even for lifetime $\tau = 1$ (Lemmas 6 and 7). Under the same restriction, HAPPY TARDIS, HAPPY MAXMINTARDIS and NONSTRICT TARDIS are all solvable in linear time (Lemma 5). In this section, we identify the minimum lifetime τ such that the problem becomes intractable for each of these problems.

3.1   NP-Completeness of HAPPY TARDIS with Lifetime 3

HAPPY TARDIS can trivially be solved in linear time when the input has lifetime $\tau \leq 2$ by Lemma 5. Here we show that the problem immediately becomes NP-complete for inputs where $\tau = 3$, even when $\mathcal{G}$ is planar.

Theorem 1. HAPPY TARDIS *is NP-complete, even restricted to instances where* $\mathcal{G}$ *is planar and lifetime is 3.*

Proof (Sketch). Our reduction is from the NP-complete problem PLANAR EXACTLY 3-BOUNDED 3-SAT, which asks whether the input Boolean formula ϕ is satisfiable [36]. We are guaranteed that ϕ is a planar formula in 3-CNF with each variable appearing exactly thrice and each literal at most twice. Let ϕ be an instance of PLANAR EXACTLY 3-BOUNDED 3-SAT consisting of clauses $\{c_1, \ldots, c_m\}$ over variables $X = \{x_1, \ldots, x_n\}$. We first create an auxiliary formula ϕ' by modifying every 2-clause of ϕ to include the special literal $\bot$. For example, the clause $(x_i \vee \neg x_j)$ becomes $(x_i \vee \neg x_j \vee \bot)$ in ϕ'. Note that ϕ' admits a satisfying assignment in which $\bot$ evaluates to False if and only if ϕ admits a satisfying assignment.

We will produce a happy temporal graph $\mathcal{G}$ which admits a TaRDiS of size exactly $k = 2n + 2m$ if and only if ϕ is satisfiable.

We create two *literal vertices* p_i^a and $\overline{p_i^a}$ (resp. n_i^a and $\overline{n_i^a}$) corresponding to the ath positive (resp. negative) appearance of the variable x_i, and connect these two vertices by an edge at time 3. Literal vertices $\bot^a$ and $\overline{\bot^a}$ correspond to $\bot$. Then for each variable x_i in ϕ we produce the *variable gadget* on vertices V_i as shown in Fig. 3 and connect it by edges at time 2 to the literal vertices $\overline{p_i^a}$ and $\overline{n_i^a}$ corresponding to variable i. This gadget has the property that any canonical TaRDiS S of size k must contain, for each $i \in [n]$, exactly two vertices from V_i, including exactly one of the four vertices $T_i^1, T_i^2, F_i^1, F_i^2$, and thereby encodes a truth assignment to the variable x_i. Note that T_i^1 (resp. F_i^1) reaches all positive (resp. negative) literal vertices for x_i, and no other literal vertices.

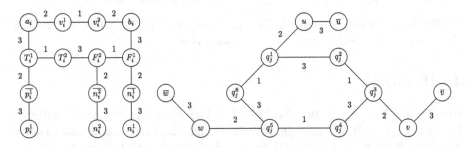

Fig. 3. Gadgets and adjacent *literal vertices* in the reduction from PLANAR EXACTLY 3-BOUNDED 3-SAT to HAPPY TARDIS. Left: the variable gadget for x_i, which appears twice negatively. Right: the clause gadget for the clause c_j. If, for example, clause $c_j = (x_5 \vee \neg x_{17} \vee x_{20})$ is the first positive appearance of x_5 and x_{20} and the second negative appearance of x_{17} in ϕ, then $u = p_5^1$, $v = n_{17}^2$ and $w = p_{20}^1$.

Then, for any three literal vertices u, v, w corresponding to the same clause c_j, each of these is connected by an edge at time 2 to one of the *clause vertices* $Q_j = \{q_j^1, \ldots, q_j^6\}$ as shown in Fig. 3. Any canonical TaRDiS S must include at least two vertices from Q_j. Further, if a canonical TaRDiS S has size k, then S includes exactly two vertices from Q_j and one of u, v, w is not reached from $S \cap Q_j$, meaning it must be reached from $S \cap V_i$ for some $i \in [n]$. In other words, $Q_j \cap S$ has size two if and only if the truth assignment corresponding to

S satisfies c_j. Note that literal vertices corresponding to the special literal $\perp$ are reachable *only* from clause vertices, and so behave identically to literals set to False, as intended.

This reduction produces an instance $(\mathcal{G}, k)$ of HAPPY TARDiS from an instance ϕ of PLANAR EXACTLY 3-BOUNDED 3-SAT such that $\mathcal{G}$ admits a TaRDiS of size at most k if and only if ϕ is satisfiable. We have membership of NP from Lemma 1. $\square$

3.2   Other Hardness Results

Theorem 2. HAPPY MAXMINTARDiS *is* Σ_2^P*-complete.*

Σ_2^P-completeness implies it is strictly harder than NP-complete problems such as SATISFIABILITY unless the polynomial hierarchy collapses to the first level. By Lemma 1, the problem is contained in Σ_2^P. Σ_2^P-hardness is proven in the arXiv version of the paper by reduction from RESTRICTED PLANAR SATISFIABILITY, a restricted variant of the canonical problem for that class. Interestingly, the proof does not easily generalize to $\tau \geq 4$. Consequently, we have only NP-hardness from Lemma 4 (NP is the class Σ_1^P of the polynomial hierarchy), leaving open the exact complexity of this restriction.

Theorem 3. NONSTRICT TARDiS *is NP-complete and W[2]-hard with respect to k for every $\tau \geq 2$. This holds even on graphs with degree at most 4.*

The proof (available in the full version) is by reduction from SET COVER, which is known to be NP-complete [9] and W[2]-hard [17].

4   NONSTRICT MAXMINTARDiS

Here we consider the restriction of NONSTRICT MAXMINTARDiS to instances with lifetime 2. We show the problem to be equivalent to the DISTANCE 3 INDEPENDENT SET (D3IS) decision problem.

Definition 4. *A distance-3-independent set (D3IS) of a static graph H is a set $S \subseteq V(H)$ such that for all distinct $u, v \in S$, $d(u, v) \geq 3$.*

The decision problem D3IS asks, for some input graph H and integer k, whether H admits a D3IS of size $\geq k$. We aim to show that a static graph H and integer k are a yes-instance of NONSTRICT MAXMINTARDiS with lifetime 2 if and only if the same graph H and integer k are a yes-instance of D3IS.

We begin by showing that existence of a maximal D3IS of size k in a graph H implies that we can find a temporal assignment $\lambda : E(H) \rightarrow \{1, 2\}$ such that a minimum TaRDiS in (H, λ) is of cardinality k. Given such a D3IS S of H, we assign $\lambda(u, v) = 1$, when $u \in S$ or $v \in S$, and $\lambda(u, v) = 2$, otherwise.

Lemma 8. *Under λ as described above, S is a minimum TaRDiS of (H, λ).*

Proof. We first show that S is a TaRDiS. We can assume without loss of generality that H is a single connected component. Suppose for contradiction some vertex u is not reachable from any vertex in S. Note that every vertex in S trivially reaches its neighbours. So, by construction of λ, u is incident only to edges at time 2. Since we have assumed that H consists of a single connected component, there must be a static path in H from each vertex in S to u. Let z be the closest vertex in S to u. Then the shortest path from z to u must have length 2 and consist of an edge assigned time 1 followed by an edge assigned time 2 (else S is not maximal). Hence the shortest path from z to u is a nonstrict temporal path and $u \in R_z$, contradicting our assumption. Hence S is a TaRDiS of the constructed instance.

We now show minimality of S. By construction of λ, every vertex $v \in S$ is temporally reachable only from its closed neighbourhood $N[v]$. No temporal path originating outside $N[v]$ can include any edge incident to v since any such path must contain an edge assigned time 2 before the final edge which is assigned time 1. Since S forms a D3IS, $N[u] \cap N[v] = \emptyset$ for all $u, v \in S$. Therefore, for (H, λ) to be temporal reachability dominated, there must at least be a vertex from the neighbourhood of each vertex in S. These are disjoint sets, so any TaRDiS must have cardinality at least k. Hence S is a minimum TaRDiS of (H, λ).   □

Definition 5. *We call a TaRDiS S on a temporal graph $\mathcal{G}$ independent if, for all vertices u, v in S with $u \neq v$, u does not reach v. Equivalently, S is independent if and only if every vertex in S is in its own sole reachability set under S.*

Lemma 9. *If a temporal graph $\mathcal{G}$ admits an independent nonstrict TaRDiS S, then S is a D3IS in the footprint graph $\mathcal{G}_\downarrow$.*

Proof. Consider two vertices $u, v \in S$ at distance $d(u, v)$ from one another in $\mathcal{G}_\downarrow$. If u and v are adjacent, then u and v reach each other, which would contradict independence of S. If $d(u, v) = 2$ then there is at least one vertex $w \in N[u] \cap N[v]$, and either $\lambda(u, w) \leq \lambda(w, v)$ or $\lambda(u, w) > \lambda(w, v)$. So one of u and v must reach the other. Hence any two vertices in S must be distance at least 3 from one another, the definition of a D3IS.   □

Lemma 10. *If some temporal graph $\mathcal{G}$ with lifetime 2 has a minimum nonstrict TaRDiS of cardinality k, then $\mathcal{G}_\downarrow$ admits a D3IS of size k.*

Proof. Our proof is constructive; given a minimum TaRDiS S, we show existence of an *independent* minimum TaRDiS S^* of equal cardinality and then apply Lemma 9.

First, we justify some simplifying assumptions about $\mathcal{G}$. Since TaRDiS can be computed independently in disconnected components of $\mathcal{G}_\downarrow$, we will assume $\mathcal{G}_\downarrow$ is connected. Further, if $E_1(\mathcal{G}) = \emptyset$ or $E_2(\mathcal{G}) = \emptyset$ we may choose any single vertex from $\mathcal{G}$ to be a minimum TaRDiS which is also independent; hence we assume $E_1(\mathcal{G}) \neq \emptyset$ and $E_2(\mathcal{G}) \neq \emptyset$. Also, recall that $SR(S, x) \neq \emptyset$ for all $x \in S$ by minimality of S.

We construct S^* by replacing every vertex x in S such that $x \notin SR(S, x)$ with some vertex x^* with the property that $R_{x^*} = R_x$ and $x^* \in SR(S, x)$, as follows. Let $y \neq x$ be a vertex in S such that y reaches x. The path from y to x cannot arrive at time 1, else S is not minimal as $R_x = R_y$ and $S \setminus \{x\}$ is a TaRDiS. Choose x^* to be the closest vertex to x in $SR(S, x)$. We know such a vertex exists by minimality of S. We claim that the path from x to x^* arrives at time 1 and so $R_x = R_{x^*}$. To see this, suppose otherwise. The path must begin with at least one edge at time 1, otherwise x^* would be reachable from y. If the path arrives at time 2, then the last vertex on the path reached at time 1 is closer to x than x^*, and is in $SR(S, x)$. Else, some other vertex in S reaches x^*.

This concludes our construction of S^* as an independent minimum TaRDiS. By Lemma 9, S^* is also a D3IS. □

Combining Lemmas 8 and 10 gives us the following theorem.

Theorem 4. NONSTRICT MAXMINTARDIS *with lifetime* $\tau = 2$ *is equivalent to* DISTANCE 3 INDEPENDENT SET.

Interestingly, the same does not hold for $\tau \geq 3$. A counterexample is shown in Fig. 2c, where the minimum TaRDiS is larger than the maximum D3IS of the footprint.

Eto et al. [22] show that D3IS is NP-complete even on planar, bipartite graphs with maximum degree 3. They also show D3IS to be $W[1]$-hard on chordal graphs with respect to the size of the distance 3 independent set. D3IS is also shown to be APX-hard on r-regular graphs for all integers $r \geq 3$ and admit a PTAS on planar graphs by Eto et al. [23]. Agnarsson et al. [1] show that D3IS is tractable on interval graphs, trapezoid graphs and circular arc graphs. Thus, these results also apply to NONSTRICT MAXMINTARDIS when $\tau = 2$.

5 Tractability

We show tractability by expressing our problems in extended monadic second-order (EMSO) logic and applying Courcelle's theorem [16].

5.1 TARDIS

We show tractability of our problems by expressing them in EMSO logic and applying the variant of Courcelle's theorem given by Arnborg et al. [4]. This result states that an optimisation problem which is definable in EMSO can be solved in linear time when parameterised by treewidth and length of the formula. Full expressions can be found in the full paper on arXiv. We provide a sketch showing some key components. Langer et al. provide definitions of first-order, MSO and EMSO logic in their survey [32].

Lemma 11. *Temporal reachability is expressible in MSO logic.*

Proof (Sketch). To encode the temporal nature of a temporal graph $\mathcal{G}$, we use an auxiliary static graph $\mathcal{S}$. Our auxiliary graph is an adaptation of the one given by Haag et al. [26, Theorem 23]. They use this graph to construct an MSO formula for TEMPORAL FEEDBACK EDGE SET. The vertices of $\mathcal{S}$ consist of the disjoint union of $V(\mathcal{G})$, $E(\mathcal{G})$, and the set of timesteps $[\tau]$. The edges of $\mathcal{S}$ consist of the following binary relations. A relation R is written as $R(e, v)$ to simplify the expression $(e, v) \in R$.

- the incidence relation inc $\subseteq E \times V$ where inc$(e, v) \iff v \in e$;
- the presence relation pres $\subseteq E \times \tau$ where pres$(e, t) \iff (e, t) \in \varepsilon$.

As shown by Haag et al., $|\mathcal{S}| \in O(\tau + |\mathcal{G}|)$ and the treewidth of $\mathcal{S}$ is bounded by a function of $\mathrm{tw}(\mathcal{G}_\downarrow) + \tau$.

The formula path(v, w) tests whether there is a temporal path from v to $w \in V$. In the strict case we use the subformula ttadj(u, v, t) given by Haag et al. [26, Theorem 23]. This uses the incidence and presence relations on $\mathcal{S}$ to test if vertices u and v are adjacent at time t. For nonstrict temporal paths, we test whether two vertices are in the same connected component of $\mathcal{G}_t$ instead of adjacency. This uses a variation of the formula conn(v, w, E') by Haag et al. which tests if there is a path using edges in the set E' from v to w. The formula for path is

$$\mathrm{path}(v, w) = \exists v_0, \ldots, v_\tau \in V : v = v_0 \wedge v_\tau = w \wedge \bigwedge_{t=0}^{\tau-1} (v_t = v_{t+1} \vee \mathrm{a}(v_t, v_{t+1}, t+1))$$

where $\mathrm{a}(v_t, v_{t+1}, t+1)$ is a place-holder for the subformula testing adjacency or connectedness for strict and nonstrict temporal paths respectively. $\qquad\square$

Lemma 12. *Both strict and nonstrict* TARDIS *are expressible in MSO.*

We use the reachability formulae given in Lemma 11 to express TARDIS in MSO. This is done by a formula which tests whether there exist k vertices such that all vertices in $\mathcal{G}$ are reachable from them.

We note that strict reachability and thus STRICT TARDIS are expressible in FO logic, which is a strict subset of EMSO. Combining the tractability result given by Arnborg et al. [4] with Lemma 12 gives the following theorem.

Theorem 5. TARDIS *is fixed-parameter tractable with respect to lifetime, k and treewidth of the footprint of the temporal graph.*

5.2 MAXMINTARDIS

We now show that MAXMINTARDIS is expressible in EMSO logic, thus proving the following theorem.

Theorem 6. MAXMINTARDIS *is fixed-parameter tractable when parameterised by lifetime, k and treewidth of the graph.*

Proof (Sketch). Our EMSO formula follows from the MSO formula for TARDIS. Since the temporal assignment is not part of the input, we must encode it as a partition of edges into sets which correspond to the time at which they are active.

Therefore, to check if an edge e is active at time t, we simply need to check if $e \in S_t$. We use variations of the formulae in Lemmas 11 and 12 to test whether a given set is a TaRDiS. For MaxMinTaRDiS it is necessarily to enforce minimality of a given TaRDiS and existence of a temporal assignment that we can check these properties on. These are done using the following subformulae over the sets X_1, X_2 of vertices and $S_1, \ldots, S_\tau$ of edges respectively:

$$\mathrm{geq}(X_1, X_2) = \exists k : \mathrm{card}(k, X_1) \wedge \neg \mathrm{card}(k+1, X_2)$$

where $\mathrm{card}(k, X)$ tests if a set X contains at least k distinct elements, and

$$\mathrm{part}(S_1, \ldots, S_\tau) = \forall e \in E : \bigvee_{1 \leq i \leq \tau} e \in S_i$$

which can be adjusted if we require a happy or simple temporal assignment. Full formulae expressing MaxMinTaRDiS are in the full version of the paper on arXiv. Hence the theorem holds.   □

6   Conclusions and Open Questions

In this paper, we introduce the TaRDiS and MaxMinTaRDiS problems and study their parameterized complexity. We show a bound on the lifetime τ and a restriction to planar inputs combined are insufficient to obtain tractability[10], and moreover tightly characterize the minimum lifetime τ for which each problem becomes intractable. Further, we show that τ, k and the treewidth of the input (temporal) graph combined are sufficient to yield tractability in all cases by leveraging Courcelle's theorem.

These results leave open the questions of the exact complexity of NonStrict MaxMinTaRDiS with lifetime $\tau \geq 3$ and Happy MaxMinTaRDiS with lifetime $\tau \geq 4$. An interesting extension of our work would be to find approximability results for these problems. From the parameterized side, it remains to be shown whether parameterization by a structural parameter of the footprint (e.g. treewidth) alone is sufficient to obtain tractability for any of the considered variants. Another interesting dimension is the comparison of NonStrict MaxMinTaRDiS and Happy MaxMinTaRDiS when τ is lower-bounded by a function of the number of edges m. With the constraint $\tau = m$ the two problems become equivalent, and their computational complexity in this case is an interesting open question. Analogously to t-Dominating Set [31], t-TaRDiS, in which t individuals must be reached provides a natural generalisation of our problem and the potential for parameterization by t.

References

1. Agnarsson, G., Damaschke, P., Halldórsson, M.M.: Powers of geometric intersection graphs and dispersion algorithms. Discret. Appl. Math. **132**(1), 3–16 (2003). https://doi.org/10.1016/S0166-218X(03)00386-X

---

[10] The result in Theorem 1 generalizes to Strict TaRDiS and NonStrict TaRDiS; D3IS and Dominating Set are NP-complete on planar graphs.

2. Akrida, E.C., Gąsieniec, L., Mertzios, G.B., Spirakis, P.G.: The complexity of optimal design of temporally connected graphs. Theory Comput. Syst. **61**(3), 907–944 (2017). https://doi.org/10.1007/s00224-017-9757-x

3. Akrida, E.C., Mertzios, G.B., Spirakis, P.G., Zamaraev, V.: Temporal vertex cover with a sliding time window. J. Comput. Syst. Sci. **107**, 108–123 (2020). https://doi.org/10.1016/j.jcss.2019.08.002

4. Arnborg, S., Lagergren, J., Seese, D.: Easy problems for tree-decomposable graphs. J. Algorithms **12**(2), 308–340 (1991). https://doi.org/10.1016/0196-6774(91)90006-K

5. Balev, S., Pigné, Y., Sanlaville, E., Schoeters, J.: Temporally connected components (2023). https://hal.science/hal-03966327

6. Bhadra, S., Ferreira, A.: Complexity of connected components in evolving graphs and the computation of multicast trees in dynamic networks. In: Pierre, S., Barbeau, M., Kranakis, E. (eds.) ADHOC-NOW 2003. LNCS, vol. 2865, pp. 259–270. Springer, Heidelberg (2003). https://doi.org/10.1007/978-3-540-39611-6_23

7. Bilò, D., D'Angelo, G., Gualà, L., Leucci, S., Rossi, M.: Blackout-tolerant temporal spanners. In: Erlebach, T., Segal, M. (eds.) ALGOSENSORS 2022. LNCS, vol. 13707, pp. 31–44. Lecture Notes in Computer Science, Springer, Cham (2022). https://doi.org/10.1007/978-3-031-22050-0_3

8. Björklund, A., Husfeldt, T., Kaski, P., Koivisto, M.: Fourier meets Möbius: fast subset convolution. arXiv e-prints p. cs/0611101 (2006). https://doi.org/10.48550/arXiv.cs/0611101. aDS Bibcode: 2006cs.......11101B

9. Book, R.V.: Richard M. Karp. Reducibility among combinatorial problems. Complexity of computer computations, Proceedings of a Symposium on the Complexity of Computer Computations, held March 20–22, 1972, at the IBM Thomas J. Watson Center, Yorktown Heights, New York, edited by Raymond E. Miller and James W. Thatcher, Plenum Press, New York and London 1972, pp. 85–103. J. Symb. Logic **40**(4), 618–619 (1975). https://doi.org/10.2307/2271828

10. Braunstein, A., Ingrosso, A.: Inference of causality in epidemics on temporal contact networks. Sci. Rep. **6**(1), 27538 (2016). https://doi.org/10.1038/srep27538

11. Casteigts, A.: A journey through dynamic networks (with excursions). Thesis, Université de Bordeaux (2018). https://hal.science/tel-01883384

12. Casteigts, A., Corsini, T., Sarkar, W.: Simple, strict, proper, happy: a study of reachability in temporal graphs (2022). https://arxiv.org/abs/2208.01720 [cs]

13. Casteigts, A., Flocchini, P., Quattrociocchi, W., Santoro, N.: Time-varying graphs and dynamic networks. In: Frey, H., Li, X., Ruehrup, S. (eds.) ADHOC-NOW 2011. LNCS, vol. 6811, pp. 346–359. Springer, Heidelberg (2011). https://doi.org/10.1007/978-3-642-22450-8_27

14. Casteigts, A., Peters, J.G., Schoeters, J.: Temporal cliques admit sparse spanners. J. Comput. Syst. Sci. **121**, 1–17 (2021). https://doi.org/10.1016/j.jcss.2021.04.004

15. Chia, M.L., Kuo, D., Tung, M.F.: The multiple originator broadcasting problem in graphs. Discret. Appl. Math. **155**(10), 1188–1199 (2007). https://doi.org/10.1016/j.dam.2006.10.011

16. Courcelle, B.: The expression of graph properties and graph transformations in monadic second-order logic. In: Handbook of Graph Grammars and Computing By Graph Transformation: Volume 1: Foundations, pp. 313–400. World Scientific (1997)

17. Cygan, M., et al.: Parameterized Algorithms. Springer, Cham (2015). https://doi.org/10.1007/978-3-319-21275-3

18. Downey, R.G., Fellows, M.R.: Fixed-parameter tractability and completeness I: basic results. SIAM J. Comput. **24**(4), 873–921 (1995). https://doi.org/10.1137/S0097539792228228
19. Enright, J., Meeks, K., Mertzios, G.B., Zamaraev, V.: Deleting edges to restrict the size of an epidemic in temporal networks. J. Comput. Syst. Sci. **119**, 60–77 (2021). https://doi.org/10.1016/j.jcss.2021.01.007
20. Enright, J., Meeks, K., Skerman, F.: Assigning times to minimise reachability in temporal graphs. J. Comput. Syst. Sci. **115**, 169–186 (2021). https://doi.org/10.1016/j.jcss.2020.08.001
21. Erlebach, T., Hall, A.: NP-hardness of broadcast scheduling and inapproximability of single-source unsplittable min-cost flow. J. Sched. **7**(3), 223–241 (2004). https://doi.org/10.1023/B:JOSH.0000019682.75022.96
22. Eto, H., Guo, F., Miyano, E.: Distance-$d$independent set problems for bipartite and chordal graphs. J. Comb. Optim. **27**(1), 88–99 (2014). https://doi.org/10.1007/s10878-012-9594-4
23. Eto, H., Ito, T., Liu, Z., Miyano, E.: Approximability of the distance independent set problem on regular graphs and planar graphs. In: Chan, T.-H.H., Li, M., Wang, L. (eds.) COCOA 2016. LNCS, vol. 10043, pp. 270–284. Springer, Cham (2016). https://doi.org/10.1007/978-3-319-48749-6_20
24. Füchsle, E., Molter, H., Niedermeier, R., Renken, M.: Delay-robust routes in temporal graphs (2022). https://doi.org/10.48550/arXiv.2201.05390 [cs]
25. Grigoryan, H.: Problems related to broadcasting in graphs. Ph.D. Concordia University (2013). https://spectrum.library.concordia.ca/id/eprint/977773/
26. Haag, R., Molter, H., Niedermeier, R., Renken, M.: Feedback edge sets in temporal graphs. Discret. Appl. Math. **307**, 65–78 (2022). https://doi.org/10.1016/j.dam.2021.09.029
27. Holyer, I.: The NP-completeness of edge-coloring. SIAM J. Comput. **10**(4), 718–720 (1981)
28. Jakoby, A., Reischuk, R., Schindelhauer, C.: The complexity of broadcasting in planar and decomposable graphs. In: Mayr, E.W., Schmidt, G., Tinhofer, G. (eds.) WG 1994. LNCS, vol. 903, pp. 219–231. Springer, Heidelberg (1995). https://doi.org/10.1007/3-540-59071-4_50
29. Kempe, D., Kleinberg, J., Kumar, A.: Connectivity and inference problems for temporal networks. In: Proceedings of the Thirty-Second Annual ACM Symposium on Theory of Computing, STOC 2000, pp. 504–513. Association for Computing Machinery, New York (2000). https://doi.org/10.1145/335305.335364
30. Klobas, N., Mertzios, G.B., Molter, H., Spirakis, P.G.: The complexity of computing optimum labelings for temporal connectivity. In: Szeider, S., Ganian, R., Silva, A. (eds.) 47th International Symposium on Mathematical Foundations of Computer Science (MFCS 2022). Leibniz International Proceedings in Informatics (LIPIcs), vol. 241, pp. 62:1–62:15. Schloss Dagstuhl - Leibniz-Zentrum für Informatik, Dagstuhl, Germany (2022). https://doi.org/10.4230/LIPIcs.MFCS.2022.62. https://drops.dagstuhl.de/opus/volltexte/2022/16860
31. Kneis, J., Mölle, D., Rossmanith, P.: Partial vs. complete domination: t-dominating set. In: van Leeuwen, J., Italiano, G.F., van der Hoek, W., Meinel, C., Sack, H., Plášil, F. (eds.) SOFSEM 2007. LNCS, vol. 4362, pp. 367–376. Springer, Heidelberg (2007). https://doi.org/10.1007/978-3-540-69507-3_31
32. Langer, A., Reidl, F., Rossmanith, P., Sikdar, S.: Practical algorithms for MSO model-checking on tree-decomposable graphs. Comput. Sci. Rev. **13–14**, 39–74 (2014). https://doi.org/10.1016/j.cosrev.2014.08.001

33. Peleg, D.: Time-efficient broadcasting in radio networks: a review. In: Janowski, T., Mohanty, H. (eds.) ICDCIT 2007. LNCS, vol. 4882, pp. 1–18. Springer, Heidelberg (2007). https://doi.org/10.1007/978-3-540-77115-9_1
34. Pybus, O., Rambaut, A., COG-UK-Consortium, et al.: Preliminary analysis of SARS-CoV-2 importation & establishment of UK transmission lineages. Virological.org (2020)
35. Tang, J., et al.: Applications of temporal graph metrics to real-world networks. In: Holme, P., Saramäki, J. (eds.) Temporal Networks. UCS, pp. 135–159. Springer, Heidelberg (2013). https://doi.org/10.1007/978-3-642-36461-7_7
36. Tippenhauer, S., Muzler, W.: On planar 3-SAT and its variants. Fachbereich Mathematik und Informatik der Freien Universitat Berlin (2016)
37. Valdano, E., Ferreri, L., Poletto, C., Colizza, V.: Analytical computation of the epidemic threshold on temporal networks. Phys. Rev. X **5**(2), 021005 (2015). https://doi.org/10.1103/PhysRevX.5.021005
38. Verheije, M.: Algorithms for domination problems on temporal graphs. Ph.D. thesis, Utrecht University (2021). https://studenttheses.uu.nl/handle/20.500.12932/41240. Accepted: 2021-08-26T18:00:14Z
39. Whitbeck, J., de Amorim, M.D., Conan, V., Guillaume, J.L.: Temporal reachability graphs (2012). https://doi.org/10.48550/arXiv.1207.7103 [cs]

Fair Scheduling Under Packet Management: Competitive Analysis of Age of Information

Chen-Rui Jien⬤ and Tung-Wei Kuo$^{(\boxtimes)}$⬤

Department of Computer Science, National Chengchi University, Taipei, Taiwan
`twkuo@cs.nccu.edu.tw`

Abstract. Maintaining up-to-date information is essential for enhancing the quality of service in mobile devices. The freshness of a mobile device is typically evaluated using the Age of Information (AoI) metric. This study considers a system where a Base Station (BS) transmits update messages to its terminals, and the goal is to design message transmission scheduling algorithms that minimize the overall AoI across all terminals. Previous studies have demonstrated that online algorithms perform poorly when the BS is required to send every message. However, in many applications, once a new message is generated, older ones can be discarded. This policy is called packet management. We prove that Round Robin (RR) is $O(1)$-competitive under packet management. We also generalize RR and consider a broader class of fair scheduling algorithms.

Keywords: Age of information · Round Robin · Competitive analysis

1 Introduction

The rapid development of 5G/6G networks has led to a significant increase in the number of mobile devices and mobile applications. The Quality of Service (QoS) of these applications heavily relies on the timely reception of update messages. It is therefore crucial for the Base Station (BS) to deliver information promptly to all connected terminals. To quantify the freshness of an information receiver, the Age of Information (AoI) metric was proposed in [10]. The AoI of a terminal is defined as the time difference between the generation of the latest received message and the current time. For instance, if the current time is 5 and the latest received message was generated at time 2, the current AoI for the terminal would be $5 - 2 = 3$. AoI has gained significant attention as it provides valuable insights into the design of scheduling algorithms in wireless networks. In this paper, we examine several scheduling algorithms through the lens of AoI.

Recently, various approaches have been explored to minimize AoI for multiple terminals that share a single channel. Queueing theory has been employed in several studies [3,13–15,18] to investigate the relationship between different service disciplines and AoI under stochastic models. Another line of research focuses on designing sampling policies on the message generator side to ensure that

K. Georgiou and E. Kranakis (Eds.): ALGOWIN 2023, LNCS 14061, pp. 117–132, 2023.
https://doi.org/10.1007/978-3-031-48882-5_9

messages are generated at appropriate times [1,2,17]. Furthermore, a considerable amount of research has been conducted on designing message transmission schedules for minimizing AoI [4–9,11,12,16]. For a comprehensive overview of AoI minimization, a detailed survey can be found in [19].

This paper specifically focuses on message transmission scheduling to minimize AoI. Previous analyses of AoI scheduling have primarily focused on stochastic models and assumed that messages are generated at a fixed rate or following Poisson processes. While these assumptions are valid in certain scenarios, such as sensor networks with a fixed sensing rate, they are generally not ideal, especially when the message generation rate adapts to changing environmental conditions. For example, a navigation application may adjust the rate of real-time traffic information updates based on traffic conditions. In this paper, we avoid making any assumptions about the message generation process to accommodate the variability and adaptability of real-world scenarios.

Several prior works have adopted a more general framework that avoids assumptions about the message generation process [5,11,12]. These works primarily focus on two aspects: the hardness of the scheduling problem and the competitive or approximation ratio of algorithms. The hardness of the scheduling problem has been studied in [5,11], while the competitive or approximation ratio of algorithms has been analyzed in [11,12]. Specifically, the competitive ratio of an algorithm $\mathcal{A}$ for minimizing an objective function obj is defined as $\max_{\mathcal{I}} \frac{obj(\mathcal{A},\mathcal{I})}{obj(\mathcal{OPT},\mathcal{I})}$, where $obj(\mathcal{A},\mathcal{I})$ is the objective value achieved by algorithm $\mathcal{A}$ on problem instance $\mathcal{I}$, and $\mathcal{OPT}$ is the optimal algorithm. An algorithm $\mathcal{A}$ is said to be c-competitive if its competitive ratio is at most c. When designing online algorithms, the goal typically revolves around designing $O(1)$-competitive algorithms.

In [5,11], the objective was to minimize the total AoI over all terminals. However, the scheduling algorithms proposed in [5,11] only consider the messages that are already stored in the BS, and newly arrived messages could only be scheduled when the algorithm is invoked again. In other words, these scheduling algorithms are offline algorithms. Subsequently, in [12], the author considered the corresponding online scheduling problem and showed that the competitive ratio of any online algorithm is $\Omega(n^{\frac{1}{5}})$, where n is the number of terminals.

1.1   Necessity of Packet Management

The above pessimistic competitive ratio can be attributed in part to the assumption that the BS must send *every* message, which may not be necessary in some applications [7–9,16]. For example, in navigation applications, once a new traffic information generated by the map server arrives at the BS, outdated traffic information does not need to be sent to the navigation applications and can be safely discarded. This policy of keeping only the newest message for each terminal at the BS is known as *packet management*. By implementing packet management, unnecessary transmission of outdated messages can be avoided, potentially leading to improved scheduling algorithms and better performance in terms of minimizing AoI.

In this paper, we address the problem of online message transmission scheduling to minimize AoI under packet management. Previous works [4,7] showed that Round Robin (RR), a well-known fair scheduling algorithm, is asymptotically optimal when the message generation processes are Bernoulli and the set of terminals is fixed. However, these assumptions are not realistic in many scenarios where terminals may join or leave the system at any time and messages may be generated according to arbitrary distributions. Therefore, we consider a more general framework that incorporates the following features:

Dynamic terminals: We allow terminals to enter or exit the system without any prior knowledge or restrictions.

Arbitrary message generation: We do not impose any assumptions on the message generation process.

Beyond RR: We generalize RR and consider a broader class of fair scheduling algorithms.

1.2 Fair Scheduling Algorithms

We define fair scheduling algorithms based on RR. The precise definitions of RR and fair scheduling algorithms can be found in Sect. 3, while we provide informal definitions here. A terminal is considered as a feasible receiver if it has a message waiting at the BS. Under RR, the BS sends one message to every feasible receiver in a circular order. This cyclic process divides time into rounds, where each round represents the time interval required for the BS to complete one cycle.

We define a scheduling algorithm $\mathcal{A}$ to be δ-Fair if it meets the following condition: Whenever a message for terminal i arrives at the BS in round r, the BS sends a message to terminal i by round $r + \delta$ under the schedule generated by $\mathcal{A}$. As a result, a δ-Fair scheduling algorithm guarantees that a terminal receives at least one message in every δ rounds (if there are messages generated for that terminal). For example, RR is 1-Fair.

It is important to note that a fair scheduling algorithm has the flexibility to send more than one message to a terminal in a single round. This enhances the design options for the scheduling algorithm and enables RR customization.

1.3 Our Results

In this paper, we prove that every δ-Fair scheduling algorithm is $O(\delta^4)$-competitive even with dynamic terminals and arbitrary message generation (Theorem 2). As a direct corollary, RR is $O(1)$-competitive.

Challenge: The total AoI of RR depends heavily on the number of feasible receivers in a round. The main challenge in analyzing δ-Fair scheduling algorithms is handling the changing set of feasible receivers due to arbitrary message generation and dynamic terminals. We overcome this challenge by lower bounding the optimal total AoI based on the number of feasible receivers in a round (Lemma 7). Another lower bound derived in this paper is due to packet management (Lemma 8).

2   Definition and System Model

We consider a network that consists of a Base Station (BS) and a set of terminals that receive messages from the BS (e.g., navigation applications that receive packets from the BS). We assume that time is indexed by $\mathbb{N}$. For terminal i, we use $t_i^{arr} \in \mathbb{N}$ to denote the time at which i arrives in the system (i.e., terminal i is connected to the BS at time t_i^{arr}) and use $t_i^{dep} \in \mathbb{N}$ to denote the time at which i leaves the system (i.e., terminal i is disconnected from the BS at time t_i^{dep}). Once terminal i arrives in the system, it starts to request information from its associated information source. For example, the information source of a navigation application may be a map server that generates real-time traffic information. Different terminals may have different information sources, and the information source associated with terminal i starts to generate messages for terminal i after time t_i^{arr}. Moreover, there is a queue Q_i at the BS that stores all the messages for i.

At each time t, at most C messages can be sent from the BS to the terminals. Thus, a schedule $\mathcal{S}$ maps every time t to a set $\mathcal{S}(t)$ of at most C terminals to which the BS sends messages at time t. We assume the transmission latency from the BS to the terminals is one unit of time. Thus, if $i \in \mathcal{S}(t)$, then the BS sends a message to i at time t, and the message is received by i at time $t+1$.

We do not make any assumption on the message generation process. Moreover, as a scheduler at the BS, we have no control over message generation times. For each message m, we use $t^{gen}(m)$ and $t^{arr}(m)$ to denote the generation time of m and the time at which m arrives at the BS, respectively. For any message m generated for terminal i, we have $t_i^{arr} < t^{gen}(m) < t^{arr}(m)$. $t^{arr}(m)$ and $t^{gen}(m)$ are available to the scheduling algorithm when m arrives at the BS. Because the information sources and the BS are usually fixed, we assume that the communication latency between an information source and the BS is also fixed. Specifically, for any terminal i and any message m for i, there is a fixed latency Δ_i such that $t^{arr}(m) - t^{gen}(m) = \Delta_i$. Upon receiving a message m for terminal i at time $t^{arr}(m)$, the BS stores m in Q_i. The BS can send m immediately at time $t^{arr}(m)$. After m is sent to i, m is then removed from Q_i.

We consider packet management so that once a new message for terminal i arrives at the BS, older messages in Q_i can be discarded without sending to the receiver. As a result, there is always at most one message in each queue Q_i.

The Age-of-Information (AoI) of terminal i at time t under schedule $\mathcal{S}$, denoted by $AoI(i, \mathcal{S}, t)$, is defined as

$$AoI(i, \mathcal{S}, t) = t - t^{gen}(\text{the last message received by } i \text{ by time } t \text{ under } \mathcal{S}).$$

For any integers a and b with $a \leq b$, define $[a, b] = \{a, a+1, a+2, \cdots, b\}$. If $a > b$, then $[a, b] = \varnothing$. A time interval that starts at time t_1 and ends at time t_2 is thus denoted by $[t_1, t_2]$. A terminal i is said to be **active** at time t if $t \in [t_i^{arr}, t_i^{dep}]$. If terminal i is not active at time t (i.e., $t \notin [t_i^{arr}, t_i^{dep}]$), then $AoI(i, \mathcal{S}, t) = 0$. When a terminal arrives in the system, its AoI is initialized to zero. For ease of exposition, we assume that once terminal i arrives in the system, it obtains a virtual message $m_{virtual}$ with $t^{gen}(m_{virtual}) = t^{arr}(m_{virtual}) = t_i^{arr}$. Thus, $AoI(i, \mathcal{S}, t_i^{arr}) = 0$.

Let D be the set of terminals. The goal is to design a message transmission schedule for the BS to minimize the total AoI. Specifically, define

$$AoI(\mathcal{S}) = \sum_{i \in D} \sum_{t=t_i^{arr}}^{t_i^{dep}} AoI(i, \mathcal{S}, t).$$

Our goal is to compute a schedule $\mathcal{S}$ that minimizes $AoI(\mathcal{S})$. We refer to this minimization problem as the MinAoI problem.

3 Fair Scheduling Algorithms

In this section, we define fair scheduling algorithms (Sect. 3.2). Because the definition of fair scheduling algorithms is based on RR, we first define RR.

3.1 Definition of RR

The pseudocode of RR can be found in Algorithm 1. We use an array L to store all terminals and assume that there is always a virtual terminal vt in the beginning of L (i.e., $L[0] = vt$). Throughout the execution of RR, there is an index variable p associated with L, and $p = 0$ initially. Let $\mathcal{RR}$ be the schedule obtained by RR. The set of receivers at time t under $\mathcal{RR}$ (i.e., $\mathcal{RR}(t)$) is determined based on p. Specifically, we say that a terminal i is a feasible receiver at time t if i is active at time t and Q_i is not empty (and thus the BS can send a message to i at time t). To construct $\mathcal{RR}(t)$, we keep advancing p and adding feasible receivers to $\mathcal{RR}(t)$ (Lines 11 and 12). The construction of $\mathcal{RR}(t)$ stops when C feasible receivers have been found (Line 10) or p has reached the end of L (Lines 13 to 16). When p reaches the end of L, p is reset to 0.

We say that RR is currently in round r if RR is traversing L for the rth time. Specifically, a round starts when $p = 0$ (Line 6) and ends when p reaches the end of L (Lines 13 and 14). In the pseudocode of RR, we increase r by one whenever $p = 0$ (Line 5). We use R_r to denote the time interval of round r (Line 14).

We only add terminals to L at the start of each round (i.e., when $p = 0$). Specifically, for any terminal i that arrives in the system in round $r - 1$, i is added to L in the beginning of round r (Lines 7 and 8). Note that because the BS can only send messages to feasible receivers (Line 11), the BS never sends a message to a terminal that is not in the system. For simplicity, we thus do not explicitly remove terminals from L even after they leave the system in the pseudocode. In practice, the BS can remove a terminal i from L if 1) the BS receives a special control message from i indicating that i is going to leave the system, or 2) the BS has not received any message related to i for a sufficiently long period of time.

Let $D_{r,\mathcal{RR}}$ be the set of terminals to which the BS sends a message during round r under $\mathcal{RR}$. Specifically, $D_{r,\mathcal{RR}} = \bigcup_{t \in R_r} \mathcal{RR}(t)$. Our design of RR has the following properties that facilitate our analysis:

Algorithm 1: Description of RR

---

1 $r \leftarrow 0, p \leftarrow 0$
2 $L \leftarrow \{vt\}$
3 **for** $t \leftarrow 1$ **to** ∞ **do**
4 $\quad$ **if** $p = 0$ **then**
5 $\quad\quad$ $r \leftarrow r + 1$
6 $\quad\quad$ $rnd\_start \leftarrow t$
7 $\quad\quad$ **forall the** i such that $t_i^{arr} < t$ and $i \notin L$ **do**
8 $\quad\quad\quad$ Append i to the end of L
9 $\quad$ $\mathcal{RR}(t) \leftarrow \varnothing$
10 $\quad$ **while** $|\mathcal{RR}(t)| < C$ **do**
11 $\quad\quad$ **if** $L[p]$ is a feasible receiver at time t **then**
12 $\quad\quad\quad$ Add $L[p]$ to $\mathcal{RR}(t)$
13 $\quad\quad$ **if** $L[p]$ is the last terminal in L **then**
14 $\quad\quad\quad$ $R_r \leftarrow [rnd\_start, t]$
15 $\quad\quad\quad$ $p \leftarrow 0$
16 $\quad\quad\quad$ **break**
17 $\quad\quad$ **else**
18 $\quad\quad\quad$ $p \leftarrow p + 1$
19 $\quad$ Send messages to terminals in $\mathcal{RR}(t)$ at time t

---

1. For any terminal $i \in D_{r,\mathcal{RR}}$, i is already in the system before round r starts.
2. Every terminal receives at most one message in each round.
3. Time can be partitioned into rounds. Specifically, $\mathbb{N} = \bigcup_{r \in \mathbb{N}} R_r$, and $R_{r_1} \cap R_{r_2} = \varnothing$ if $r_1 \neq r_2$.

For any non-empty time interval $T = [a, b]$, define $start(T) = a$ and $end(T) = b$. Observe that when $|R_r| = 1$, $D_{r,\mathcal{RR}}$ may be empty. This happens if there is no feasible receiver at the beginning of round r. However, when $|R_r| > 1$, we have $|\mathcal{RR}(t)| = C$ for any $t \in [start(R_r), end(R_r) - 1]$. Thus, we have the following result.

Fact 1. *For any* $r \in \mathbb{N}$, $C(|R_r| - 1) \leq |D_{r,\mathcal{RR}}| \leq C|R_r|$. *Thus, if* $|R_r| > 1$, $|D_{r,\mathcal{RR}}| = \Theta(C|R_r|)$.

3.2   Definition of Fair Scheduling Algorithms

The definition of fair scheduling algorithms is based on the rounds yielded by RR. Let δ be any non-negative integer. An algorithm $\mathcal{A}$ is δ-Fair if it satisfies the following constraint for any problem instance: For any round r, if a message m for terminal i arrives at the BS in round r (i.e., $t^{arr}(m) \in R_r$), then the BS, under the schedule produced by $\mathcal{A}$, sends a message to terminal i in round $r + k$ for some $0 \leq k \leq \delta$. In other words, after the BS receives a message m for terminal i, the BS must send some message m' to terminal i within δ rounds.

Note that due to packet management, m and m' may be different messages. We stress that under a δ-Fair scheduling algorithm, the BS can send multiple messages to the same terminal in a single round.

4 Analysis of Fair Scheduling Algorithms

In this section, we prove the following main theorem of this paper.

Theorem 2. *Every δ-Fair scheduling algorithm is $O(\delta^4)$-competitive for the MinAoI problem.*

Because RR is 1-Fair, we have the following corollary.

Corollary 3. *RR is $O(1)$-competitive for the MinAoI problem.*

4.1 Objective Function Transformation: From AoI to Pseudo AoI

Let m be the last message received by terminal i under schedule $\mathcal{S}$ by time t. We then have $AoI(i, \mathcal{S}, t) = t - t^{gen}(m)$. To prove Theorem 2, we often consider $t - t^{arr}(m)$ instead of $t - t^{gen}(m)$. Specifically, define

$$A(i, \mathcal{S}, t) = t - t^{arr}(\text{the last message received by } i \text{ by time } t \text{ under } \mathcal{S}).$$

We call $A(i, \mathcal{S}, t)$ the **pseudo AoI** of terminal i at time t under $\mathcal{S}$. Observe that for any active terminal that has received some message from the BS, the difference between its AoI and pseudo AoI is Δ_i.

For any $X \subseteq D$, any time interval T, and any schedule $\mathcal{S}$, define

$$A(X, \mathcal{S}, T) = \sum_{i \in X} \sum_{t \in T} A(i, \mathcal{S}, t)$$

and

$$AoI(X, \mathcal{S}, T) = \sum_{i \in X} \sum_{t \in T} AoI(i, \mathcal{S}, t).$$

We may consider the sum of (pseudo) AoI over the entire time horizon (i.e., $T = [0, \infty]$); if so, we simply write $A(X, \mathcal{S})$ and $AoI(X, \mathcal{S})$ instead of $A(X, \mathcal{S}, [0, \infty])$ and $AoI(X, \mathcal{S}, [0, \infty])$. Like the definition of $AoI(\mathcal{S})$, we define $A(\mathcal{S}) = A(D, \mathcal{S})$. Finally, we abuse the notation slightly and define $A(i, \mathcal{S}, T)$ as $A(\{i\}, \mathcal{S}, T)$ and $AoI(i, \mathcal{S}, T)$ as $AoI(\{i\}, \mathcal{S}, T)$.

Let $\mathcal{OPT}$ be the optimal schedule. Because $t^{arr}(m) - t^{gen}(m) = \Delta_i$ is fixed, it should not be too surprising to see that to prove Theorem 2, it suffices to minimize the pseudo AoI. Due to space limit, we omit the proof of the following theorem.

Theorem 4. *For any $r \geq 1$ and any schedule $\mathcal{S}$, if $A(\mathcal{S}) \leq r \cdot A(\mathcal{OPT})$, then $AoI(\mathcal{S}) \leq 2r \cdot AoI(\mathcal{OPT})$*

Let $\mathcal{S}_\delta$ be the schedule obtained by any δ-Fair scheduling algorithm. By Theorem 4, to prove Theorem 2, it suffices to prove

$$A(\mathcal{S}_\delta) = O(\delta^4) A(\mathcal{OPT}). \tag{$*$}$$

4.2   Lower Bounds of $A(\mathcal{OPT})$

To prove Eq. (∗), we introduce a few lower bounds of $A(\mathcal{OPT})$. Our first lower bound focuses on the total pseudo AoI of $D_{r,\mathcal{RR}}$ during round r under $\mathcal{OPT}$. Note that because the pseudo AoI of any terminal is zero initially and the transmission latency from the BS to every terminal is one, we have the following fact.

Fact 5. *For any schedule $\mathcal{S}$, any terminal i and any time t such that $t_i^{arr} + 1 \leq t \leq t_i^{dep}$, we have $A(i, \mathcal{S}, t) \geq 1$.*

Claim 6. *Let T be any time interval with $|T| \geq 4$ and X be any set of terminals that arrive in the system before T starts and leave the system after T ends. If $|X| \geq C\lfloor \frac{|T|}{2} \rfloor$, then*

$$A(X, \mathcal{OPT}, T) = \Omega(|X||T|^2).$$

Proof. Let T' be the time interval that starts at the beginning of T and has a size of $\min\left(\lfloor \frac{|X|}{2C} \rfloor, |T|\right)$. Because $|X| \geq C\lfloor \frac{|T|}{2} \rfloor$ and $|T| \geq 4$, we have $\lfloor \frac{|X|}{2C} \rfloor = \Omega(|T|)$ and thus $|T'| = \Omega(|T|)$. For any schedule, the number of terminals in X that cannot receive any message during T' is at least $|X| - C|T'| \geq |X| - C\lfloor \frac{|X|}{2C} \rfloor \geq \frac{|X|}{2}$. For each of these terminals, the cumulative pseudo AoI during T' is at least $1 + 2 + 3 + \cdots + |T'| = \Omega(|T'|^2) = \Omega(|T|^2)$. Thus, $A(X, \mathcal{OPT}, T) = \Omega\left(|X||T|^2\right)$. □

The next lower bound is an application of Fact 5 and Claim 6.

Lemma 7. *For any round k,*

$$A(D_{k,\mathcal{RR}}, \mathcal{OPT}, R_k) = \Omega\left(|D_{k,\mathcal{RR}}||R_k|^2\right).$$

Proof. We divide the proof into two cases.

  Case 1: $|R_k| < 8$. By the design of RR, all the terminals in $D_{k,\mathcal{RR}}$ arrive in the system before round k starts. Thus, by Fact 5, $A(D_{k,\mathcal{RR}}, \mathcal{OPT}, R_k) = \Omega(|D_{k,\mathcal{RR}}|) = \Omega\left(|D_{k,\mathcal{RR}}||R_k|^2\right)$.

  Case 2: $|R_k| \geq 8$. Let T_1 be the first half of R_k with $|T_1| = \lceil \frac{|R_k|}{2} \rceil \geq 4$. Let $T_2 = R_k \backslash T_1$ be the second half of R_k. Let X be the set of terminals to which the BS sends a message during T_2 under $\mathcal{RR}$. Specifically, $X = \bigcup_{t \in T_2} \mathcal{RR}(t)$. Observe that because $|R_k| \geq 8$, we have $|T_2| \geq 4$ and thus $[start(T_2), end(T_2) - 1]$ is non-empty. By the design of RR, for any $t \in [start(T_2), end(T_2) - 1]$, $|\mathcal{RR}(t)| = C$. This implies that $|X| = \Theta(|D_{k,\mathcal{RR}}|)$.

  Next, we claim that

$$|X| \geq C\lfloor \frac{|T_1|}{2} \rfloor. \tag{1}$$

Note that $|R_k| = \lceil \frac{|R_k|}{2} \rceil + \lfloor \frac{|R_k|}{2} \rfloor$. Thus, $|T_2| = \lfloor \frac{|R_k|}{2} \rfloor$. By the design of RR, we then have $|X| \geq C(|T_2| - 1) = C(\lfloor \frac{|R_k|}{2} \rfloor - 1) \geq C\lfloor \frac{|T_1|}{2} \rfloor$, where the last inequality follows from $|T_1| = \lceil \frac{|R_k|}{2} \rceil$ and $|R_k| \geq 8$.

By the design of RR, every terminal in X arrives in the system before round k starts. Moreover, since the BS sends a message to every terminal in X during T_2, terminals in X cannot leave the system during T_1. By Eq. (1) and Claim 6, $A(X, \mathcal{OPT}, T_1) = \Omega(|X||T_1|^2)$. Because $|X| = \Theta(|D_{k,\mathcal{RR}}|)$ and $|T_1| = \Theta(|R_k|)$, we then have $A(D_{k,\mathcal{RR}}, \mathcal{OPT}, R_k) \geq A(X, \mathcal{OPT}, T_1) = \Omega(|X||T_1|^2) = \Omega(|D_{k,\mathcal{RR}}||R_k|^2)$. □

The next lower bound is due to packet management.

Lemma 8. *Let $\mathcal{S}$ be any schedule. If terminal i receives a message m at time t under $\mathcal{S}$, then*

$$A(i, \mathcal{OPT}, [t^{arr}(m), t]) = \Omega(A(i, \mathcal{S}, t)^2).$$

Proof. Let $T = [t^{arr}(m), t]$. Due to packet management, terminal i cannot receive any message newer than m by time t under any schedule. Thus, for any time τ in T, the pseudo AoI of terminal i at time τ under $\mathcal{OPT}$ is at least $\tau - t^{arr}(m)$. As a result,

$$A(i, \mathcal{OPT}, T) \geq \sum_{\tau \in T}(\tau - t^{arr}(m)) = 0 + 1 + 2 + 3 + \cdots + (t - t^{arr}(m))$$

$$= \Omega((t - t^{arr}(m))^2) = \Omega(A(i, \mathcal{S}, t)^2).$$

□

4.3 Partition of $[t_i^{arr} + 1, t_i^{dep}]$

For any terminal i, we partition the time interval $[t_i^{arr}+1, t_i^{dep}]$ based on terminal i's message receiving times under $\mathcal{S}_\delta$. To simplify the proof of Eq. (∗), we adopt the following assumption.

Assumption 9. *The BS sends at most one message to every terminal in every round under $\mathcal{S}_\delta$.*

This assumption can be satisfied at the cost of increasing the pseudo AoI. Specifically, if the BS sends multiple messages to terminal i in round r, we can retain only the first message transmission to i and eliminate any subsequent transmissions to i in round r. We will prove that Eq. (∗) holds even under Assumption 9.

Let $t_i^{rec}(m, \mathcal{S}_\delta)$ be the time at which message m is received by i under $\mathcal{S}_\delta$. For any round r, if the BS sends a message m_r to terminal i in round r under $\mathcal{S}_\delta$, define $T_{i,r}$ as the time interval that ends at time $t_i^{rec}(m_r, \mathcal{S}_\delta)$ and starts after i receives the message prior to m_r. Specifically, assume that m_r is the jth message received by i under $\mathcal{S}_\delta$. Let m_{prev} be the $(j-1)$th message received by i under $\mathcal{S}_\delta$ (if $j = 1$, then m_{prev} is the virtual message received at time t_i^{arr}). Define

$$T_{i,r} = [t_i^{rec}(m_{prev}, \mathcal{S}_\delta) + 1, t_i^{rec}(m_r, \mathcal{S}_\delta)],$$

and
$$T_{i,r}^+ = [t^{arr}(m_{prev}), t_i^{rec}(m_r, \mathcal{S}_\delta)].$$

Note that by Assumption 9, m_r is unique and m_{prev} is sent before round r. If the BS does not send any message to i in round r under $\mathcal{S}_\delta$, $T_{i,r} = T_{i,r}^+ = \varnothing$.

Let m_{last} be the last message received by i under $\mathcal{S}_\delta$. If i does not receive any message under $\mathcal{S}_\delta$, then m_{last} is the virtual message received at time t_i^{arr}. Define
$$T_{i,last} = [t_i^{rec}(m_{last}, \mathcal{S}_\delta) + 1, t_i^{dep}],$$

and
$$T_{i,last}^+ = [t^{arr}(m_{last}), t_i^{dep}].$$

Assume that i receives messages in rounds $r_1, r_2, \cdots, r_k$ under $\mathcal{S}_\delta$ ($r_1 < r_2 < \cdots < r_k$). Thus, $T_{i,r_1}, T_{i,r_2}, \cdots, T_{i,r_k}$ and $T_{i,last}$ partition $[t_i^{arr}+1, t^{dep}]$. Although $T_{i,r_1}^+, T_{i,r_2}^+, \cdots, T_{i,r_k}^+$ and $T_{i,last}^+$ are not mutually disjoint, the next lemma shows that it is safe to sum up these time intervals' pseudo AoI.

Lemma 10. *Let i be any terminal and let $\mathcal{T}_i = \{T_{i,r}^+ | r \in \mathbb{N}, T_{i,r}^+ \neq \varnothing\}$. For any time interval $T \in \mathcal{T}_i$, T intersects at most 4 other intervals in $\mathcal{T}_i$. Therefore, any time t appears in at most 5 time intervals in $\mathcal{T}_i$ and thus*

$$\sum_{i \in D} \left(\left(\sum_{r \in \mathbb{N}} A(i, \mathcal{OPT}, T_{i,r}^+) \right) + A(i, \mathcal{OPT}, T_{i,last}^+) \right) = O(1)A(\mathcal{OPT}).$$

Proof. Let $i \in D$ and assume that i receives messages in rounds $r_1, r_2, \cdots, r_k$ under $\mathcal{S}_\delta$ ($r_1 < r_2 < \cdots < r_k$). It suffices to show that for any T_{i,r_j}^+, among $T_{i,r_1}^+, T_{i,r_2}^+, \cdots, T_{i,r_j-1}^+$, it can only intersect $T_{i,r_{j-2}}^+$ and $T_{i,r_{j-1}}^+$. For the sake of contradiction, assume that T_{i,r_j}^+ intersects $T_{i,r_{j-3}}^+$. Let m_{-3}, m_{-2}, m_{-1}, and m be the messages received by i in rounds r_{j-3}, r_{j-2}, r_{j-1} and r_j under $\mathcal{S}_\delta$, respectively. Because T_{i,r_j}^+ intersects $T_{i,r_{j-3}}^+$, we have $t^{arr}(m_{-1}) = start(T_{i,r_j}^+) \leq end(T_{i,r_{j-3}}^+) = t_i^{rec}(m_{-3}, \mathcal{S}_\delta)$. This implies $t^{arr}(m_{-2}) < t^{arr}(m_{-1}) \leq t_i^{rec}(m_{-3}, \mathcal{S}_\delta)$, which is impossible due to packet management. Specifically, due to packet management, the BS should send m_{-2} instead of m_{-3} to i in round r_{j-3} under $\mathcal{S}_\delta$. $\qquad\square$

Define
$$D_{r,\delta} = \{i | \text{the BS sends a message to terminal } i \text{ in round } r \text{ under } \mathcal{S}_\delta\},$$

and
$$D_r^{dep} = \{i | \text{terminal } i \text{ leaves the system in round } r\}.$$

Observe that $T_{i,r}$ is non-empty if and only if $i \in D_{r,\delta}$. The proof of the following lemma, which is based on the bounds established in Sect. 4.2, is postponed to the end of this paper.

Lemma 11. *For any round r,*

$$\sum_{i \in D_{r,\delta}} A(i, \mathcal{S}_\delta, T_{i,r}) + \sum_{i \in D_r^{dep}} A(i, \mathcal{S}_\delta, T_{i,last})$$

$$= O\left(\sum_{i \in D} A(i, \mathcal{OPT}, T_{i,r}^+) + \sum_{i \in D_r^{dep}} A(i, \mathcal{OPT}, T_{i,last}^+)\right)$$

$$+ O\left(\delta^2 |D_{r,\delta}| + \delta^2 |D_r^{dep}| + \delta^3 \max_{r-\delta \leq k \leq r} A(D, \mathcal{OPT}, R_k)\right).$$

4.4 Proof of Eq (∗)

$$A(\mathcal{S}_\delta) = \sum_{r \in \mathbb{N}} \left(\sum_{i \in D_{r,\delta}} A(i, \mathcal{S}_\delta, T_{i,r}) + \sum_{i \in D_r^{dep}} A(i, \mathcal{S}_\delta, T_{i,last})\right)$$

$$\overset{\text{by Lemma 11}}{=} O\left(\sum_{r \in \mathbb{N}} \left(\sum_{i \in D} A(i, \mathcal{OPT}, T_{i,r}^+) + \sum_{i \in D_r^{dep}} A(i, \mathcal{OPT}, T_{i,last}^+)\right)\right)$$

$$+ O\left(\sum_{r \in \mathbb{N}} \left(\delta^2 |D_{r,\delta}| + \delta^2 |D_r^{dep}| + \delta^3 \max_{r-\delta \leq k \leq r} A(D, \mathcal{OPT}, R_k)\right)\right)$$

$$\overset{\text{by Fact 5}}{=} O\left(\delta^2 \sum_{r \in \mathbb{N}} \left(\sum_{i \in D} A(i, \mathcal{OPT}, T_{i,r}^+) + \sum_{i \in D_r^{dep}} A(i, \mathcal{OPT}, T_{i,last}^+)\right)\right)$$

$$+ O\left(\sum_{r \in \mathbb{N}} \left(\delta^3 \max_{r-\delta \leq k \leq r} A(D, \mathcal{OPT}, R_k)\right)\right)$$

$$\overset{\text{by Lemma 10}}{=} O(\delta^2) A(\mathcal{OPT}) + O\left(\delta^3 \sum_{r \in \mathbb{N}} \max_{r-\delta \leq k \leq r} A(D, \mathcal{OPT}, R_k)\right)$$

$$= O(\delta^4) A(\mathcal{OPT}),$$

where the last equality holds because R_ks partition the time horizon and each round is considered $O(\delta)$ times in the summation.

4.5 Proof of Lemma 11

For any non-empty $T_{i,r}$, define $t_{i,r}^*$ as the smallest time t in $T_{i,r}$ such that $A(i, \mathcal{S}_\delta, t) > A(i, \mathcal{OPT}, t)$; if such a time t does not exist, then $t_{i,r}^*$ is defined as $end(T_{i,r}) + 1$. We then partition $T_{i,r}$ into two time intervals,

$$T_{i,r}^A = [start(T_{i,r}), t_{i,r}^* - 1]$$

and
$$T_{i,r}^B = [t_{i,r}^*, end(T_{i,r})].$$

Note that if $t_{i,r}^* = start(T_{i,r})$, then $T_{i,r}^A = \varnothing$ and $T_{i,r}^B = T_{i,r}$; if $t_{i,r}^* = end(T_{i,r})+1$, then $T_{i,r}^A = T_{i,r}$ and $T_{i,r}^B = \varnothing$. Clearly, for any non-empty $T_{i,r}$, we have

$$A(i, \mathcal{S}_\delta, T_{i,r}^A) \le A(i, \mathcal{OPT}, T_{i,r}^A). \tag{2}$$

For any terminal i, define $t_{i,last}^*$ as the smallest time t in $T_{i,last}$ such that $A(i, \mathcal{S}_\delta, t) > A(i, \mathcal{OPT}, t)$; if such a time t does not exist, then $t_{i,last}^*$ is defined as $end(T_{i,last}) + 1$. We then partition $T_{i,last}$ into two time intervals,

$$T_{i,last}^A = [start(T_{i,last}), t_{i,last}^* - 1]$$

and
$$T_{i,last}^B = [t_{i,last}^*, end(T_{i,last})].$$

Clearly, for any terminal i, we have

$$A(i, \mathcal{S}_\delta, T_{i,last}^A) \le A(i, \mathcal{OPT}, T_{i,last}^A). \tag{3}$$

For any non-empty $T_{i,r}$, recall that i receives a message at time $start(T_{i,r})-1$ under $\mathcal{S}_\delta$. We further define $a_{i,r}$ as the pseudo AoI of i at time $start(T_{i,r}) - 1$ under $\mathcal{S}_\delta$. For any non-empty $T_{i,r}$, we then have

$$A(i, \mathcal{S}_\delta, T_{i,r}) = (a_{i,r} + 1) + (a_{i,r} + 2) + \cdots + (a_{i,r} + |T_{i,r}^A| + |T_{i,r}^B|)$$
$$= O\left(a_{i,r}^2 + |T_{i,r}^A|^2 + |T_{i,r}^B|^2\right). \tag{4}$$

For any terminal i, define $a_{i,last}$ as the pseudo AoI of i at time $start(T_{i,last}) - 1$ under $\mathcal{S}_\delta$. For any terminal i, we then have

$$A(i, \mathcal{S}_\delta, T_{i,last}) = (a_{i,last} + 1) + (a_{i,last} + 2) + \cdots + (a_{i,last} + |T_{i,last}^A| + |T_{i,last}^B|)$$
$$= O\left(a_{i,last}^2 + |T_{i,last}^A|^2 + |T_{i,last}^B|^2\right). \tag{5}$$

Thus, to prove Lemma 11, it suffices to prove the following three claims.

Claim 12. *For every round r and every terminal $i \in D_{r,\delta}$, we have*

$$a_{i,r}^2 = O(A(i, \mathcal{OPT}, T_{i,r}^+)).$$

For every terminal i, we have

$$a_{i,last}^2 = O(A(i, \mathcal{OPT}, T_{i,last}^+)).$$

Claim 13. *For every round r and every terminal $i \in D_{r,\delta}$, we have*

$$|T_{i,r}^A|^2 = O(A(i, \mathcal{OPT}, T_{i,r}^A)).$$

For every terminal i, we have

$$|T_{i,last}^A|^2 = O(A(i, \mathcal{OPT}, T_{i,last}^A)).$$

Claim 14. *For every round* r, *we have*

$$\sum_{i \in D_{r,\delta}} |T_{i,r}^B|^2 = O\left(\delta^2 |D_{r,\delta}| + \delta^2 \max_{r-\delta \leq k \leq r} A(D, \mathcal{OPT}, R_k)\right),$$

and

$$\sum_{i \in D_r^{dep}} |T_{i,last}^B|^2 = O\left(\delta^2 |D_r^{dep}| + \delta^3 \max_{r-\delta \leq k \leq r} A(D, \mathcal{OPT}, R_k)\right).$$

Proof of Claim 12. Let m be the message received by i at time $start(T_{i,r}) - 1$ under $\mathcal{S}_\delta$. If m is the virtual message received at time t_i^{arr}, then $a_{i,r} = 0$ and Claim 12 clearly holds. Otherwise, let $t = start(T_{i,r}) - 1$. By Lemma 8, we have $A(i, \mathcal{OPT}, [t^{arr}(m), t]) = \Omega(a_{i,r}{}^2)$, which combined with $[t^{arr}(m), t] \subseteq T_{i,r}^+$ implies the first part of Claim 12.

Next, we prove the second part of Claim 12. Let m be the message received by i at time $start(T_{i,last}) - 1$ under $\mathcal{S}_\delta$. If m is the virtual message received at time t_i^{arr}, then $a_{i,last} = 0$ and Claim 12 clearly holds. Otherwise, let $t = start(T_{i,last}) - 1$. By Lemma 8, we have $A(i, \mathcal{OPT}, [t^{arr}(m), t]) = \Omega(a_{i,last}{}^2)$, which combined with $[t^{arr}(m), t] \subseteq T_{i,last}^+$ implies the second part of Claim 12. $\square$

Proof of Claim 13. By Eq. (2), for every terminal $i \in D_{r,\delta}$, we have

$$A(i, \mathcal{OPT}, T_{i,r}^A) \geq A(i, \mathcal{S}_\delta, T_{i,r}^A) = \Omega(|T_{i,r}^A|^2),$$

where the last equality follows from the fact that i never receives a message during $T_{i,r}^A$ under $\mathcal{S}_\delta$. This completes the proof of the first part of Claim 13.

By Eq. (3), for every terminal i, we have

$$A(i, \mathcal{OPT}, T_{i,last}^A) \geq A(i, \mathcal{S}_\delta, T_{i,last}^A) = \Omega(|T_{i,last}^A|^2).$$

This completes the proof of the second part of Claim 13. $\square$

Proof Claim 14. Let $D_{r,\delta,B}$ be the set of terminals i in $D_{r,\delta}$ such that $T_{i,r}^B \neq \varnothing$ (i.e., $t_{i,r}^* \in T_{i,r}$). Let $i \in D_{r,\delta,B}$. We first show that $t_{i,r}^*$ must be in round k for some $k \geq r - \delta$. For the sake of contradiction, assume that $k \leq r - \delta - 1$. Let m_{prev} be the message received by i at time $start(T_{i,r}) - 1$ under $\mathcal{S}_\delta$. Due to packet management, when i receives m_{prev} under $\mathcal{S}_\delta$, i's pseudo AoI under $\mathcal{S}_\delta$ cannot be greater than its pseudo AoI under $\mathcal{OPT}$. Thus, by the definition of $t_{i,r}^*$, it must be the case that, under $\mathcal{OPT}$, i receives some message m^* newer than m_{prev} at time $t_{i,r}^*$, but i does not receive m^* by time $t_{i,r}^*$ under $\mathcal{S}_\delta$. Thus, by the design of $\mathcal{S}_\delta$, the BS must then send some message newer than m_{prev} by round $k + \delta$. Because $k \leq r - \delta - 1$, we have $k + \delta \leq r - 1$, which implies that, under $\mathcal{S}_\delta$, i receives a message during $[t_{i,r}^* + 1, end(R_{r-1}) + 1] \subseteq [start(T_{i,r}), start(R_r)] \subseteq [start(T_{i,r}), end(T_{i,r}) - 1]$. However, by the definition of $T_{i,r}$, it is impossible for i to receive any message during $[start(T_{i,r}), end(T_{i,r}) - 1]$ under $\mathcal{S}_\delta$. Thus, $t_{i,r}^*$ is in round k for some $k \geq r - \delta$.

We then have

$$|T_{i,r}^B| \leq \left(\sum_{k=r-\delta}^{r} |R_k| \right) + 1 \leq \left((\delta+1) \max_{r-\delta \leq k \leq r} |R_k| \right) + 1 \tag{6}$$

Note that the plus one in the above inequality is due to the fact that $end(T_{i,r}^B)$ may equal $start(R_{r+1})$, which happens when the BS sends a message to terminal i at the end of round r. Next, we divide the proof of the first part into two cases.

Case 1: For all k in $[r-\delta, r]$, $|R_k| = 1$. In this case, we have

$$\sum_{i \in D_{r,\delta}} |T_{i,r}^B|^2 = \sum_{i \in D_{r,\delta,B}} |T_{i,r}^B|^2 \stackrel{\text{by Eq. (6)}}{\leq} \sum_{i \in D_{r,\delta,B}} \left(\left((\delta+1) \max_{r-\delta \leq k \leq r} |R_k| \right) + 1 \right)^2$$

$$= |D_{r,\delta,B}| (\delta+2)^2 = O\left(\delta^2 |D_{r,\delta}| \right).$$

Case 2: There is an integer k^* in $[r-\delta, r]$ such that $|R_{k^*}| > 1$. We first claim that $|D_{r,\delta,B}| = O(\max_{r-\delta \leq k \leq r} |D_{k,\mathcal{RR}}|)$. This is because

$$|D_{r,\delta,B}| \leq C|R_r| \leq C \max_{r-\delta \leq k \leq r} |R_k| = O\left(\max_{r-\delta \leq k \leq r} |D_{k,\mathcal{RR}}| \right), \tag{7}$$

where the last equality is due to the assumption of this case and Fact 1. Thus,

$$\sum_{i \in D_{r,\delta}} |T_{i,r}^B|^2 = \sum_{i \in D_{r,\delta,B}} |T_{i,r}^B|^2 \stackrel{\text{by Eq. (6)}}{\leq} \sum_{i \in D_{r,\delta,B}} \left(\left((\delta+1) \max_{r-\delta \leq k \leq r} |R_k| \right) + 1 \right)^2$$

$$\stackrel{\text{by Eq. (7)}}{=} O\left(\max_{r-\delta \leq k \leq r} |D_{k,\mathcal{RR}}| \right) \left(\left((\delta+1) \max_{r-\delta \leq k \leq r} |R_k| \right) + 1 \right)^2$$

$$= O\left(\delta^2 \left(\max_{r-\delta \leq k \leq r} |D_{k,\mathcal{RR}}| \right) \left(\max_{r-\delta \leq k \leq r} |R_k| \right)^2 \right).$$

Observe that for any round r and $\delta \geq 1$, if $k^* = \text{argmax}_{r-\delta \leq k \leq r}|D_{k,\mathcal{RR}}|$, then $k^* = \text{argmax}_{r-\delta \leq k \leq r}|R_k|$. Thus,

$$\sum_{i \in D_{r,\delta}} |T_{i,r}^B|^2 = O\left(\delta^2 \max_{r-\delta \leq k \leq r} |D_{k,\mathcal{RR}}||R_k|^2 \right) \stackrel{\text{by Lemma 7}}{=} O\left(\delta^2 \max_{r-\delta \leq k \leq r} A(D_{k,\mathcal{RR}}, \mathcal{OPT}, R_k) \right)$$

$$= O\left(\delta^2 \max_{r-\delta \leq k \leq r} A(D, \mathcal{OPT}, R_k) \right),$$

which completes the proof of the first part of Claim 14.

Next, we prove the second part of Claim 14. Let $D_{r,B}^{dep}$ be the set of terminals i in D_r^{dep} such that $T_{i,last}^B \neq \varnothing$. Let $i \in D_{r,B}^{dep}$. By a similar argument used in the first part of the proof, $t_{i,last}^*$ must in round k for some $k \geq r - \delta$. Thus,

$$|T_{i,last}^B| \leq \left(\sum_{k=r-\delta}^{r} |R_k| \right) \leq \left((\delta+1) \max_{r-\delta \leq k \leq r} |R_k| \right). \tag{8}$$

Moreover, because under $\mathcal{OPT}$, every terminal $i \in D_{r,B}^{dep}$ receives a message in R_k for some k in $[r - \delta, r]$, we have

$$|D_{r,B}^{dep}| \leq C \left(\sum_{k=r-\delta}^{r} |R_k| \right). \tag{9}$$

Next, we divide the proof of the second part into two cases.

Case 1: For all k in $[r - \delta, r]$, $|R_k| = 1$. In this case, we have

$$\sum_{i \in D_r^{dep}} |T_{i,last}^B|^2 = \sum_{i \in D_{r,B}^{dep}} |T_{i,last}^B|^2 \overset{\text{by Eq. (8)}}{\leq} \sum_{i \in D_{r,B}^{dep}} \left((\delta + 1) \max_{r-\delta \leq k \leq r} |R_k| \right)^2 = O\left(\delta^2 |D_r^{dep}| \right).$$

Case 2: There is an integer k^* in $[r - \delta, r]$ such that $|R_{k^*}| > 1$. We first claim that $|D_{r,B}^{dep}| = O(\delta \max_{r-\delta \leq k \leq r} |D_{k,\mathcal{RR}}|)$. This is because

$$|D_{r,B}^{dep}| \overset{\text{by Eq. (9)}}{\leq} C \left(\sum_{k=r-\delta}^{r} |R_k| \right) \leq C(\delta + 1) \max_{r-\delta \leq k \leq r} |R_k| = O\left(\delta \max_{r-\delta \leq k \leq r} |D_{k,\mathcal{RR}}| \right), \tag{10}$$

where the equality is due to the assumption of this case and Fact 1. Thus,

$$\sum_{i \in D_r^{dep}} |T_{i,last}^B|^2 = \sum_{i \in D_{r,B}^{dep}} |T_{i,last}^B|^2 \overset{\text{by Eq. (8)}}{\leq} \sum_{i \in D_{r,B}^{dep}} \left((\delta + 1) \max_{r-\delta \leq k \leq r} |R_k| \right)^2$$

$$= |D_{r,B}^{dep}| \left((\delta + 1) \max_{r-\delta \leq k \leq r} |R_k| \right)^2 \overset{\text{by Eq. (10)}}{=} O\left(\delta \max_{r-\delta \leq k \leq r} |D_{k,\mathcal{RR}}| \right) \left((\delta + 1) \max_{r-\delta \leq k \leq r} |R_k| \right)^2$$

$$= O\left(\delta^3 \max_{r-\delta \leq k \leq r} |D_{k,\mathcal{RR}}||R_k|^2 \right) \overset{\text{by Lemma 7}}{=} O\left(\delta^3 \max_{r-\delta \leq k \leq r} A(D_{k,\mathcal{RR}}, \mathcal{OPT}, R_k) \right)$$

$$= O\left(\delta^3 \max_{r-\delta \leq k \leq r} A(D, \mathcal{OPT}, R_k) \right),$$

which completes the proof of the second part of Claim 14. □

Acknowledgements. This work was supported in part by the Ministry of Science and Technology of Taiwan under Contract MOST 111-2221-E-004-003-MY2. This work was also financially supported by the "Research Center for Chinese Cultural Metaverse in Taiwan" of National Chengchi University (NCCU) from The Featured Areas Research Center Program within the framework of the Higher Education Sprout Project by the Ministry of Education (MOE) in Taiwan.

References

1. Bedewy, A.M., Sun, Y., Kompella, S., Shroff, N.B.: Age-optimal sampling and transmission scheduling in multi-source systems. In: Proceedings of the Twentieth ACM International Symposium on Mobile Ad Hoc Networking and Computing, pp. 121–130 (2019)
2. Bedewy, A.M., Sun, Y., Kompella, S., Shroff, N.B.: Optimal sampling and scheduling for timely status updates in multi-source networks. IEEE Trans. Inf. Theory **67**(6), 4019–4034 (2021)

3. Farazi, S., Klein, A.G., Brown, D.R.: Average age of information in multi-source self-preemptive status update systems with packet delivery errors. In: 2019 53rd Asilomar Conference on Signals, Systems, and Computers, pp. 396–400. IEEE (2019)
4. Han, B., Zhu, Y., Jiang, Z., Sun, M., Schotten, H.D.: Fairness for freshness: optimal age of information based OFDMA scheduling with minimal knowledge. IEEE Trans. Wireless Commun. **20**(12), 7903–7919 (2021)
5. He, Q., Yuan, D., Ephremides, A.: Optimal link scheduling for age minimization in wireless systems. IEEE Trans. Inf. Theory **64**(7), 5381–5394 (2017)
6. Hsu, Y.P., Modiano, E., Duan, L.: Age of information: design and analysis of optimal scheduling algorithms. In: 2017 IEEE International Symposium on Information Theory (ISIT), pp. 561–565. IEEE (2017)
7. Jiang, Z., Krishnamachari, B., Zheng, X., Zhou, S., Niu, Z.: Timely status update in wireless uplinks: analytical solutions with asymptotic optimality. IEEE Internet Things J. **6**(2), 3885–3898 (2019)
8. Kadota, I., Sinha, A., Uysal-Biyikoglu, E., Singh, R., Modiano, E.: Scheduling policies for minimizing age of information in broadcast wireless networks. IEEE/ACM Trans. Netw. **26**(6), 2637–2650 (2018)
9. Kadota, I., Uysal-Biyikoglu, E., Singh, R., Modiano, E.: Minimizing the age of information in broadcast wireless networks. In: 2016 54th Annual Allerton Conference on Communication, Control, and Computing (Allerton), pp. 844–851. IEEE (2016)
10. Kaul, S., Yates, R., Gruteser, M.: Real-time status: how often should one update? In: 2012 Proceedings IEEE INFOCOM, pp. 2731–2735. IEEE (2012)
11. Kuo, T.W.: Minimum age of information TDMA scheduling: Approximation algorithms and hardness results. IEEE Trans. Inf. Theory **66**(12), 7652–7671 (2020)
12. Kuo, T.W.: Competitive analyses of online minimum age of information transmission scheduling. In: IEEE INFOCOM 2022-IEEE Conference on Computer Communications Workshops (INFOCOM WKSHPS), pp. 1–8. IEEE (2022)
13. Moltafet, M., Leinonen, M., Codreanu, M.: On the age of information in multi-source queueing models. IEEE Trans. Commun. **68**(8), 5003–5017 (2020)
14. Najm, E., Telatar, E.: Status updates in a multi-stream M/G/1/1 preemptive queue. In: IEEE Infocom 2018-IEEE Conference On Computer Communications Workshops (Infocom Wkshps), pp. 124–129. IEEE (2018)
15. Pappas, N., Gunnarsson, J., Kratz, L., Kountouris, M., Angelakis, V.: Age of information of multiple sources with queue management. In: 2015 IEEE international conference on communications (ICC), pp. 5935–5940. IEEE (2015)
16. Sun, J., Jiang, Z., Krishnamachari, B., Zhou, S., Niu, Z.: Closed-form whittle's index-enabled random access for timely status update. IEEE Trans. Commun. **68**(3), 1538–1551 (2019)
17. Sun, Y., Cyr, B.: Sampling for data freshness optimization: non-linear age functions. J. Commun. Netw. **21**(3), 204–219 (2019)
18. Yates, R.D., Kaul, S.K.: The age of information: real-time status updating by multiple sources. IEEE Trans. Inf. Theory **65**(3), 1807–1827 (2018)
19. Yates, R.D., Sun, Y., Brown, D.R., Kaul, S.K., Modiano, E., Ulukus, S.: Age of information: an introduction and survey. IEEE J. Sel. Areas Commun. **39**(5), 1183–1210 (2021)

Run for Cover: Dominating Set via Mobile Agents

Prabhat Kumar Chand$^{(\boxtimes)}$ [iD], Anisur Rahaman Molla[iD],
and Sumathi Sivasubramaniam[iD]

Indian Statistical Institute, Kolkata, India
pchand744@gmail.com, molla@isical.ac.in, sumathivel89@gmail.com

Abstract. Research involving computing with mobile agents is a fast-growing field, given the advancement of technology in automated systems, e.g., robots, drones, self-driving cars, etc. Therefore, it is pressing to focus on solving classical network problems using mobile agents. In this paper, we study one such problem– finding small dominating sets of a graph G using mobile agents. Dominating set is interesting in the field of mobile agents as it opens up a way for solving various robotic problems, e.g., guarding, covering, facility location, transport routing, etc. In this paper, we first present two algorithms for computing a *minimal dominating set*: (i) an $O(m)$ time algorithm if the robots start from a single node (i.e., gathered initially), (ii) an $O(\ell\Delta\log(\lambda) + n\ell + m)$ time algorithm, if the robots start from multiple nodes (i.e., positioned arbitrarily), where m is the number of edges and Δ is the maximum degree of G, ℓ is the number of clusters of the robots initially and λ is the maximum ID-length of the robots. Then we present a $\ln(\Delta)$ approximation algorithm for the *minimum* dominating set which takes $O(n\Delta\log(\lambda))$ rounds.

Keywords: Dominating Set · Mobile Agents · Distributed Network Algorithms · Approximation Algorithms · Time Complexity · Memory Complexity · Maximal Independent Set

1 Introduction

Research on autonomous mobile agents (we interchangeably use the terms **agent** and **robot** throughout the paper) has become an area of significant interest in the field of distributed computing. As autonomous agents become part of everyday life (in the form of robots, drones, self-driving cars, etc.,) the area becomes more and more relevant. On the other hand, the dominating set problem is a well-researched classical graph problem. A dominating set D of a graph $G = (V, E)$ is a subset of the nodes V such that for any $v \notin D$, v has a neighbour in D. Finding a dominating set has several practical applications. For example, in wireless communications, the dominating set of the underlying network is useful in finding efficient routes within ad-hoc mobile networks. They are also useful in problems such as *document summarising*, and for designing *secure systems* for *electrical grids*, to mention a few.

© The Author(s), under exclusive license to Springer Nature Switzerland AG 2023
K. Georgiou and E. Kranakis (Eds.): ALGOWIN 2023, LNCS 14061, pp. 133–150, 2023.
https://doi.org/10.1007/978-3-031-48882-5_10

Covering problems, such as vertex covers, maximal independent sets (MIS), and dominating sets, also have real-world applications in the field of mobile agents. For example, a minimum dominating set can form the charge stations or parking places for autonomous mobile robots. The maximal independent sets can be used to solve the same but also ensure that any two robots are not close in real life. Both MIS and dominating sets can find a place in the guarding problem, i.e., placing mobile robots such that robots guard (cover) an entire polygon. In the mobile robot setting, MIS has been explored in [4,8,22]. However, in these works, the robots have some amount of visibility (they have some knowledge of the graph) while ours have zero knowledge. While both MIS and dominating sets are of great interest, in this paper, we limit ourselves to solving the dominating set problem in the field of mobile robots. We note, however, that for the minimal dominating set case, our produced dominating sets are also maximal independent sets.

While the problem is a classic problem in graph theory, several attempts have been made to solve it in distributed computing research as well [5,7,15,16].

In the field of mobile robots, we believe ours is the first attempt to solve the dominating set problem. Our algorithms rely on the ideas used for *dispersion* to achieve a solution for the dominating set problem. Dispersion, first introduced by the authors in [1] has been well studied for various configurations of robots (see [11–13,20]). The problem is briefly: on an n node graph G, in which there is a configuration of robots $\mathcal{R}, |\mathcal{R}| \leq n$, we want to ensure that there is at most one robot on each node. We take advantage of the fact that most dispersion protocols involve the exploration of G, and develop algorithms for calculating dominating sets. In the next subsection, we mention our major results.

1.1   Our Results:

In this paper, we show how to compute a minimal dominating set and an approximate minimum dominating set on an anonymous graph using mobile robots. Let G be a connected and anonymous graph of n nodes and m edges with maximum degree Δ. Suppose n robots (with distinct IDs) are distributed arbitrarily over the nodes of G. We develop algorithms for the robots to work collaboratively and identify small dominating sets of G. In particular, our results are:

- an $O(m)$ time algorithm for the robots to compute a minimal dominating set on G when all robots are gathered at a single node initially. The set of dominating nodes also forms a MIS.
- an $O(\ell\Delta \log(\lambda) + n\ell + m)$ time algorithm for the robots to compute a minimal dominating set on G when the robots are placed arbitrarily at ℓ nodes initially.
- an $O(n\Delta \log(\lambda))$ time algorithm for a $\ln(\Delta)$ approximation solution to the minimum dominating set on G, where λ is the maximum ID-length of the robots.

All our algorithms require that the robots have at most $O(\log(n))$ bits of memory. In a recent work in [10], the authors solved a related problem called the Distance-2-Dispersion problem (See Sect. 1.2 for details) which also produces a MIS in special cases (when the number of robots is greater than the number of nodes in the graph) in $O(m\Delta)$ rounds with $O(\log(\Delta))$ bits of memory in each robot.

1.2   Related Works

Finding small dominating sets for graphs is one of the most fundamental problems in graph theory which along with its variants has been extensively studied for the last four decades. The dominating set problem and the set cover problem are closely related and the former one can be regarded as a special case of the latter. To find a minimum set cover for arbitrary graphs has been shown to be NP-hard [6,9].

There have been a few studies on the dominating set and related problems for various distributed models. In [7], Jia et al. gave the first efficient distributed implementation of the dominating set problem in the CONGEST model. Their randomised algorithm, which is the refinement of the greedy algorithm adapted from [17] takes $O(\log(n)\log(\Delta))$ rounds and provides a $\ln(\Delta)$ - optimal dominating set in expectation (Δ is the maximum degree among the n nodes of the graph). It has at most a constant number of message exchanges between any two nodes. In [23], Evan Sultanik et al. gave a distributed algorithm for solving a variant of the art gallery problem equivalent to finding a minimal dominating set of the minimal visibility graphs. Their algorithm runs in a number of rounds on the order of the diameter of the graph producing solutions that are within a constant factor of optimal with high probability. In [16], Kuhn and Wattenhofer gave approximation algorithms for minimum dominating sets using LP relaxation techniques. Their algorithm computes an expected dominating set of size $(k\Delta^{\frac{2}{k}}\log(\Delta))$ times the optimal and takes $O(k^2)$ rounds for any arbitrary parameter k. Each node sends $O(k^2\Delta)$ messages, each of size $O(\log(\Delta))$. With k chosen as some constant, this algorithm provides the first non-trivial approximation to the minimal dominating set which runs in a constant number of rounds. Fabian Kuhn et al. in [15] gave time lower bounds for finding minimum vertex cover and minimum dominating set in the context of the classical *message passing* distributed model. They showed that the number of rounds required in order to achieve a constant or even only a poly-logarithmic approximation ratio is at least $\Omega(\sqrt{\frac{\log(n)}{\log(\log(n))}})$ and $\Omega(\sqrt{\frac{\log(\Delta)}{\log(\log(\Delta))}})$. In [5] the authors gave deterministic approximation algorithms for the minimum dominating set problem in the CONGEST model with an almost optimal approximation guarantee. They gave two algorithms with an approximation ratio of $(1+\epsilon)(1+\log(\Delta+1))$ running respectively in $O(2^{O(\sqrt{\log(n)\log(\log(n))})})$ and $O(\Delta\operatorname{polylog}(\Delta) + \operatorname{polylog}(\Delta)\log^\star(n))$ for $\epsilon > \frac{1}{\operatorname{polylog}(\Delta)}$. The paper also explores the problem of connected dominating sets using these algorithms, giving a $\ln(\Delta)$ - optimal connected dominating set.

In our paper, we compute minimal dominating set and approximate minimum dominating set on an arbitrary anonymous graph with the help of mobile robots with limited memory. Our algorithms use a key procedure called *dispersion* that re-positions $k \leq n$ mobile robots (which initially were present arbitrarily on a n-node graph G) to a distinct node of G such that one node has at most one robot. Dispersion of mobile robots is a well-studied problem in distributed robotics in different settings. It is introduced in [1] and saw its development over the years through several papers [2,11–13,18–21]. To date, [14] provides the best-known result for solving dispersion in $O(m + k\Delta)$ rounds and using $\log(k + \Delta)$ bits memory per robot (k is the number of robots).

In a recent work by Kaur et al. [10], the authors formulated and solved the Distance-2-Dispersion (D-2-D) problem in the context of mobile robots on an anonymous graph G, which is a closely related problem to ours. In the Distance-2-Dispersion problem, each of the k robot settles at some node satisfying these two conditions: (i) two robots cannot settle at adjacent nodes (ii) a robot can only settle at the node already occupied by another robot if and only if there's no more unoccupied node that satisfies condition (i). They showed that, with $O(\log(\Delta))$ bits of memory per robot, the (D-2-D) problem can be solved in $O(m\Delta)$ rounds, Δ being the highest degree of the graph. Their algorithm requires no pre-requisite knowledge of the parameters m, n and Δ. Additionally, they show that if the number of robots $k \geq n$ (number of vertices in G), the nodes with settled robots form a maximal independent set for G.

2   Model and Problem Definition

Graph: The underlying graph $G(V, E)$ is connected, undirected, unweighted and anonymous with $|V| = n$ nodes and $|E| = m$ edges. The nodes of G do not have any distinguishing identifiers or labels. The nodes do not possess any memory and hence cannot store any information. The degree of a node $v \in V$ is denoted by δ_v and the maximum degree of G is Δ. Edges incident on v are locally labelled using port numbers in the range $[1, \delta_v]$. A single edge connecting two nodes receives independent port numbering at the two end. The edges of the graph serve as *routes* through which the robots can commute. Any number of robots can travel through an edge at any given time.

Robots: We have a collection of n robots $\mathcal{R} = \{r_1, r_2, ..., r_n\}$ residing on the nodes of the graph. Each robot has a unique ID in the range $[0, n^c]$, where $c \geq 1$ is arbitrary; and has $O(\log(n))$ bits to store information. Two or more robots can be present (*co-located*) at a node or pass through an edge in G. However, a robot is not allowed to stay on an edge. A robot can recognise the port number through which it has entered and exited a node.

Communication Model: We consider a synchronous system where the robot are synchronised to a common clock. We consider the local communication model where only co-located robots (i.e., robots at the same node) can communicate among themselves.

Time Cycle: Each robot r_i, on activation, performs a *Communicate −*
Compute − Move (CCM) cycle as follows.

- **Communicate:** r_i may communicate with other robots present at the same
  node as itself.
- **Compute:** Based on the gathered information and subsequent computations,
  r_i may perform all manner of computations within the bounds of its memory.
- **Move:** r_i may move to a neighbouring node using the computed exit port.

A robot can perform the CCM task in one time unit, called *round*. The **time**
complexity of an algorithm is the number of rounds required to achieve the
goal. The **memory complexity** is the number of bits required by each robot
to execute the algorithm.

Definition 1 (Problem Definition).
*Consider an undirected, connected n-node simple anonymous graph G with
n mobile robots placed over the nodes of G arbitrarily. Let Δ denote the highest
degree of a node in G.*

Minimal Dominating Set. *The robots, irrespective of their initial placement,
rearrange and colour themselves in such a way that i) there is a robot at each
node of G ii) there is a self-identified subset of robots, coloured black, on $D \subseteq G$
which forms a minimal dominating set for G.*

Approximate Minimum Dominating Set. *The robots, irrespective of how
they are initially placed, rearrange and colour themselves in such a way that a
dominating set for G of size at most $\alpha|D^*|$ is identified, where D^* is a minimum
dominating set. Here α is the approximation ratio to the minimum dominating
set.*

*Our goal is to design algorithm for solving the above problems as fast as
possible and keeping α as small as $\ln(\Delta)$.*

3   Preliminaries: DFS Traversal and PROCEDURE_MYN

In this section, we present two subroutines that we use in our algorithms. The
first one is a simple depth-first search (DFS) traversal that allows the robots
to explore the entire graph and disperse at the same time. The second one is a
procedure that allows two robots on neighbouring nodes to meet each other if
required.

3.1   DFS Traversal Protocol

The DFS Traversal Protocol is used frequently as a subroutine in several mobile
robot problems. Our paper uses the same DFS protocol as described in [14].

Assume that all the n robots are initially docked at a node which we call the *root* node. The high-level idea is to traverse the graph, node by node while posting one robot at each node. The DFS protocol begins at the *root* where the robot with the least ID settles. The remaining robots leave the *root* via a computed exit port to land at a new node. The next smallest ID robot settles at the new node while the remaining $n - 2$ robots leave the node to continue exploration. The robot group may need to backtrack when it encounters a settled robot or when all ports of a node have been explored. DFS completes when every robot settles. With the end of DFS, the robots achieve dispersion. The protocol takes $O(m)$ rounds. A full description of the protocol can be found in the full paper [3].

3.2   Procedure_MYN (Meet-Your-Neighbor)

Since the port ordering of nodes is different, it can be tricky to ensure that two robots on neighbouring nodes meet. Also, it is difficult to time the movement of robots and guarantee that two neighbours meet without access to a global clock. Since, it can be essential for two robots to pass information to each other, arranging ways to ensure such a meeting can be beneficial. Procedure_MYN is helpful in ensuring that a robot is able to communicate with all its neighbours at least once when required. We use the pairing procedure Procedure_MYN to ensure that during a scan for neighbours, a robot meets all its neighbours. For this, the algorithm essentially exploits the bits representing the IDs of the robots. Let λ denote the largest ID among all the n robots. Therefore, the robots use a $\log(\lambda)$ bit field to store the IDs. Procedure_MYN runs in phases. Each phase consists of Δ rounds and there are a total of $\log(\lambda)$ phases. Each phase corresponds to a bit in the field (with robots having IDs less than $\log(\lambda)$ bits padding the rest with 0s). The steps in a phase are simple, starting with the rightmost bit, if the bit is 1, the robot uses Δ rounds to visit all its neighbours. If the bit is 0, the robot waits at its node for visitors. Clearly, since all robots have unique IDs, for any two pairs of neighbouring robots, there exists at least one round in which the robots have different bits and meet. More details in the full paper [3]. Clearly, the procedure takes no more than $O(\Delta \log(\lambda))$ rounds to ensure that a robot meets with all its neighbours.

Hence,

Lemma 1. Procedure_*MYN* ensures that a robot meets all its neighbours at least once and takes no more than $O(\Delta \log(\lambda))$ rounds.

4 Algorithm for Minimal Dominating Set

In this section, we show that we can achieve a minimal dominating set for both the rooted and arbitrary initial configuration. In the rooted case, initially, all robots are gathered at a single root, while in the arbitrary case, the robots are gathered in clusters across the graph.

4.1 Single Source Initial Configuration

Let us first consider the case where all the mobile agents are initially housed at a single node of the graph. We refer to such a configuration as a single source or *rooted initial configuration*. We design an algorithm for the mobile agents to work collaboratively to compute a minimal dominating set of G. In particular, agents identify a subset D of the vertices V such that D is a minimal dominating set of G. Given n agents that start from a single source, our algorithm takes $O(m)$ rounds to find such a D, where m is the number of edges in the graph. Agents are not required to know any graph parameters.

To solve the dominating set problem in the rooted initial configuration, we modify the standard DFS traversal (see Sect. 3.1) to allow the agents to simultaneously traverse and compute the dominating set D.

To ensure that the robots know if they are part of the dominating set for G in the end, each robot is *coloured* accordingly. The robots that occupy the nodes $D \subset V$ are coloured "black" to distinguish them from other mobile robots. Thus, the set of mobile robots coloured black forms the dominating set for G. To ensure proper colouring, each robot uses an additional variable $r_i.colour$ along with the ones used for executing the DFS Traversal. $r_i.colour$ is used to classify the nature of the robot with respect to the dominating set. Each robot, at a given time, has one out of the three colours - *black*, *grey* and *white*. Initially, all robots are *white* in colour. Robots change their colour to *black* once it becomes a member of the dominating set. Robots that are adjacent to a black coloured robot are coloured *grey*.

We will now describe our algorithm in detail. As mentioned before, our algorithm for creating a dominating set follows a modified version of the depth-first algorithm described in Sect. 3.1. We do so by the addition of an extra step each time a robot explores a new node, to decide a robot's colour.

As in the DFS, the collection of robots $\mathcal{R} = \{r_1, r_2, \ldots, r_n\}$ start the algorithm from the $root \in V$. The robots leave the smallest ID robot r_1 at $root$, where r_1 settles and colours itself *black*. In general, the robots navigate the graph via the DFS protocol with the extra step of deciding the colour of the robot that settles. This is decided as follows. Each time the robots decide to settle a robot a the node u, they visit all neighbours of u. If they find a *black* settled robot among u's neighbours, then the robot settling at u colours itself *grey*, else it colours itself *black*. However, the robot that has just arrived at a new empty node with its *parent* coloured *black* can immediately become *grey*. The remaining robots move via the smallest port available at u to the next node according to the DFS traversal protocol (see, Sect. 3.1) and the algorithm continues.

The unsettled robots scan their neighbour for *black* robots only in the *forward* phase. The algorithm stops when the last unsettled robot that started from *root* settles and colours itself. The nodes of G, which we notate by D, that have a *black* robot placed, now form a dominating set for the graph G. An illustrative example of the same has been provided in Fig. 1.

Algorithm 1. DOMINATING SET - SINGLE SOURCE (ALGORITHM FOR ROBOT r_i)

Require: An n-node anonymous graph with n mobile agents docked at *root*.
Ensure: Agents settle over the nodes and identify a minimal dominating set.

1: Let the robots $\{r_1, r_2, \ldots, r_i, \ldots, r_n\}$ be docked at a node *root*. Robot r_i maintains the following list of variables: $\langle r_i.id, r_i.parent, r_i.child, r_i.state, r_i.colour \rangle$, where $r_i.colour$ is initially set to *white*, $r_i.parent$, $r_i.child$ are set to *null* and $r_i.state$ is set to *forward*.
2: **while** r_i is unsettled **do**
3:     **if** r_i is not the minimum ID robot among the unsettled robots **then**
4:        move according to DFS Traversal Protocol 3.1
5:     **else**
6:        **if** the current node is empty **then**
7:           set $r_i.settle \leftarrow 1$ and inform the other unsettled robots to stay stationary
8:           move to and check the colour of its parent robot and return
9:           **if** parent is black **then**
10:              sets $r_i.colour \leftarrow grey$
11:           **else**
12:              visits each neighbour of the current node and if there is at least one *black* in its neighbour, set $r_i.colour \leftarrow grey$ or else set $r_i.colour \leftarrow black$
13:              inform the remaining unsettled node about the completion of colouring
14:           **end if**
15:     **else**
16:           move according to DFS Traversal Protocol 3.1 to find an empty node
17:        **end if**
18:     **end if**
19: **end while**
20: remain stationary at the current node for the rest of the algorithm
21: The nodes where each *black*-coloured robot is stationed form the dominating set D of G.

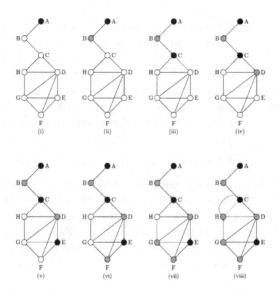

Fig. 1. Illustration of Mobile Robots identifying a Minimal Dominating Set. The robots start at the *root* node A. The minimum ID robot settles at A and colours itself as *black*. The rest of the robots follow the DFS and ends up at node *B*, where the next minimum ID robot in the group settles and colours itself as *grey* (since it comes from a *black* parent). The rest of the robots now stops at the next node in the DFS, node C. The settled robot at C scans the neighbourhood (teal coloured edges) and finds no *black* robot and hence colours itself as *black*. The algorithm continues along the DFS route (blue-directed edges) shown from (iv) to (vii), settles and colours robots accordingly till it reaches the final configuration (viii). The red edge denotes a *backtrack*. After the configuration of (viii) is reached, no new node is discovered and the algorithm stops after completing the DFS of the graph.

Analysis

Lemma 2. *Algorithm 4.1 ensures that each robot is associated with a distinct node in G and that the subset, D, of robots coloured black forms a minimal dominating set of G.*

Proof. During the course of the algorithm, which begins with a group of unsettled robots at a specially designated node called *root*, the robots get settled one by one in increasing order of the IDs, at some distinct node of G. The DFS protocol ensures that the entire graph is explored and each node in G contains a settled robot. Since each settled robot gets immediately coloured as black or grey, Algorithm 4.1 leaves no robot with the colour *white*. The *black*-coloured robots, D, form the dominating set, whereas the *grey* robots are the ones that are adjacent to one or more robots included in the dominating set. Note that a robot is coloured grey if and only if there exists a neighbour that was coloured black. Since there are no white robots at the end of the protocol, D is a dominating set of G.

We now prove that D represents a minimal dominating set for the graph G. For contradiction, let us assume that after the end of the algorithm, we can remove a *black* node (robot) r_x from D without disrupting it's dominating set property. Therefore, D is still a dominating set for G without r_x. Now, since the algorithm executes sequentially, the parent and every neighbourhood of r_x is *grey* after the end of the algorithm. It leaves the node r_x uncovered by any black node. Therefore D does not form a dominating set for G with r_x excluded. □

Lemma 3. *Algorithm 4.1 executes in $O(m)$ rounds.*

Proof. The algorithm essentially executes a depth-first search, in which it settles the n robots, one by one. The depth-first search takes up $O(m)$ rounds. In addition to that, once a robot r_i settles at a specific node u, it takes a maximum of $O(\delta_i)$ rounds, where δ_i is the degree of the node u, to search for robots among its neighbours, to decide its own colour. Therefore, the algorithm takes $O(m + \sum(\delta_i)) = O(m)$ rounds to execute. □

Memory per Robot. Each robot stores its ID which takes $O(\log(n))$ bit space. Along with that, the parent and child pointers take $O(\log(\Delta))$ bit memory each. Other variables take up a constant number of bits. Therefore, the memory complexity is $O(\log(n + \Delta)) = O(\log(n))$ bits.

Combining it with Lemma 2 and Lemma 3 and we have the following theorem.

Theorem 1. *Let G be an n-node arbitrary, connected and anonymous graph with m edges. Let n mobile robots with distinct IDs in the range $[0, n^c]$, where c is constant, be placed at a single node, known as the rooted initial configuration. Then, a minimal dominating set for G can be found in $O(m)$ rounds using Algorithm 4.1 with $O(\log(n))$ bits of memory at each robot.*

As a by-product, the Algorithm 4.1 computes a maximal independent set (MIS). In fact, the set D is also a MIS for G. Thus we get the following result on MIS.

Theorem 2 (Maximal Independent Set). *Let n mobile robots be initially placed at a single node of an n-node anonymous graph G with m edges. Then there is an algorithm (cf. Algorithm 4.1) for the robots to compute a maximal independent set of G in $O(m)$ rounds and with $O(\log(n))$ bits memory per robot.*

Proof. A robot receives a *black* colour after ensuring that no neighbour is coloured black. This ensures that no two adjacent nodes host *black* robots guaranteeing D to be an independent set. Now, let's assume that we can add a black node v to D while maintaining its independent set property. Since, the robot at v was initially *grey*, it must have had a *black* neighbour at some node u. Therefore, we happen to have two adjacent nodes u and v that are resided by *black* robots, contradicting the fact that D is an independent set. Therefore, no new black node can be added to the independent set D, making it a maximal independent set (MIS). □

4.2 Multi Source Initial Configuration

In the multi-source (or arbitrary) case, the n robots $\{r_1, r_2, \ldots, r_n\}$ start as $\ell < n$ clusters, placed arbitrarily at ℓ different nodes of G. Once again, our algorithm for constructing dominating sets is inspired by the DFS procedure for dispersion [14]. In this section, we show how we can achieve a minimal dominating set for such a configuration.

The robots first perform dispersion using the method described in Kshemkalyani [14]. Briefly, their algorithm allows each of the ℓ clusters to begin DFS independently. If a DFS meets no other DFS, then it executes to completion as in the rooted case. If not, their algorithm ensures that if two (or more) DFSs meet while dispersing, they are all merged into the DFS with the largest number of settled robots. That is if DFS i meets DFS j and i has more settled robots at the time of meeting, then j is collapsed and all of j's robots join in executing i's DFS. This act of gathering all of j into i is called *subsumption*. Thus, when two DFSs meet, the shorter DFS gets subsumed by the larger one. Note that this means that once dispersion is achieved, there may be several DFS trees.

Let us assume then, after the end of the algorithm, there are $\ell^* \leq \ell$ independent DFSs that never met (each with its own unique *root*). Each DFS is identified by a unique label *treelabel* (which is the ID of the smallest robot in the tree). Our procedure to create the minimal dominating set consists of two steps i) elect a global leader robot r^* ii) with r^* as root, use an adaption of Algorithm 4.1 to achieve a minimal dominating set. Note that the dispersion algorithm in [14] takes $O(m)$ rounds. To ensure coordination, each robot waits to begin the leader election protocol after $cn\Delta$ rounds for a sufficiently large constant c from the start of dispersion.

Leader Election: We first use the PROCEDURE_MYN (see Sect. 3) to ensure that all robots first meet their neighbours. When a robot meets a robot from a different ID, they share their *treelabels* with one another. When a robot receives a lower *treelabel* value, it updates its own *treelabel* to the lower value. After PROCEDURE_MYN has been executed, each robot, starting from the leaf nodes in a DFS (say DFS i) now sends its newly updated *treelabel* value to the root of DFS i ($root_i$) via its *parent* pointers. The root of the DFS i, $root_i$, waits for $O(n)$ rounds as it receives different values of *treelabel* continuously from its leaf nodes (*up-casting*). The $root_i$ now compares the minimum *treelabel* values received from its children with its own *treelabel* and decides on the minimum *treelabel*. It then sends it along through its children into each and every node of its, in the DFS (*down-casting*). All the robots in DFS i are now updated with the lowest *treelabel* value. This marks the end of a phase. After the end of ℓ (although ℓ^* is sufficient, its value is unknown) such phases, it is guaranteed that each of the n robots in G now has a consistent *treelabel* value. The final *treelabel* value is the minimum among the ℓ^* DFSs, however, it may not represent the minimum ID robot, as it may be consumed by a larger DFS during the dispersion process happening earlier. After the end of the protocol, the robot that has the globally decided minimum *treelabel* continues the algorithm. We identify the leader robot with the minimum *treelabel* value as r^*.

Creating Minimal Dominating Set: With $r^\star$ as a leader, it first creates a new DFS of the graph G with the node containing $r^\star$ as the *root* node. Since the robots are dispersed across each and every node of G, the nodes of G are now distinguishable owing to the distinct IDs of the mobile robots in the nodes. $r^\star$ starts from the root and rewrites the *parent* and *child* pointers of each robot as its traverses across the whole graph G in a depth-first manner. Moving to an empty node implies that $r^\star$ has arrived at the *root*. In such cases, $r^\star$ modifies its own variables accordingly. The other details regarding the DFS can be found in Sect. 3.1. After the end of this process, which takes an additional $O(m)$ rounds, the newly assigned pointers of the robots now represent a DFS of G with $r^\star$ (node) as the root.

Initially, all the robots are coloured *white* by default. The identification of the dominating set takes place in similar lines as with the rooted case described in the previous Sect. 4.1. The algorithm begins with $r^\star$ colouring itself black. $r^\star$ then moves the next node (say, node u resided by a robot r_u) following the newly created DFS. Upon the arrival of $r^\star$ at u, r_u scans each of its neighbours to check if there is a black robot. If there are no black robots, r_u colours itself as *black* otherwise if there is at least one black robot in the neighbourhood of u, r_u colours itself *grey*. After r_u has changed its colour from *white*, it informs $r^\star$ as $r^\star$ now moves to the next node following the DFS. The process continues similarly with each new node of degree δ_i, requiring $O(\delta_i)$ rounds for a robot to its scan its neighbour and colour itself accordingly. The algorithm terminates as soon as $r^\star$ completes the DFS of G.

Therefore, combining the results from the previous section (Sect. 4.1, DFS traversal and PROCEDURE_MYN), we get the following main result.

Theorem 3. *Let G be an n-node anonymous graph with the maximum degree Δ. Let n mobile robots with distinct IDs in the range $[0, n^c]$, where c is constant, be initially placed arbitrarily among ℓ nodes of G in ℓ clusters. Then, a minimal dominating set for G can be found in $O(\ell\Delta \log(\lambda) + n\ell + m)$ rounds using Algorithm 4.2 with $O(\log(n))$ bits memory per robot. λ is the maximum ID-string length of the robots.*

Proof. Algorithm 4.2 first disperses the n robots over the n nodes using the algorithm in [14] , which takes $O(m)$ rounds. We then elect a leader among the robots. There are at most ℓ DFS trees (as it starts with ℓ clusters initially). Each DFS tree uses PROCEDURE_MYN to communicate with the neighbouring DFS (if any). Once the leaf nodes receive a new communication from a different DFS, it sends the information to the root of its DFS; which may take $O(n)$ rounds. In the worst case PROCEDURE_MYN may be executed ℓ times to elect the leader. From Lemma 1 we know that PROCEDURE_MYN takes $O(\Delta \log(\lambda))$ rounds. Thus, the leader election requires $O(\ell(\Delta \log(\lambda) + n))$ rounds. The leader robot then finds a minimal dominating set while forming a single DFS tree using at most $O(m)$ rounds. Finally, the dominating set identification takes another $O(m)$ rounds. Therefore, the time complexity of Algorithm 4.2 is $O(m + \ell(\Delta \log(\lambda) + n) + m) = O(m + \ell\Delta \log(\lambda) + n\ell)$ rounds. □

5   Algorithm for ln(Δ)-Approximation Minimum Dominating Set

In this section, we describe an approximation algorithm that gives us a dominating set with a size that is optimal within a factor of $\ln(\Delta)$ in the mobile agent setting. In the previous algorithms, our methodology was based on scanning only the 1-hop neighbourhood of a robot to assign a robot one of the two colours - *black* or *grey*. The set of *black* coloured robots formed the dominating set for G. Although these previous algorithms (*rooted*) ran in $O(m)$ rounds, the approximation ratio of the dominating set size produced with these algorithms to the optimal (minimum) dominating set could be huge. For example, if we consider a star graph with the robots starting at one of the leaves, then all leaf nodes become included in the dominating set (Fig. 2). Although that dominating set is minimal, it is far from optimal. The optimal in the case of a star graph is the single non-leaf node at the centre. Therefore, the approximation ratio in such a case can be as large as $O(n)$. In this section, we adapt the well-known greedy distributed algorithm [17], to provide a better approximation solution for the dominating set problem in the mobile agent setting.

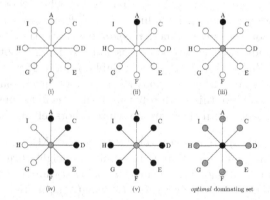

Fig. 2. When the robots start at a leaf node (node A), our previous algorithm (Algorithm 4.1) produces a minimal dominating set identified by the black nodes as in (v) by executing through (ii), (iii) and (iv). The figure right next to (v) on the other hand, shows an optimal dominating set. Therefore, for an n node graph, the size of a minimal dominating set could be as bad as $O(n)$ compared to the optimal.

In [17], the authors give a greedy distributed algorithm (referred to in the paper as "*distributed database coverage heuristic* (DDCH)") for calculating a dominating set with an approximation ratio of $\ln \Delta$ to the optimal set size. The same is reintroduced for a synchronous communication model where the nodes can communicate with each other without moving [7]. The authors also refined the algorithm to a randomized version obtaining a better-expected running time. We essentially adopt the greedy distributed algorithm to our own model. The challenge is of course as follows: in the earlier distributed setting, nodes are allowed to communicate with their neighbours within the span of a round, whereas the robots in our model cannot communicate with each other unless they are at the same node. While the robots can gather information by visiting neighbouring robots, however, it is difficult to time the movement of robots and guarantee that two neighbours meet without access to a global clock. However, with the help of PROCEDURE_MYN introduced in the previous section, a successful adaptation of the greedy algorithm is possible. More details follow.

For this protocol, we assume that the n mobile robots of set, $\mathcal{R} = \{r_1, r_2, \ldots, r_n\}$ start from a dispersed position on graph G. That is, they are initially dispersed among the n nodes of the graph G with each robot at a distinct node of G. If the robots are arbitrarily placed over G initially, the robots could be re-positioned using the dispersion algorithm described in [14]. As in our previous sections, each robot is assigned a variable colour to keep track of its colour, which can take one of three values *white, grey* or *black*. Let $D \subset G$ be the set of black robots at the end of the protocol, and D forms the dominating set of G. A white robot is one that is not (yet) covered by any robot in the dominating set. The *grey* robots represent robots that are already covered by some robot in D. Initially, all the robots are coloured *white*.

Let *span* of a robot r_i, $w(r_i)$, be the number of white robots in the direct $(1 - hop)$ neighbourhood of r_i, including r_i itself. Each robot r_i uses an extra variable $r_i.span$ for the *span* values. $r_i.span$ has both the ID and the span count. The basic idea of the protocol is as follows. Each robot calculates the maximum span value within its $2 - hop$ neighbourhood. If r is the robot that has the maximum span within $2 - hops$ then r colours itself black and informs its neighbours. To achieve this, each robot performs the following four stages (of $2\Delta \log(\lambda)$ rounds each) until there are no white robots left in the graph:

1. r_i **calculates its span** $r_i.span$: The PROCEDURE_MYN, described in the previous section guarantees that r_i meets all its neighbouring robots within $O(\Delta \log(\lambda))$ rounds ("meeting" includes r_i being stationary and a neighbouring robot arriving at r_i during these $O(\Delta \log(\lambda))$ rounds). Inside the first $O(\Delta \log(\lambda))$ rounds, the robot r_i communicates with its immediate neighbours and evaluates $r_i.span$.

2. r_i **gets to know the highest** *span* **value within its immediate neighbours**
   Inside the next $O(\Delta \log(\lambda))$ rounds, r_i communicates with its immediate neighbours to know the highest *span* value within its neighbourhood. If $r_j.span$ is the highest span value among immediate neighbours, $r_i.span$ gets replaced by $r_j.span$. For identical *span* values, a robot with a lower ID is selected.

3. r_i **gets to know the highest** *span* **value within its** $2 - hop$ **neighbours**
   In the next $O(\Delta \log(\lambda))$ rounds of the algorithm, r_i visits all its immediate neighbours once again to check if there are any new updated span values (possibly from a neighbour's neighbour).

4. **if r_i coloured itself black, then it informs its neighbours.**
   After the completion of the first three stages, r_i has the information of the highest span and the robot that has the highest span in its $2-hop$ neighbourhood. If r_i itself is the robot with the highest span, it colours itself *black*. Any robot that receives *black* colour then takes additional $O(\Delta \log(\lambda))$ rounds to go to its neighbours and colour any *white* robot in their neighbour as *grey*.

Note that once a robot colours itself *black*, its colour does not change. All robots then reset their *span* values and the next phase of $O(\Delta \log \lambda)$ begins. The algorithm runs till each robot r_i has no more *white* robots in their neighbourhood.

Lemma 4. *Let r_i and r_k be two robots at a distance of 2 hops from each other. Then, the value of $r_k.span$ can be communicated to r_i within $O(\Delta \log(\lambda))$ rounds.*

Proof. Since r_i and r_k are at a distance of 2 hops from each other, there exists a sequence of robots (nodes) (r_i, r_{i_1}, r_k) from r_i to r_k. In the first $O(\Delta \log(\lambda))$ rounds, r_i can communicate with r_{i_1} to get the value of $r_{i_1}.span$. In the meanwhile, r_{i_1} also collects the value of $r_k.span$ in the same $O(\Delta \log(\lambda))$ round. Therefore, in the second sub-phase of $O(\Delta \log(\lambda))$ rounds, when r_i communicates with r_{i_1} again, r_i receives the value of $r_k.span$ through r_{i_1} or the vice-versa.   □

Algorithm 2. $\ln(\Delta)$ OPTIMAL DOMINATING SET (ALGORITHM FOR ROBOT r_i)

1: **while** there are white robots in the neighbourhood **do**
2:    **for** $i = 1$ to $O(\Delta \log \lambda)$ **do**   ▷ Stage 1
3:        Each robot $r_i \in \mathcal{R}$ computes its span $r_i.span$ using compute span PROCEDURE_MYN.
4:        **if** $r_i.span$ is zero **then**
5:            Then r_i stops executing the protocol. But will provide information if requested.
6:        **end if**
7:    **end for**
8:    **for** $i = 1$ to $O(\Delta \log \lambda)$ **do**   ▷ Stage 2
9:        Each robot $r_i \in \mathcal{R}$ communicates its span $r_i.span$ its neighbours.
10:   **end for**
11:   **for** $i = 1$ to $O(\Delta \log \lambda)$ **do**   ▷ Stage 3
12:       Each robot $r_i \in \mathcal{R}$ computes the maximum span within 2-hops.
13:   **end for**
14:   **if** $r_i.span$ is highest among all robots in the $2-hop$ neighbourhood **then**,   ▷ Stage 4
15:       r_i colours itself as *black*
16:       **for** $i = 1$ to $O(\Delta \log \lambda)$ **do**
17:           r_i meets each neighbour and colours any *white* robot as *grey* (use PROCEDURE_MYN)
18:       **end for**
19:   **end if**
20:   Reset $r_i.span$ for all $r_i \in \mathcal{R}$.
21: **end while**

Lemma 5. *Algorithm 5 computes a dominating set D which is a* $\ln(\Delta)$ *approximation to the optimal size dominating set* D^* *for the graph G.*

Proof. Our protocol emulates the greedy distributed algorithm in [7] by ensuring that the node with the highest span within a two-hop neighbourhood becomes a part of the dominating set. Hence the $\ln(\Delta)$ approximation follows directly from the approximation results in [7,24]. □

Lemma 6. *Algorithm 5 takes* $O(n\Delta\log(\lambda))$ *rounds to execute.*

Proof. There are four stages within a single while loop in Algorithm 5. The first stage starts by calculating the span of each robot which takes $O(\Delta\log(\lambda))$ rounds. In the next two stages of $O(\Delta\log(\lambda))$ rounds, the robots communicate their *span* to all the robots with a distance of $2 - hops$. In the final stage, when a robot gets a colour *black* (the robot with the highest span in its $2 - hop$ neighbourhood), it can take another $O(\Delta\log(\lambda))$ rounds to instruct its neighbouring robots to colour themselves as *grey*. So, a single while loop from *span* calculation till colouring robots as *grey*; takes no more than $O(\Delta\log(\lambda))$ rounds. As the execution of a single while loop gives us at least one *black* robot, in the worst case, the algorithm needs at most $O(n)$ iterations of the while loop. Thus, giving us a complexity of $O(n\Delta\log(\lambda))$ rounds. □

Theorem 4. *Let G be an n-node arbitrary, connected and anonymous graph with a maximum degree* Δ. *Let n mobile robots with distinct IDs are placed in a dispersed initial configuration. Then, a* $ln(\Delta)$-*approximation solution to the minimum dominating set for the graph G can be found in* $O(n\Delta\log(\lambda))$ *rounds using Algorithm 5 with* $O(\log(n))$ *bits of memory per robot, where* λ *is the maximum length of the ID-string of the robots.*

Proof. From Lemma 5, we know that Algorithm 5 provides a $ln(\Delta)$ approximation solution. And from Lemma 6 we know that it takes at most $O(n\Delta\log(\lambda))$ rounds to execute. Thus, the theorem. □

6   Conclusion and Future Work

In this paper, we solved the problem of finding the dominating set of a graph G using mobile agents. When the agents start at a single source, we are able to find a minimal dominating set in $O(m)$ rounds. On the other hand, for the multi-source starting configuration, the robots obtained a minimal dominating set in $O(\ell\Delta\log(\lambda) + n\ell + m)$ rounds. Additionally, the dominating sets obtained by these two algorithms also serve as a maximal independent set for the graph G. In the last section, we described an approximation algorithm that gave us a dominating set with a size that is optimal within a factor of $\ln(\Delta)$. The approximation algorithm had a running time of $O(n\Delta\log(\lambda))$ rounds.

In future work, it would be interesting to investigate the lower bounds - in terms of time, memory and number of robots being used, for the dominating set problem in the same distributed model. It would be interesting to see if it's possible to produce dominating sets that are also connected, i.e., connected dominating sets. It would also be exciting to explore other classical graph problems, such as ruling sets, colouring etc., And of course, given practical real-world concerns, adaption of the algorithms for faulty robots is an important aspect to be considered for the future as well.

References

1. Augustine, J., Moses Jr., W.K.: Dispersion of mobile robots: a study of memory-time trade-offs. In: ICDCN (2018)
2. Chand, P.K., Kumar, M., Molla, A.R., Sivasubramaniam, S.: Fault-tolerant dispersion of mobile robots. In: CALDAM (2023)
3. Chand, P.K., Molla, A.R., Sivasubramaniam, S.: Run for cover: dominating set via mobile agents. arXiv preprint arXiv:2309.02200 (2023)
4. Das, R., Sharma, A., Sau, B.: Maximum independent set formation on a finite grid by myopic robots. arXiv preprint arXiv:2207.13403 (2022)
5. Deurer, J., Kuhn, F., Maus, Y.: Deterministic distributed dominating set approximation in the congest model. In: PODC, pp. 94–103 (2019)
6. Garey, M.R., Johnson, D.S.: Computers and Intractability: A Guide to the Theory of NP-Completeness. W. H. Freeman and Co., New York (1990)
7. Jia, L., Rajaraman, R., Suel, T.: An efficient distributed algorithm for constructing small dominating sets. Distrib. Comput. 15(4), 193–205 (2002)
8. Kamei, S., Tixeuil, S.: An asynchronous maximum independent set algorithm by myopic luminous robots on grids. arXiv preprint arXiv:2012.03399 (2020)
9. Karp, R.M.: Reducibility among combinatorial problems. In: Complexity of Computer Computations (1972)
10. Kaur, T., Mondal, K.: Distance-2-dispersion: dispersion with further constraints. In: NETYS (2023)
11. Kshemkalyani, A.D., Ali, F.: Efficient dispersion of mobile robots on graphs. In: ICDCN (2019)
12. Kshemkalyani, A.D., Molla, A.R., Sharma, G.: Fast dispersion of mobile robots on arbitrary graphs. In: ALGOSENSORS (2019)
13. Kshemkalyani, A.D., Molla, A.R., Sharma, G.: Dispersion of mobile robots using global communication. J. Parallel Distrib. Comput. 161, 100–117 (2022)
14. Kshemkalyani, A.D., Sharma, G.: Near-optimal dispersion on arbitrary anonymous graphs. In: OPODIS (2021)
15. Kuhn, F., Moscibroda, T., Wattenhofer, R.: What cannot be computed locally! In: PODC (2004)
16. Kuhn, F., Wattenhofer, R.: Constant-time distributed dominating set approximation. In: PODC (2003)
17. Liang, B., Haas, Z.: Virtual backbone generation and maintenance in ad hoc network mobility management. In: IEEE INFOCOM (2000)
18. Molla, A.R., Mondal, K., Moses Jr., W.K.: Efficient dispersion on an anonymous ring in the presence of weak byzantine robots. In: ALGOSENSORS (2020)
19. Molla, A.R., Mondal, K., Moses Jr., W.K.: Byzantine dispersion on graphs. In: IPDPS (2021)
20. Molla, A.R., Moses Jr., W.K.: Dispersion of mobile robots: the power of randomness. In: TAMC (2019)

21. Pattanayak, D., Sharma, G., Mandal, P.S.: Dispersion of mobile robots tolerating faults. In: ICDCN (2021)
22. Pramanick, S., Samala, S.V., Pattanayak, D., Mandal, P.S.: Filling mis vertices of a graph by myopic luminous robots. In: ICDCIT (2023)
23. Sultanik, E., Shokoufandeh, A., Regli, W.: Dominating sets of agents in visibility graphs: distributed algorithms for art gallery problems. In: AAMAS (2010)
24. Wattenhofer, R.: Chapter 12, lecture notes: principles of distributed computing (2004). https://disco.ethz.ch/courses/ss04/distcomp/

Author Index

K. Georgiou and E. Kranakis (Eds.): ALGOWIN 2023, LNCS 14061, p. 151, 2023.
https://doi.org/10.1007/978-3-031-48882-5

Printed in the United States
by Baker & Taylor Publisher Services